Democracy, Revolution, and History

THE WILDER HOUSE SERIES IN POLITICS, HISTORY, AND CULTURE

The Wilder House Series is published in association with the Wilder House Board of Editors and the University of Chicago.

A complete list of titles appears at the end of this book.

David Laitin and George Steinmetz, Editors

DEMOCRACY, REVOLUTION, and HISTORY

edited by THEDA SKOCPOL

with the assistance of
GEORGE ROSS
TONY SMITH
JUDITH EISENBERG VICHNIAC

Cornell University Press

Ithaca and London

First published 1998 by Cornell University Press
First printing, Cornell Paperbacks, 1999

Printed in the United States of America

Cornell University Press strives to use environmentally responsible suppliers and materials to the fullest extent possible in the publishing of its books. Such materials include vegetable-based, low-VOC inks, and acid-free papers that are recycled, totally chlorine-free, or partly composed of nonwood fibers. Books that bear the logo of the FSC (Forest Stewardship Council) use paper taken from forests that have been inspected and certified as meeting the highest standards for environmental and social responsibility. For further information, visit our website at www.cornellpress.cornell.edu.

Library of Congress Cataloging-in-Publication Data

Democracy, revolution, and history / edited by Theda Skocpol.
    p. cm. — (The Wilder House series in politics, history, and culture)
Includes index.
ISBN 0-8014-3377-0 (cloth : alk. paper)
ISBN 0-8014-8626-2 (pbk. : alk. paper)
1. Social history. 2. Social class—History. 3. Democracy—
History. 4. Dictatorship—History. 5. Revolutions—History.
6. Moore, Barrington, 1913– Social origins of dictatorship and
democracy. I. Skocpol, Theda. II. Series.
HN13.D38 1998
306'.09—dc21   98-3181

Cloth printing   10 9 8 7 6 5 4 3 2 1
Paperback printing   10 9 8 7 6 5 4 3 2 1

Barry and Betty Moore, June 1944

Contents

III. GLOBAL AND NATIONAL POLITICS
SINCE MID-CENTURY

Preface

Barrington Moore, Jr., has never sought acolytes or disciples; and if any tried to pop up in his seminars, he squelched them abruptly. There are therefore no self-declared "Moorists" on the contemporary academic scene. But there is no dearth of people profoundly shaped by Barrington Moore's work and example. Many, of course, have been influenced simply by reading Moore's wonderful writings. Others, like the editors and contributors to this volume, have been fortunate to know him directly as his associates or (in most cases) his students. Many former Moore students are now senior established scholars, who tend to be a lot like Barry: crossers of disciplinary boundaries; oriented to comparative and historical research; and committed to tackling substantive questions. They tend to be almost instinctively allergic to general models that obliterate the differences among societies across time and space. There is thus a distinctive Moore-inspired approach to contemporary social science, even if there is no orthodox Moore School.

A plan to gather essays by Moore's associates and former students has been around for some time. At first, we aimed to put together a volume that would reflect the full variety of Moore's own *oeuvre,* but in due course it became clear that a volume focused upon Moore's most influential book, *Social Origins of Dictatorship and Democracy,* made more sense. Such a collection allows us to address central tendencies in historical comparative politics over the last generation—for *Social Origins,* and scholarship provoked by it, have been at the center of such intellectual tendencies.

The shift of emphasis meant that, alas, a number of high-quality essays had to be set aside. In the spirit of completing a compact and coherent book, several would-be contributors graciously cooperated with this decision. We thankfully acknowledge such help in the larger endeavor from Victoria Bonnell, David Plotke, Dina Spechler, Martin Spechler, Jon Wiener, and Robert Paul Wolff. Another member of the community of Moore-inspired scholars, Hal Benenson, died during the final stages of preparation of this volume. We remain terribly saddened by this loss, and honor the memory of Hal's friendship and scholarship.

Prefaces usually conclude with thanks to a long list of financial supporters. We have no such debts for this volume, although we greatly appreciate the support and patience of David Laitin, editor of the Wilder House Series at Cornell University Press; of the reviewers of this manuscript at various stages; and of all those at Cornell University Press who have helped in the publication process.

Our greatest debt, however, is to Barry Moore himself—mentor, model, and friend. Without Barry, we would all be much lesser scholars, teachers, and people. We also cherish the memory of Betty Moore, who nurtured our careers at Barry's side. Recollections of hard work and sparing praise in rigorous Harvard seminars motivate us still. Yet we are equally sustained by memories of companionship on the ski slopes and images of sunny days on the *Amy Q* and other delightful waterbound conveyences. In these places and more, as much as in the classroom, we have engaged with Barry in the recurring—and ongoing—conversations about the things that really matter.

GEORGE ROSS, THEDA SKOCPOL,
TONY SMITH, AND JUDITH EISENBERG VICHNIAC

Cambridge, Massachusetts

Democracy, Revolution, and History

Barrington Moore's *Social Origins* and Beyond: Historical Social Analysis since the 1960s

GEORGE ROSS, THEDA SKOCPOL, TONY SMITH
AND JUDITH EISENBERG VICHNIAC

The publication in 1966 of Barrington Moore's *Social Origins of Dictatorship and Democracy: Lord and Peasant in the Making of the Modern World* helped to inspire new agendas of research and reflection in macroscopic social science.[1] Here was a book of epochal vision and rigorous comparative inquiry, a work that explored morally compelling questions about the societal underpinnings of freedom and oppression, probing for the roots of democracy, revolutions, communism, and fascism in modern world history. Not only through its arguments, but still more through the force of its intellectual and methodological example, *Social Origins* opened new vistas for scholars in the United States and beyond.

Such a judgment about *Social Origins of Dictatorship and Democracy* is more apparent in retrospect than it may have been at the moment when the book first appeared. Even then, however, some reviewers foretold the book's likely impact. As J.H. Plumb presciently put it in the *New York Times Book Review:* "This is a profoundly important book, as much for what it attempts as for what it achieves. . . . Throughout the book, there is the constant play of a mind that is scholarly, original and imbued with the rarest gift of all, a deep sense of human reality. . . . I expect that this book will influence a whole generation of young American historians and lead them to problems of the greatest significance."[2] Plumb's prognostication was echoed by C. Vann Woodward, who wrote that "Barrington Moore, Jr., undertakes in this big and

---

[1] Barrington Moore, Jr., *Social Origins of Dictatorship and Democracy: Lord and Peasant in the Making of the Modern World* (Boston: Beacon Press, 1966).

[2] J. H. Plumb, "How It Happened," *New York Times Book Review* 71 (1966).

closely argued book to map the historical routes that the major nations of the West and East have taken to reach the stage of modern industrial society. . . . His book is a landmark in comparative history and a challenge to scholars of all lands who are trying to learn how we arrived at where we now are."[3]

Despite its ambitious scope—mapping social, economic, and political transformations over several hundred years in England, France, the United States, Germany, Japan, and India—*Social Origins of Dictatorship and Democracy* was not produced by any huge, lavishly funded, "multidisciplinary" research team. It was, instead, the achievement of a classically educated scholar working alone in his study.[4]

A Life of Scholarship

An austere person with a rigorously disciplined style of scholarly work, Barrington Moore, Jr. was born in 1913 and grew up in New York City and Newport, Rhode Island. He mastered Greek and Latin during his undergraduate years at Williams College and studied for a Ph.D. in sociology at Yale University under the guidance of Albert Galloway Keller. During World War II, Moore served as a strategic analyst to aid the U.S. military effort, yet thereafter he spent his entire career in academia as a teacher and research scholar. He taught in the interdisciplinary Social Science Division at the University of Chicago from 1945 to 1947. Then he moved to Harvard University, where he has been affiliated with the Russian Research Center, remaining largely aloof from departmental concerns and collegial politics. Over the years, Moore taught small seminar-style classes of Harvard undergraduate and graduate students, working only with carefully selected handfuls of young people whom he felt could master the challenges of classical social theory and broad comparative-historical investigations. Meanwhile, he pursued his personally engrossing scholarly agenda, working in close partnership with his wife, Elizabeth (or, more commonly, Betty) C. Moore.

Betty's parents had immigrated to the United States from Japan early in the twentieth century. Although of modest means, they reared and educated five children (of which Betty was the third). Betty earned an M.A. in linguistics from Berkeley, where she began teaching after World War II broke out. Following Pearl Harbor, she had to move from the West Coast and ended up working in the same office of the Department of Justice where Barrington was employed. They were married in 1944. After nearly forty-eight years of marriage, Betty Moore died on Valentine's Day 1992.

[3] C. Vann Woodward, "Comparative Political History," *Yale Review* 56 (1967).

[4] Dennis Smith, *Barrington Moore: A Critical Appraisal* (Armonk, N.Y.: M. E. Sharpe, 1983), p. 3. This is an excellent overview of Moore's life and scholarship.

In a talk he gave in the late 1980s, Barry described his books as based on "family labor." Betty edited every book manuscript from the second draft to completion and attended meticulously to the host of tasks that always surround publication. In an agreement reached before Barry published his first book, Betty was the sole recipient of all royalties that his writings received. The couple maintained a lifestyle that complemented their heavy work regimen. They cooperated on daily household routines and shared preferences about ideas, colleagues, and friends. Although a city girl, Betty also came to share Barry's love of skiing and sailing, their main diversions when not engaged in scholarly work.

Although Moore became a "Russian specialist" of sorts, he never took a narrow approach even to topics that fell within that specialty. Moore's works on the Soviet Union and its Communist dictatorship brought comparative and theoretical perspectives to bear on this globally important national case.[5] What is more, throughout his scholarly career, both long before and long after the appearance of *Social Origins,* Moore has produced encompassing reflections on the human condition. Back in the 1940s, he published articles on "The Relation Between Social Stratification and Social Control" and "A Comparative Analysis of the Class Struggle."[6] In 1958, Moore published a remarkable collection called *Political Power and Social Theory,* which brought together seven iconoclastic "studies," including "Totalitarian Elements in Pre-Industrial Societies," "The New Scholasticism and the Study of Politics," "Reflections on Conformity in Industrial Society," and "On the Notions of Progress, Revolution, and Freedom." Finally, of course, there have been Moore's wide-ranging books—not only *Social Origins of Dictatorship and Democracy* published in 1966, but also *Reflections on the Causes of Human Misery and on Certain Proposals to Eliminate Them* published in 1972, and *Injustice: The Social Bases of Obedience and Revolt* published in 1978.[7]

Barrington Moore, Jr., never operated during his career as did such other influential social scientists as Talcott Parsons, Gabriel Almond, Samuel P. Huntington, or Immanuel Wallerstein. Moore virtually never traveled to professional scholarly meetings, and he did not agree to manage professional

[5] For examples, see Barrington Moore, Jr., "The Influence of Ideas on Policies as Shown in the Collectivization of Agriculture in Russia," *American Political Science Review* 41, no. 3 (1947): 733–43; Moore, *Soviet Politics—The Dilemma of Power: The Role of Ideas in Social Change* (Cambridge, Mass.: Harvard University Press, 1954); and Moore, *Terror and Progress USSR: Some Sources of Change and Stability in the Soviet Dictatorship* (Cambridge, Mass.: Harvard University Press, 1954).

[6] Barrington Moore, Jr., "The Relation between Social Stratification and Social Control," *Sociometry* 5, no. 3 (1942): 230–50; and Moore, "A Comparative Analysis of the Class Struggle," *American Sociological Review* 10, no. 1 (February 1945): 31–37.

[7] Barrington Moore, Jr., *Reflections on the Causes of Human Misery and on Certain Proposals to Eliminate Them* (Boston: Beacon Press, 1972); and Moore, *Injustice: The Social Bases of Obedience and Revolt* (White Plains, N.Y.: M. E. Sharpe, 1978).

events or run for offices in scholarly associations. Dismissive of grand conceptual schemes in social science, Moore would not engage in disputes over theoretical paradigms; and he made no effort at all to recruit a "school" of followers. Indeed, students had to make a special effort to work with this idiosyncratic and demanding teacher, and they could not expect him actively to "sponsor" them on job markets. What students learned from Moore was a style of inquiry and an inspiring set of values about the life of scholarship. Students and colleagues alike were challenged to rethink assumptions and investigate historical and social changes more deeply.

At first glance, Moore's idiosyncratic career and his "ivory tower" orientation would not seem to be the stuff from which a turning point in the broader world of contemporary scholarship could emanate. Obviously, social and intellectual forces bigger than Moore himself were at work in the 1960s and 1970s. Yet these tendencies resonated with, and were in part shaped by, Moore's scholarly achievements—above all in *Social Origins of Dictatorship and Democracy.*

A Turn toward Historical and Comparative Inquiry

Visitors to the U.S. academic world of the 1950s and early 1960s discovered prestigious social-scientific disciplines and scholars who had come into their own in the heady years of U.S. preeminence and university expansion after World War II. In the social sciences, research empires had been established and faculty salaries increased; courses for undergraduates had gained places in college curricula formerly devoted to natural sciences and the humanities; and proliferating Ph.D. programs were spewing out graduates to fill new professorial positions opening up across the country (and, indeed, across the globe). As academic high priests who were connected to the managers of national economic prosperity in a Keynesian age, economists were the chief beneficiaries of all of this excitement in social science. Yet foreign-area–specialists, sociologists, and "political scientists" (as they now called themselves) also did very well.

The academic social sciences that rode this postwar wave were, on the whole, ahistorical and largely accepting of the status quo in the United States. As C. Wright Mills pointed out in his 1959 manifesto, *The Sociological Imagination,* U.S. academics were attracted either to "grand theory" or to "abstracted empiricism."[8] They tried, that is, to theorize about all times and places at once or to carry through statistically based empirical research about narrowly defined social problems in the contemporary United States. In retro-

[8] C. Wright Mills, *The Sociological Imagination* (New York: Oxford University Press, 1959).

spect, this was perhaps to be expected. With many research dollars from foundations and government suddenly at stake, social analysts were trying to prove that they were scientists just like investigators of the natural world. Geopolitically and economically, America temporarily sat astride the globe, and the West was locked in a bitter Cold War with the Communist East. There were masses of facts to be learned and organized with the aid of new investigative and computational techniques available to empirical researchers working at home or abroad. Theorists—such as the structure-functionalists who reasoned about "modernization" and "comparative development"—sought to generalize in as encompassing a manner as possible about a world in which it was expected (or at least hoped) that all paths would lead up the mountaintop where the United States of America already sat. Scholars might well speak of "problems" in the United States and subject them to careful scrutiny, yet their studies were either purely academic or else oriented to carefully circumscribed reformist purposes.

Taking issue with this perspective, C. Wright Mills was bitingly critical of the dominant modes of knowing and reasoning he saw in early postwar U.S. social science. He decried conceptual elaboration for its own sake and suggested that devotion to technical sophistication could lead away from tackling significant research problems. In contrast to the deformities of the academic status quo, Mills held out the promise of social science as a critical and historically oriented way of developing rational knowledge about societal structures, historical transformations, and the capacities of human actors to maneuver within and against them. Calling for a modern renewal of "the classical tradition" of social inquiry, Mills asked scholars to take up questions with a pressing relevance to the human condition, past and present. Scholars should, he felt, use historical evidence and comparative reasoning to explore power relations and processes of social change. Scholars should debate hypotheses, theories and techniques, not for their own sake, but in close relation to important substantive inquiries. And the prime audiences for such a critical, historical social science should be students and the thinking public, not managers seeking merely to make the status quo more efficient.

Had he lived, we can be certain that Mills would have wholeheartedly applauded the publication in 1966 of Barrington Moore's *Social Origins,* a book that embodied and helped to realize Mills's vision for social inquiry. For Mills and Moore were kindred scholarly spirits. Moore was one of a couple dozen colleagues that Mills thanked for going over the manuscript of *The Sociological Imagination.* Moore's early studies of the Soviet Union were among the few works that Mills cited as positive contemporary examples of social science in the classical tradition. *The Sociological Imagination* primarily criticized contemporary social science works—such as those by Talcott Parsons and Paul Lazersfeld—while mentioning only a handful of positive examples, works by Franz Neumann, David Riesman, Max Weber, and John Kenneth Galbraith, as well as by Barrington Moore, Jr.

The best indication that Mills would have applauded *Social Origins* comes from juxtaposing Mills's prescriptions, especially in the pivotal chapter of *The Sociological Imagination* on "Uses of History," with what Moore actually wrought in his magnum opus. "We need the variety provided by history even to ask sociological questions properly, much less to answer them," Mills wrote. We "must study the available range of social structures, including the historical as well as the contemporary. If we do not take into account the range . . . our statements cannot be empirically adequate."[9] And we must look over vast stretches of time, too: "A-historical studies usually tend to be static or very short-term studies of limited milieux. That is only to be expected, because we more readily become aware of larger structures when they are changing, and we are likely to become aware of changes only when we broaden our view to include a suitable historical span."[10] *Social Origins of Dictatorship and Democracy* realized this vision much more fully than any contemporary social science work that Mills had been able to cite positively in 1959. For Barrington Moore's monumental study probed the causal and moral realities of "alternative routes" to ways of organizing political power in the modern world—to liberal democracy, fascism, and communism. *Social Origins* tackled morally compelling questions about human freedom, human suffering, and the costs of modernization. Its author moved back and forth between hypotheses and empirical historical evidence, using comparisons across six nations: England, France, the United States, Germany, Russia, Japan, and India. And the book examined historical transformations from the 1300s to the twentieth century.

Social Origins played an important role in spurring new styles of historical and comparative-historical social science in U.S. academia. It is, of course, difficult to substantiate such a claim, because much more than a single book (or a single scholar) mattered. One could name many scholars, of widely differing theoretical and political orientations, who had a hand in creating renewed historical and comparative-historical tendencies from the 1960s: Reinhard Bendix, Samuel P. Huntington, Charles Tilly, S. N. Eisenstadt, Michael Walzer, Seymour Martin Lipset, and Immanuel Wallerstein are among the names that would appear on such a list along with Moore's.

More fundamentally, there would never have been substantial and sustainable historical "turns" within mainstream academic social science had it not been for the conjuncture of demography, geopolitics, and societal disruptions in the 1960s and after. Civil Rights and student movements shook domestic complacency inside the United States, as America fought on the ultimately

[9] Mills, *Sociological Imagination*, pp. 146–47.
[10] Ibid., p. 149.

losing side of the war in Vietnam. By the 1970s, the United States was no longer as dominant compared to other advanced industrial nations as it had been right after World War II. Such developments abroad and at home raised questions about the adequacy of the grand theories and narrowly empirical studies that Mills had decried and opened possibilities for new macroscopic and critical approaches to scholarship. What is more, these real-world changes coincided with the arrival in U.S. universities of swollen cohorts of young people, many of whom were attracted to learning, teaching, and doing critical, historically oriented social science. These younger (now middle-aged) scholars of the "sixties generation" have been the ones to create full-blown professional research programs and shared intellectual agendas within American social science from the 1970s onward. Critically minded and historically oriented developments in the U.S. social sciences eventually came to be embodied in the Comparative and Historical Section (founded in 1982–83) of the American Sociological Association; the Conference Group on the Political Economy of Advanced Industrial Societies in political science (founded in 1978); journals such as *Politics and Society* (founded in 1970), *Theory and Society* (founded in 1974), and *Studies in American Political Development* (founded in 1986); and the Politics and History Section of the American Political Science Association (launched in 1989).

Although many people and forces came together to spur the rise and institutionalization of comparative and historical social science during the 1970s and 1980s, Barrington Moore's scholarship, especially in *Social Origins,* played a pivotal role in catalyzing the underlying intellectual developments. Moore articulated no theoretical or methodological recipes. What he did instead was to study and write about pressingly relevant big questions from an autonomously critical perspective. The origins, cost, and fate of liberal democracy versus authoritarianism in the modern world mattered greatly when Moore wrote *Social Origins.* Moore both appreciated and held up to critical scrutiny the value claims of the West about progress and freedom in European and U.S. history. Writing at a time when many young scholars were intellectually experimenting with Marxism as a way to declare independence against reigning academic orthodoxies, Moore both used and sharply revised Marxian hypotheses about democracy and revolutions in modern world history. He blended Marxist, Weberian and other theoretical approaches. And he insisted upon careful and wide-ranging comparative-historical investigation of an empirical and causal nature, but one that was not at all narrow minded.

At the time of its publication, many people considered *Social Origins* a thoroughly radical work, a sharp break with general modernization theories and with empiricist social science. But in fact *Social Origins* revised and revitalized, rather than abandoned, previous social science traditions. It explored "modernization" as a matter of alternative routes, not evolutionary necessity.

It refurbished the theoretical eclecticism and imagination of macroscopic and comparative social science. Above all, it broadened the meaning of evidence and analysis to encompass the "historical scope of conception and full use of historical materials" so passionately advocated by C. Wright Mills.

Social Origins of Dictatorship and Democracy thus could end up inspiring and provoking many others, especially younger scholars, who never met or were not personally influenced by Barrington Moore. Others whom Moore taught or intellectually touched went on to produce kindred scholarly works and, in some cases, to do the sorts of institution building for historical and comparative social science that he himself never attempted. The point is that Moore's exemplary book opened pathways and debates that revitalized, rather than destroyed or distracted from, passionate social science research—research on big, morally relevant questions, addressed through reason and broad-ranging evidence, not just interpretation or technique.

The Roots of Dictatorship and Democracy

Those early appreciative reviewers, such as J. H. Plumb and C. Vann Woodward, who suggested that *Social Origins of Dictatorship and Democracy* would be more influential because of its example and the questions it raised than because of the answers it offered, were certainly on the mark. Over the three decades since the appearance of *Social Origins,* its explanatory theses about the roots of dictatorship and democracy have been repeatedly reexamined by scholars willing to undertake comparative and historical investigations of as bold a scope as Moore himself undertook (or even bolder). It would take more than an essay, indeed more than a book, to explore all of the lines of theoretical debate and comparative-historical research on these matters that *Social Origins* helped to inspire—or provoke.[11] Still, pointing to the essays in part I of this book as well as to various books published in recent decades, we can note the highlights of several lines of research inspired by the major causal arguments of *Social Origins.*

At the core of *Social Origins of Dictatorship and Democracy* was a thesis about the socioeconomic underpinnings of illiberal and antidemocratic regimes, ranging from bureaucratic monarchies in premodern Europe and Asia through fascist authoritarian regimes in the twentieth century. In his case studies, Moore always attended to the interplay of a variety of institutional,

---

[11] Jonathan Wiener, "Review of Reviews: The Barrington Moore Thesis and Its Critics," *History and Theory* 15 (1976): 146–75 assesses the reviews that immediately reacted to *Social Origins* after its publication, and suggests some of the agendas of research that the book opened up.

socioeconomic, and conjunctural factors. Yet his distinctive explanatory emphasis was on dominant-class coalitions—between relatively "weak" commercial-capitalist groups (including urban bourgeoisies and market-oriented farmers) and "labor-repressive" landed upper classes. Moore argued that such coalitions built up, and relied upon, centralized and repressive state authority to keep lower classes at work and politically quiescent. In some historical cases, such as France, Russia, and China, repressive dominant-class coalitions and the agrarian-bureaucratic regimes that they underpinned were overthrown by revolutions, which in turn opened the way either for a gradual transition to liberal democracy (France) or for Communist dictatorships (Russia and China), depending on whether commercial capitalist bourgeoisies were present or not. But in other cases such as Germany and Japan, Moore argued, repressive dominant-class coalitions held on, promoting a turn toward fascism. Moore saw only England as a case that historically escaped the grip of these repressive coalitions led by labor-repressive landlords; and he attributed England's special trajectory to the steady rise of market-oriented agriculture and landlords from the sixteenth century onward. Even the United States, in Moore's view, was stamped during modernization by a labor-repressive landed upper class. For Moore sees the southern U.S. slaveholders, and the only partially successful Civil War against them, as pivotal for the subsequent uneven course of U.S. democratic development.

Although Barrington Moore took considerable intellectual inspiration from classic Marxist theoretical ideas about class relations and the social underpinnings of politics, he did so with a new twist: *Social Origins* made a distinctive contribution by emphasizing not the political roles of capitalist bourgeoisies or the wage-earning proletariat, but instead the role of "lord and peasant in the making of the modern world." Moore stressed that peasant communities, rebelling from below, had provided the "dynamite" to bring down agrarian-bureaucratic old orders in France, Russia, and China. And he viewed labor-repressive forms of commercial agriculture, along with the upper landed classes that benefitted from such relationships, as mainstays of those prerevolutionary old regimes that had been brought down by revolutions from below in such places as Bourbon France, Tsarist Russia, and Imperial-through-Republican China.

Such analytical emphases on peasants and landlords flourished after *Social Origins* in a burgeoning comparative-historical literature on the causes of revolutions. The studies of agrarian classes and social relations in revolutions that Moore helped to inspire are too many to name, yet prominent among them would certainly be Charles Tilly's *The Vendée* (1967), Jeffery Paige's *Agrarian Revolution* (1975), James Scott's *The Moral Economy of the Peasant* (1976), Theda Skocpol's *States and Social Revolutions* (1979), and Timothy

Wickham-Crowley's *Guerrillas and Revolution in Latin America* (1992).[12] It is fair to say that all of these works, while differing with Moore's arguments about the overall roots and consequences of revolutions, have nevertheless built upon and in many ways reconfirmed the value of his emphasis on peasants, rather than urban proletarians, as the key popular actors in social revolutions from below in the modern world.

More broadly, however, much of the comparative-historical scholarship on democracy and authoritarianism since *Social Origins* has taken issue with many of Moore's key arguments. For example, Moore downplayed the role of urban classes in struggling for democracy in the modern world. But their role has reemerged in such recent grand comparative and historical studies as *Liberalism, Fascism, or Social Democracy: Social Classes and the Political Origins of Regimes in Interwar Europe* by the late Gregory M. Luebbert; *Capitalist Development and Democracy* by Dietrich Rueschemeyer and Evelyne and John Stephens; *Working-Class Formation: Nineteenth-Century Patterns in Western Europe and the United States* by Ira Katznelson and Aristide Zolberg; and *Shaping the Political Arena: Critical Junctures, the Labor Movement, and Regime Dynamics in Latin America* by Ruth Berins Collier and David Collier.[13] The authors of these works explicitly and warmly acknowledge their intellectual debts to Barrington Moore's *Social Origins.* They agree that political regime transformations in the modernizing world must be understood in relationship to historically shifting class alliances. Yet they show convincingly that urban middle and working classes are pivotal partners, along with agrarian classes, in such alliances. If our purpose is to understand the conditions for the emergence, or survival, of liberal democratic polities, then we must not downplay as much as Moore did, the orientations and activities of urban classes and their organizations.

Among the "organizations" that Moore deemphasized in the grand sweep of *Social Origins* were political parties. All of the works just mentioned investi-

---

[12] Charles Tilly, *The Vendée: A Sociological Analysis of the Counterrevolution of 1793* (New York: Wiley, 1967); Jeffery M. Paige, *Agrarian Revolution: Social Movements and Export Agriculture in the Underdeveloped World* (New York: Free Press, 1975); James C. Scott, *The Moral Economy of the Peasant: Rebellion and Subsistence in Southeast Asia* (New Haven: Yale University Press, 1976); Theda Skocpol, *States and Social Revolutions: A Comparative Analysis of France, Russia, and China* (New York: Cambridge University Press, 1979); and Timothy Wickham-Crowley, *Guerrillas and Revolution in Latin America: A Comparative Study of Insurgents and Regimes since 1956* (Princeton: Princeton University Press, 1992).

[13] Gregory M. Luebbert, *Liberalism, Fascism, or Social Democracy: Social Classes and the Political Origins of Regimes in Western Europe* (New York: Oxford University Press, 1991); Dietrich Rueschemeyer, Evelyne Stephens, and John Stephens, *Capitalist Development and Democracy* (Chicago: University of Chicago Press, 1992); Ira Katznelson and Aristide R. Zolberg, eds., *Working-Class Formation: Nineteenth-Century Patterns in Western Europe and the United States* (Princeton: Princeton University Press, 1986); and Ruth Berins Collier and David Collier, *Shaping the Political Arena: Critical Structures, the Labor Movement, and Regime Dynamics in Latin America.* (Princeton: Princeton University Press, 1991).

gate systems of electorally based political parties as institutional arrangements that mediate and help to shape class politics and interclass alliances. As Gregory Luebbert demonstrates with special clarity, class alliances during European modernization could form, or fail to form, not only because of the sorts of economic interests that Moore emphasizes in *Social Origins,* but also because of the institutional arrangements of electoral politics and the arrays of political parties that emerged historically in each nation. In her contribution to this volume, Theda Skocpol makes an analytically similar point about the United States. She argues that Moore could have more effectively sustained his thesis about the contributions of the U.S. Civil War to the emergence of modern American democracy if he had more carefully considered the organizational patterns and competitive electoral dynamics of U.S. political parties in the late nineteenth century. U.S. parties were patronage oriented and geared to mobilizing majorities of male voters across classes in the North; thus party competition in the late nineteenth century fueled the expansion of social spending for Union veterans and survivors, along with policies favoring big business. In his chapter on the United States in *Social Origins,* Moore correctly stresses that much of the democratic potential of the Civil War struggle against slavery was lost at the end of Reconstruction, when the Union armies retreated from the South and left the freedmen in poverty and defenseless against repressive political violence. Moore nevertheless believes that the U.S. Civil War contributed to liberal democratic development in the United States. And he is right, Skocpol maintains, if one takes into account the popular roots and social-welfare consequences of Republican Party hegemony in the late nineteenth and early twentieth century. Theoretically speaking, Moore was not prepared to do this, but his class-analytic approach can be supplemented with due attention to the institutional arrangements of politics, including electoral and party structures.

Political parties, of course, need not be electorally oriented. Among the most influential parties in modern world history have been disciplined Leninist parties, ideologically oriented organizations designed to contest for state power, often in authoritarian settings—and also designed to wield state power in dictatorial ways. In chapter 5, Edward Friedman uses a reexamination of China and India to question Moore's relative blindness in *Social Origins* to the obstacles that Leninist organizations and strategies of modernization would create for both democracy and economic development in the twentieth-century Third World. Friedman argues that post-British-colonial India has done much better, both economically and democratically than Moore seemed to expect in 1966, when his argument about national development in the twentieth century implied that only violent, peasant-based revolutions from below could clear the way to national economic development. Tellingly, in *Social Origins* Moore took his analysis of the Chinese Revolution (and his brief discussions of the Russian Revolution) only up to the point of the fall of the old regimes. He did not probe, as Friedman does, into what happened to politics and national economic development after social revolutions occurred. After all, peasants were not the ones who took state power. National authority was seized by Leninist parties who proceeded to rule dictatorially, overriding opposition while pursuing ideologically inspired strategies of national development that were often quite detrimental to the popular groups whose revolts had originally cleared their way to power.

Another line of analysis has gained prominence in studies that confront again the most fundamental questions raised in *Social Origins* about the roots of liberal versus authoritarian tendencies in modern politics. A number of Moore-inspired scholars, including several with essays in this volume, have shifted attention from the socioeconomic and class factors stressed by Moore toward the roles of geopolitics, war, and associated bureaucratic state institutions in blocking, or opening up, historical possibilities for the emergence of liberal and democratic politics. Perhaps the most ambitious attempt to reengage and revise the core of the theoretical and comparative-historical argument of *Social Origins of Dictatorship and Democracy* has been made by Brian Downing, the author of *The Military Revolution and Political Change: Origins of Democracy and Autocracy in Early Modern Europe,* based on a Ph.D. thesis that won the Gabriel Almond Dissertation Award of the American Political Science Association in 1992.[14] The central arguments of Downing's book are presented in his contribution to this volume, an essay which resonates in many ways with Charles Tilly's essay immediately following it, "Where Do Rights Come From?"

In slightly different but ultimately complementary ways, Downing and Tilly show that geopolitical constraints and possibilities were crucial for early modern European states, whose monarchs had to figure out ways to raise people and money to fight ever more intensive wars. The circumstances of warfare, and the bureaucratic and representative institutions through which monarchs and various social classes bargained over ways of raising resources, profoundly influenced the political paths along which various early modern European nations traveled. Some, such as Britain and the Netherlands, avoided or cut short authoritarian-bureaucratic developments. Others, such as France and Prussia, ended up building strong centralized bureaucracies and standing armies as monarchs overrode social opposition at home to amass resources for wars, especially land wars, with neighboring states. Downing and Tilly certainly do not neglect to analyze class relationships, including the relationships

[14] Brian M. Downing, *The Military Revolution and Political Change: Origins of Democracy and Autocracy in Early Modern Europe* (Princeton: Princeton University Press, 1992).

in agriculture that Barrington Moore taught us all to treat as critical. Yet these authors examine the interrelationships of geopolitical and economic developments and treat state-building monarchs as key actors in relationship to merchants, landlords, and peasant communities. As Downing shows especially convincingly, nationally varied institutional legacies from the feudal era patterned many of the maneuvers, conflicts, and alliances of the various class and political actors. At the same time, these actors reconstructed European states in liberal or authoritarian directions and fought the recurrent naval and land wars that punctuated the entire history of early modern Europe.

Significantly, Moore himself today accepts much of this reworking of his comparative analysis of early modern Europe. In a step that shows how open Moore remains to new ideas, including those that challenge his own earlier conclusions, he penned an endorsement for Downing's book. "When the manuscript of this book came to my attention," Moore says, "I intended to do no more than skim it to see if I could help a young scholar unknown to me. Instead, I found myself reading every word straight through to the end. The author's emphasis on the role of the instruments of violence and repression in inhibiting liberal and democratic trends is new to scholarship and quite convincing. Here is comparative history at its best. This book takes a big step beyond my *Social Origins of Dictatorship and Democracy*."[15] At the end of his essay here, Downing himself pays tribute to the enduring strengths of Moore's contributions in *Social Origins,* suggesting that the "class-based arguments of the origins of dictatorship and democracy need to be complemented with ones recognizing the importance of military organization, geopolitics, and resource mobilization." Downing acknowledges that *Social Origins* has served as a source of inspiration for his work and that of many others. In short, even those who disagree with certain of Moore's central theses see themselves as scholarly partners with him in a grand search for an understanding of liberal and authoritarian tendencies in the modern world. And Moore sees his critics that way, too.

Groups and Identities in Politics

The great historical sweep of Barrington Moore's work tends to relativize questions about the social construction of ideologies, identities, and interests—the focus of the essays in part II of this book. At various points Moore speculates broadly about the generality of practices in which groups define themselves against, and to the exclusion and denigration of, others. Demonizing the other as part of group strategies for self-advancement is a regular and

---

[15] See Moore's endorsement on the jacket flap of Downing's *Military Revolution.*

ineradicable dimension of human society, at least from the standpoint of a realist like Moore. And the broader Weberian question of the social origins of the "action orientations" of important groups is an important one. But from the vantage point of centuries-long social developments, the processes creating a group's conception of itself in relation to outsiders can be taken as "givens." Large social groups with a roughly common relationship to on-going structures construct identities, common interests and conflicting definitions of others which, however one explains their precise origins, are visible as social facts to the diligent researcher. For the most part, what interested Moore was what happened, over long periods of time, once such groups had consolidated.

The outline of *Social Origins* is interesting from this point of view. The crucible of the most important modern modes of governance—liberal, fascist, or communist—lay in variations of coalition and conflict that developed among premodern, particularly agrarian, social groups confronted by capitalist modernization. Agrarian interests and identities were constructed in quite different ways depending upon the evolving structures of agriculture in the face of marketization. For example, elites controlling plantation systems, like the Junkers or the slaveholders of the American South, were likely to carry premodern and illiberal ideas into the modern era if their interests could be sustained during the transition to capitalism. Where this occurred, the seeds for illiberal political modernity could be sown: undemocratic modernization from above became likely. At such a time, liberal propensities of the bourgeoisie could be blunted. Then, when these premodern ideas inevitably confronted twentieth-century ideologies of popular participation, the latter ideologies could be distorted into fascism; residues of premodern illiberal ideas could be used to encourage populist mobilization. Where precapitalist agrarian structures were different, however, or where agrarian groups were fundamentally changed by the coming of capitalism, it was possible for liberal political options to triumph, though often at the cost of violent crises. Finally, agrarian elites could block the emergence of capitalism altogether; then the basis for communist revolution, a different form of modernization from above, was created.

Ideas, self-definitions and concepts of interests based upon structures of economic production, are all essential to the Moore analysis. The outcomes that Moore sought to explain were the triumph of particular systems of political thought and institutions which encouraged societies and groups within them toward particular political "action orientations." And at the heart of these outcomes lay the implications of ideologically defined class interests, ideas about the desired shape of society, the proper way to live and the nature of groups perceived as the enemies of such things. The particular ideas of the Junkers, for example, the *noblesse de robe,* the English gentry, Brahmins, or Chinese scholar officials are vital to Moore's explanation of long-term developmental trajectories. Moore simply refrains from unduly problematizing the social construction of these ideas in order to focus upon other matters.[16]

In *Social Origins*, Moore had little to say about intellectuals and ideological revolutionary movements in the making of modern political upheavals and authoritarian regimes. Of course, he mentioned the Jacobins in the French Revolution and the Communists in the Russian and Chinese Revolutions. Yet Moore said little about who these people were and why they saw politics and nation building as they did. Going over many of the same cases of revolutionary change that Moore discussed in *Social Origins*, Michael Walzer's contribution to this volume directly probes the activities and ideas of the ideological vanguards. Walzer also explores the interactions of classes and ideological leaderships, offering the provocative hypothesis that liberal and democratic outcomes were possible only when the class "partners" in the making of revolutions were able to assert themselves against Jacobin or Leninist vanguards that wanted to remake the world in terms of ideological visions. Walzer offers an alternative way to think about why the Jacobins fell from power in France while Communists continued to dominate predominantly agrarian post-revolutionary societies in Russia and China.

The other two essays in this section go even further than Walzer toward problematizing the social construction of discourses of groups' interests. Rebecca Scott's concern is the social construction of the notion of race, understood in relation to class interests. Labeling and stigmatizing particular groups as racial minorities is an ancient custom, as Moore himself remarks in his discussions of caste in India. It has obviously become a burning contemporary issue as transnational population migrations tied to capitalist development and colonization have created multicolored populations in societies claiming to be democratic. Racial stigmatization is a form of social exclusion that contradicts democratic assumptions, and its prevalence creates explosive conflict situations.

Scott's point of departure is the observation that race can be defined in a wide range of different ways. She uses comparative analytical tools similar to Moore's to explore relatively short moments at the end of the nineteenth century in the sugar producing agrarian economies of Louisiana and Cuba. The structure of class conflict and alliances, and the consequent outcomes in terms of the social definition of race, turn out to be different in each setting. In Louisiana, planta-

---

[16] One should not exaggerate this point, however. In *Injustice*, a classic that has not been sufficiently discussed, Moore considers Marxist claims about the processes of interest definition among workers by empirical investigation of the German working class. Moore finds that the Marxist schema concerning the construction of working-class interests from underlying social structures is profoundly misleading. The claims for working-class radicalism turn out to come largely from intellectual leftists and organizational elites.

tion elites pursuing postbellum economic survival confronted the possibility of unified black and white resistance to a low-wage sharecropping system. To cope, they played on virulent racism to divide and rule, thereby making their own small contribution to the consolidation of apartheid in the American South. In Cuba, resistance to continued Spanish colonization created a very different definition of race, softened by black and white unification in a struggle against an outside enemy. Later occupation by the Americans brought with it attempts to import an American definition of race, but they were not completely successful. Scott's interest in the variability of definitions of race leads her to a fascinating preoccupation with the contingency of historical development and the possibility of alternative outcomes. This resonates with Moore's most abiding concerns.

Judith Eisenberg Vichniac is interested in an analogous puzzle. How did it happen, given relatively similar historical origins, that social definitions and citizenship rights of French and German Jews ended up being so different by the end of the nineteenth century? In both cases Jewish communities began as excluded, stigmatized minorities. In France, however, Jews achieved virtual equality as citizens, despite the persistence of cultural anti-Semitism. In decentralized Germany, the trajectory of Jewish assimilation was roughly similar to France until the nineteenth century, when the illiberal and xenophobic nationalism that underlay final national unification again stimulated strong anti-Semitism and recast Jews as not true Germans, a situation preparing the way for the horrors of the twentieth century.

Vichniac's comparative historical analysis follows that of *Social Origins* rather closely. But her purpose, that of exploring the ways in which French and German national development led to varying definitions of Jewish minorities, is quite different. The patterns of class coalition and conflict that modernized France, with the Revolution at their center, consecrated a universalistic Republican political philosophy that made it very difficult to label particular social groups as non-French and to exclude them. Despite persistent anti-Semitism in French society, this philosophy protected and integrated Jews. The patterns which modernized and centralized Germany led to very different outcomes with the failure of bourgeois revolution and the consequent weakness of liberal democratic concepts of citizenship. At a later point German Jews could not invoke firm citizenship claims against ambient anti-Semitism. Instead they became an invisible minority and an eventual target.

When *Social Origins* made its initial impact, it was unorthodox to think that deep social structures and political values might interact to block the development of democracy. Many scholars supposed that modernization and industrialization would inevitably lead to social progress. Moore's arguments were a sobering reminder that not all economically developing nations establish "modern" institutions or tolerant, democratic values. Today, we should remain sobered in the face of new claims about the "end of history" and the inevitable total triumph of democracy. As the third millennium unfolds, new bearers of illiberal notions, and new structural obstacles to democracy, may well become apparent. And as the essays in part II demonstrate, to understand them it is necessary to combine a long-term analysis of structural transformations with an understanding of group identities, outlooks, and discourses.

Global and National Politics since Mid-Century

Part III of this book deals with the impact of international forces on the course of domestic political developments, a concern peripherally present in Moore's work but not central to it. Like most works in comparative social science, Moore's *Social Origins* made the working assumption that long-established societies are best conceived of as complex organisms composed of inherited values and practices. In these societies, organized socioeconomic interests and political institutions have come to interact with one another to a degree that gives them a distinct identity. Except insofar as one country's people may try to emulate the achievements of another, societies can best be understood as effectively existing in worlds unto themselves. In such circumstances, only the most powerful foreign influences can hope to shape the dynamic of local events, as Moore's review of British India in *Social Origins* illustrates. Hence the rationale of the division of *Social Origins* into chapters on specific countries faced with the global dilemma of modernizing agrarian societies.

Over the last quarter century, however, American social science has become more interested in what is often called the "intersection" of comparative and international studies, arenas where forces whose character is only fully apparent when studied globally interact with forces whose identity is best understood in terms of a discrete society. To be sure, Moore recognizes that a challenge such as that of economic modernization is global, and as a consequence that events in one country—successful industrialization, for example—will produce efforts in other countries to duplicate in their own way the achievements of the first. But for Moore, as for most traditional comparativists, such defensive modernization will occur according to the logic of the social structure of the country undertaking it (whence his famous distinction among democratic, fascist, and communist roads to development). It is altogether characteristic of Moore's writings—as of comparativism in general—that he treats international phenomena (be it class conflict, nationalism, or ideology) essentially as they manifest themselves in terms of specific peoples and not as forces whose identity should be studied at the international level, independently of their local identities.

By contrast, in the essays of part III, the authors variously credit worldwide forces with a greater affect on local social and political developments than Moore's categories of analysis easily allow. From the points of view of Peter Gourevitch, George Ross, and Tony Smith, the international arena is one of intense interstate competition wherein rival parties constantly adjust their own behavior—often with unintended consequences—in light of what they believe it to be to their competitive advantage to do.

In the view of all of these essays, the end of the Cold War has been especially important in revealing the importance of transnational forces on the economic, social, and political development of distinct peoples. For Gourevitch, looking at Japanese and American economic management styles, and for Ross, analyzing the way the European Community (renamed the European Union in 1993) responded to its competitive position in the world economy in the mid-1980s, critical country-specific developments reflect the dynamic of the world economy.

For Gourevitch, the end of the Cold War means that even more than before, political economists will study not so much the difference between capitalism and central planning as the differences within capitalism itself. He turns to the Japanese style of industrial management to see how it has led Americans to conceive of their own productive system and its competitive position internationally. Of course, in important ways Gourevitch sustains leading assumptions of Moore's work. He finds that Americans have been slow to duplicate often superior Japanese ways because of resistance within the American cultural, class, and management systems to kinds of procedures that are distinctively Japanese. America's ability to borrow from the Japanese is strongly conditioned, in other words, by America's own history and culture, a point that reinforces the truism that Japan and America are two quite distinct societies, as Moore would readily agree. Thus, Moore's insistence on the primacy of the internal (or country-specific) forces over international ones is not so much rejected as it is supplemented by Gourevitch's exploration of interactions among industrial powers in a dynamic world economy.

A somewhat different approach appears in the essay by George Ross. Along with Gourevitch, Ross is concerned with the sociopolitical consequences of international economic change—here insofar as it has affected the process of European unification. Ross identifies a global capitalist economy whose often anarchic contortions created a powerful international "environment" acting on what is now called the European Union. Ross moves even further from Moore's categories of analysis than Gourevitch, by studying the actions of supranational agencies. Ross particularly focuses on the role of the European Commission in promoting fundamental socioeconomic and political changes in the member states of the Union. His ultimate concern, however, rejoins Moore's—asking how these changing sociopolitical structures affect the progress or decline of democracy.

According to Ross, a set of conditions came together in the middle of the 1980s to revive movement toward economic integration under the terms of the Single Act adopted in 1986–87 and the 1992 Treaty of Maastricht, which proposed the step-by-step creation of economic and monetary union. These conditions included the impact of international economic competition on Europe; the willingness of leading member states in the European Union to cede sovereignty to cope with the challenge; and visionary leadership from heads of the European Commission. As national resistance to increased European integration since 1993 has demonstrated, the various nation-states are still alive and kicking—just as most comparativists would expect. Yet transfers of sovereignty between particular nations and the European Union have become an extremely important factor in contemporary European politics. Understanding these transfers, and conflicts about them, requires more appreciation of international relations and supranational processes than comparative analysis customarily musters.

Ross concludes on a realistic and pessimistic note which brings his analysis back toward the spirit of *Social Origins*. Leaders of sovereign European nations have divested themselves of some state capacities and functions in response to clear economic challenges. In the process, however, they have also passed difficult domestic problems to a level of governance where standards of democracy fall far short of those historically achieved within the nations of Europe. The structural problems and political opportunities that have created special openings for European integration may, therefore, also turn out to render telling blows against Europe's precious democratic legacies.

Tony Smith's essay recasts Moore's trichotomy among fascist, communist, and democratic roads to modernity by seeing them not so much as alternatives but as competitors with one another in the contest to give governmental form to nationalist demands for a state based on popular sovereignty. Thus, in every industrial and semi-industrial country in the world by the 1930s, rival fascist, communist, and democratic movements jockeyed with each other (and often with traditional authoritarian movements as well) for power in a struggle that, as the Spanish Civil War revealed, was soon every bit as much international as it was local. In World War II, democratic and communist forces broke the power of fascism. Subsequently, it was the American occupation of Germany and Japan and the conversion of these two countries into open-market democracies that eventually contributed to the victory of the American-led democracies over Soviet communism.

Once again, however, Moore's analysis is not rejected but rather supplemented by an approach insisting on the ability of a foreign military occupation to change in meaningful ways local societies. Smith finds that Japan and Germany assuredly remain distinctively themselves today, as Moore would assume. But Smith also concludes, uncharacteristically for traditional comparative analysis, that the impact of the American occupation had more than a marginal influence on the postwar character of these two important countries, which in turn had a key impact on the character of the international system as a force in its own right in the struggle between East and West.

What these essays suggest is that for too long comparativists with their country-specific studies have adopted an unfortunately narrow "every tub on its own bottom" approach to historical change. They have tended to pay insufficient attention to the worldwide diffusion of ideas, techniques, and institutional forms that have proceeded according to a dynamic that country-specific studies cannot adequately appreciate.

Certainly the essays assembled here do not exhaust the possible range of subjects to be explored at the intersection of comparative and international studies. Nationalism, for example, has both its international and its country-specific dimensions and it would be inappropriate to reduce either to the terms of the other. So too, feminism is coming to be a worldwide force whose character and influence should not be studied solely at the level of individual countries. Or consider the current turn against statism and corporatism in the economic organization of peoples. Like the diffusion of Keynesian thinking a generation earlier, this change in economic analysis and management has acquired an international ideological character that has had profound reper-cussions on domestic social and political forces wherever it takes hold.

To be sure, Moore, and traditional comparativists in general, are correct to insist that these worldwide forces had a part of their origin in the experience of specific peoples before they became internationalized. Moreover, Moore is also quite right to hold that such international forces subsequently take root in different environments in distinctive ways depending on the unique character of local social structures that must be studied in their own terms. An insistence on the molding power of worldwide forces over local events in no way means that the careful analysis of individual societies in terms of their own laws of movement can be dispensed with as, for example, "world-systems" thinking and the "dependency" approach to political development far too often sup-pose. If the authors here mean to supplement Moore's manner of analysis by their own emphasis on the independent and powerful influence of worldwide forces on local developments, they by no means intend to deny the importance of understanding the character of concrete social and political systems and their extraordinary capacity to transmute the most powerful of international influences into local terms.

Companions in the Search for Truth

In Moore's own continued activities, as well as through the further scholar-ship his work has inspired, we know the truth of the reflections that he offered in 1966 at the end of the preface to *Social Origins*. Commenting on the challenges of doing morally engaged comparative history, Moore invoked a "parallel with the explorer of unknown lands," who

> is not called upon to build a smooth and direct highway for the next band of travelers. Should he be their guide, he is thought to acquit himself adequately if he avoids the time-consuming backtracks and errors of his first exploration, courteously refrains from leading his companions through the worst of the underbrush, and points out the more dangerous pitfalls as he guides them warily past. If he makes a clumsy misstep and stumbles into a trap, there may even be some in the party who not only enjoy a laugh at his expense, but may also be willing to give him a hand to set him forth on his way once more. It is for such a band of companions in the search for truth that I have written this book.[17]

Moore recruited many such companions—even though the journeys he led them on were very arduous. Some of Moore's fellow explorers went back to discover better paths through the terrain Moore himself had first crossed, while others started from Moore's end point to forge new routes over unexplored regions.

As this volume suggests, because so many people have been inspired by Moore's arguments and example, the paths that go forward, or around again, from Moore's landmark achievement in *Social Origins of Dictatorship and Democracy* lead in many of the most promising directions in theory and research in the historical social sciences that have been opened up since the 1960s. The journeys of Moore's companions, as well as the journeys of those they have guided in turn, continue to go forward today. These ventures promise to lead toward new truths for many years to come.

[17] Moore, *Social Origins*, pp. xvii–xviii.

PART I

THE ROOTS OF DICTATORSHIP AND DEMOCRACY

CHAPTER 2

War and the State in
Early Modern Europe

BRIAN M. DOWNING

Some thirty years ago, Barrington Moore, Jr., published a powerful comparative study of the origins of democracy, fascism, and communism.[1] Rich in historical detail and aloof from the functionalism of the period, it constituted a big step beyond existing models of political change. The logic of *Social Origins* draws from social history, a school of thought stemming from Marxism and economic history that stresses the importance of underlying economic and social forces for political changes: a rising gentry in the English Civil War, an emboldened bourgeoisie in the French Revolution. Owing to the diminished respect for the reigning scholarly orthodoxy brought on by World War I and the Depression, social history became highly influential during the interwar years, a critical period in the intellectual development of a generation of scholars.

In the following decades, social history shed much light on the origins of revolution, social movements, and political change. It became a new orthodoxy. But perhaps social history's influence came at the expense of a line of inquiry sketched by Max Weber, Otto Hintze, and Hans Delbrück, emphasizing the importance of military organization in history.[2] Drawing from their

---

[1] *Social Origins of Dictatorship and Democracy: Lord and Peasant in the Making of the Modern World* (Boston: Beacon Press, 1966). I thank Barrington Moore, Jr., for commenting on my work, indeed for inspiring my work. His scholarship has been a formidable standard for me, and now so is his magnanimity.

[2] Max Weber, *Economy and Society*, 2 vols., Guenther Roth and Claus Wittich, eds. (Berkeley and Los Angeles: University of California Press, 1978); Otto Hintze, *Die Hohenzollern und ihr Werk* (Berlin: Paul Parey, 1915); *Staat und Verfassung: Gesammelte Abhandlungen zur allge-*

example, I will explore the role military forces have played in the unfolding of democracy and dictatorship. I shall argue that warfare in the early modern period decisively patterned constitutional and autocratic outcomes as states responded not simply to warfare, but to the intensity of warfare and the degree of domestic resource mobilization. Six cases will be analyzed: Brandenburg-Prussia, France, England, Sweden, the Netherlands, and Poland. These countries were involved in varying levels of warfare, from the relatively light warfare of England to the extremely heavy, protracted conflicts of Prussia. They also had different political outcomes: the preservation of a constitutional state, its destruction and replacement with autocracy, and the loss of sovereignty. All six countries had roughly similar political arrangements at the outset of the early modern period, what shall be called here medieval constitutional government. In this political system, found throughout most of Europe excluding Russia and Castilian Spain, political power was shared, more or less equally, by the crown's chancery and the representative assembly of the nobility, burghers, and clerics, known variously as parliament, estates, cortes, and landtag. It is this nexus between the crown's executive and the estates' financial power where we find critical internal battles for the direction, form, and control of the state, as it responded to modern warfare.

An important impetus to political change stemmed from innovations in warfare spreading across Europe. The military revolution shifted the means of destruction from decentralized, self-equipped feudal armies, in the direction of large, centrally supplied ones—a portentous transition that shifted military matters almost exclusively onto the shoulders of the central state. Military innovations presented enormous pressures on states to find new means to finance these fantastically expensive war machines. This is the key to both conflict within the dualist political system and the rise of autocracy in early modern Europe.

Brandenburg-Prussia

It is convenient but inaccurate to view Prussia as always having been a military-centered state, "an army with a country" as the expression went. But the course of Prussian and German history meanders widely from the medieval period to the outset of the early modern period, from the rigid authority of the Teutonic Knights to the constitutional state of the sixteenth century, which in

---

meinen Verfassungsgeschichte Fritz Hartung, ed. (Leipzig: Koehler & Amelang, 1941); *Regierung und Verwaltung: Gesammelte Abhandlungen zur Staats-, Rechts-, und Sozialgeschichte Preussens,* Gerhard Oestreich ed. (Göttingen: Vandenhoeck & Ruprecht, 1967); Hans Delbrück, *History of the Art of War within the Framework of Political History,* 4 vols. (Westport, Conn.: Greenwood Press, 1975–1985).

critical ways resembled Whig England and hardly seemed a foundation for military absolutism. With the outbreak of the Thirty Years' War (1618–1648), the relative tranquility of the Baltic littoral was rudely shattered. Brandenburg was occupied by foreign troops, systematically exploited, and forced to cooperate with whichever army was currently camped there. Even after the Peace of Westphalia, tensions between Sweden and Poland placed Brandenburg in a most dangerous geopolitical position between two formidable powers.

In 1653, with war imminent, the Great Elector was able to cajole from the divided parliament sufficient funding for a modest army, in exchange for the confirmation of privileges, tax exemptions, and official recognition of serfdom. What had seemed to the estates to be an equitable quid pro quo actually shifted power irretrievably to the Elector by providing him the ultimate arbiter of constitutional conflicts, a standing army. The army cast the deciding vote in 1657 when the estates refused further funding. The crown proclaimed its right to levy taxes without the approval of the estates and began to deploy the army as collector. Protest became markedly more timid and was answered by terse references to the need for expediency.[3] Accounting to parliament was part of a past when the international order allowed such niceties. Neither the great issues of the day, nor even the small ones, would any longer be decided by parliamentary speeches and majority decisions.

The Great Elector's defeat of the estates is a familiar story that recounts only part of the destruction of constitutionalism in Prussia. The decline of the estates had as concomitant the rise of the cornerstone of Prussian military-bureaucratic absolutism, the *Generalkriegskommissariat*. In the middle of the seventeenth century it was charged with the administration, supply, and recruitment of the army; and, at least until the peace with Poland in 1660, it had the extraordinary mission of collecting tax revenues and budgeting its growing bureaus. But with new war against France in 1672, the Generalkriegskommissariat regained these functions, developed institutional autonomy from the privy council, and began its penetration into local government, and later into virtually every component of civil society and individual life.

The Generalkriegskommissariat established a complex administrative apparatus with its central command in Berlin.[4] Its original duties of collecting taxes were soon expanded into administrative and judicial areas. The state assumed control of aspects of the judiciary, attained a preponderant voice in determining the mayors, supervised the police forces, and otherwise managed

---

[3] See Fritz Hartung, *Deutsche Verfassungsgeschichte vom 15. Jahrhundert bis zur Gegenwart* (Leipzig: B. G. Teubner, 1914), pp. 59–61; Gustav Schmoller, "Die Entstehung des preußischen Heeres von 1640 bis 1740," in Otto Büsch and Wolfgang Neugebauer, eds., *Moderne Preußische Geschichte, 1648–1947: Eine Anthologie*, Band II (Berlin: Walter de Gruyter, 1981), pp. 751–58.

[4] Ott. Hintze, "Der Commissarius und seine Bedeutung in der allgemeinen Verwaltungsgeschichte," in *Staat und Verfassung: Gesammelte Abhandlungen zur allgemeinen Verfassungsgeschichte*, Fritz Hartung, ed. (Leipzig: Koehler & Amelang, 1941), pp. 233–35.

town affairs. The peasantry was inducted into a system of active and reserve duty (*Kantonsystem*). Local government in the countryside fared no better. Whereas local affairs had been handled by regional bodies (*Kreisdirektoren*), these were absorbed by state commissars into the *Landräte*, which acted as Berlin's overseer in the provinces (managing the police, maintaining bridges and roadways, and surveilling the local nobles) but which, ironically, also afforded the nobles a measure of articulation and politicking. The Landräte provided a forum for the expression and protection of local interests vis-à-vis the state, especially during times of state weakness. It is necessary to bear this in mind to prevent conceptualizing the seventeenth-century Prussian state as an early form of totalitarianism. Despite the preponderance of state power, a measure of politics went on, especially at the local level. The state relied heavily on the nobility and allowed a measure of local control as long as control over taxation and the army was in its hands. Absolutism was never absolute.[5]

The mobilization of the population and economic resources begun by the Great Elector was the first phase of the state's assumption of a managerial position vis-à-vis civil society. The dearth of resources in Prussia required the scope and intensity of this managerialism to be extensive. Accordingly, the state began to squeeze out scarce resources, to determine more efficient methods of extraction, and also to develop or seize additional resources— commercial enterprises or adjacent territories. These resources would add to the coffers of the state and its institutional core, the army, through its bu- reaucratic arm, the Generalkriegskommissariat. The principal reason for eco- nomic management lay in war and preparation for it. Engineers, architects, and scientists were organized into a state academy through which the state could better stimulate and control the Prussian economy. The state built roads, bridges, and canals to facilitate communication and troop movements. English agricultural techniques (*verbesserte Englische Wirtschaft*) were studied by the appropriate ministry, and practiced on the crown's demesne before being introduced onto the manors of the kingdom. Protection of the nascent textile and metallurgical industries began as early as 1684 and continued throughout the next centuries as new industries critical to military power emerged. State ownership of industry and investment in new factories, banks, and mines were routine.[6]

[5] See Reinhart Koselleck, *Preußen zwischen Reform und Revolution: Allgemeines Landrecht, Verwaltung und soziale Bewgung von 1791 bis 1848* (Stuttgart: Ernst Klett Verlag, 1967); Robert M. Berdahl, "The Stände and the Origins of Conservatism in Prussia," *Eighteenth Century Studies* 6 (1973): 298–321; Robert M. Berdahl, *The Politics of the Prussian Nobility: The Development of a Conservative Ideology, 1770–1848* (Princeton: Princeton University Press, 1988), passim; Hartung, *Deutsche Verfassungsgeschichte*, pp. 67–68.

[6] W. O. Henderson, *Studies in the Economic Policy of Frederick the Great* (London: Frank Cass, 1963), pp. 2–7, 17–37, 157–59; Geoffrey Parker, *The Military Revolution: Military Innovation and the Rise of the West, 1500–1800* (Cambridge: Cambridge University Press, 1988), pp. 148–49; Hartung, *Deutsche Verfassungsgeschichte*, pp. 65–72; Hans-Heinrich

Managerialism had many intriguing aspects. Beginning in the early eighteenth century, and continuing into the next, the state enacted numerous laws and regulations aimed at preserving the social position of the peasantry. These *Bauernschutz* laws aimed to protect the peasant from increased demands of his lord in the latter's attempts to expand his manors at the expense of the peasantry. Driving a peasant from his small plot was treated with the same gravity as if the lord had driven him to desert from his regiment. The aim of these laws was not ultimately the protection of the peasantry, or even the prevention of aggrandizement by the nobility; rather they aimed at preserving a social and economic order that extracted revenues from the peasantry to pay for the military, an order that had to be maintained in a dangerous geopolitical situation. The Great Elector and his successors directed the resources of the state to matters of public sanitation, the suppression of quackery, and even to modest efforts at public education, activities which preceded similar efforts elsewhere in Europe by a full century. Owing to its extensive stockpiles of grain in the event of war, the state was able to regulate food prices. Thus to some extent, the origins of the welfare state lie in war.[7]

Resource mobilization for wars of the seventeenth century was quite high in Brandenburg-Prussia. This destroyed the constitutional state and set into motion the development of military-bureaucratic absolutism, closely allied to the nobility and the beholden middle classes. Fundamental political change in military-bureaucratic absolutisms comes only from massive peasant revolution, complete military defeat, fiscal collapse, or deep alienation of elite social classes—dangerous political situations that Prussia (but as will be seen, not France) was able to avoid. Nineteenth-century reforms brought a measure of constitutional propriety, but, in essence, Germany remained a military-bureaucratic state until the collapse of the old regime at the close of the First World War.

France

Brandenburg-Prussia and France, oddly enough for such long-standing enemies, have much in common. By the end of the seventeenth century they

Müller, "Domänen und Dömanenpächter in Brandenburg-Preussen im 18. Jahrhundert," in Büsch and Neugebauer, eds., 1: 316–59; Hugo Rachel, "Merkantilismus in Brandenburg-Preußen," in Büsch and Neugebauer, eds., 2: 951–93; for the nineteenth century see Ulrich Peter Ritter, "Preußische Gewerbeförderung in früh-industrieller Zeit," in Büsch and Neugebauer, eds., 2: 1031–87.

[7] Ott. Büsch, *Militärsystem und Sozialleben im Alten Preussen, 1713–1807: Die Anfänge der sozialen Militarisierung der preußisch-deutschen Gesellschaft* (Berlin: Walter de Gruyter, 1962), pp. 72–73; Martin A. Kitchen, *Military History of Germany from the Eighteenth Century to the Present* (Bloomington: Indiana University Press, 1975), pp. 12–13; Reinhold August Dorwart, *The Prussian Welfare State before 1740* (Cambridge, Mass.: Harvard University Press), 1971, pp. 77–90.

resembled each other in significant ways. Each had faced serious wars in the mid-seventeenth century, which required domestic resource mobilization. Each had set aside constitutionalism and built centralized state structures that levied and collected taxes without the approval of the estates. French political change came with the Thirty Years' War (1618–48), which began as a dispute between the estates of Bohemia and the Holy Roman Empire, but swiftly escalated into a conflict raging across much of Europe. France, however, avoided direct involvement during the first half of the war, limiting itself to subsidizing the Swedes, whose timely landing in Pomerania (1630) stalemated Habsburg forces, and, for the moment, secured French interests.

When Spain soundly defeated the Swedes at Nördlingen in 1634, France had to enter the war or face the prospect of Habsburg hegemony, if not rule. But its army had grown only slowly since the religious wars of the previous century. The army was small, ill-trained, and ill-equipped compared to the Hapsburg forces now just to the east. Enormous revenues were necessary to pay, train, and supply a modern army, and the absence of allies, vast commercial wealth, or topographical obstacles to invaders dictated that money be extracted from domestic sources. Military expenditures went up by two-thirds in the year after Nördlingen.[8]

New taxes and political institutions came into direct and fierce conflict with the estates, *parlements*, and town councils of French constitutionalism. The agent of systematic extraction was the corps of intendants that had begun to appear in the provinces in the late sixteenth century, but whose numbers, functions, and unpopularity shot up dramatically as extraction accelerated. In 1636 the intendants used the military to collect forced loans in the *pays d'elections;* two years later, new taxes earmarked for the army were forcibly levied and collected in the *pays d'états* as well as in the *pays d'elections*. Five years later, a sales tax was levied without approval from the estates, effectively ending the constitutional distinctions of the fifteenth-century tax system in the two *pays*. The ruthless efficiency of the intendants is attested to by the increase in French military expenditures, rising sharply from 41 million livres in 1630 to 108 million in 1636.[9]

---

[8] Richard Bonney, *Political Change in France under Richhiew and Mazarin 1624–1661* (Oxford: Oxford University Press, 1978), pp. 42ff; and R. J. Bonney, *The King's Debts: Finance and Politics in France, 1589–1661* (Oxford: Clarendon Press, 1981), pp. 172–73.

[9] R. J. Bonney, *The King's Debts: Finance and Politics in France, 1589–1661* (Oxford: Oxford University Press, 1981), pp. 172–73; Parker, *The Thirty Years' War*, p. 150; Bonney, *Political Change*, pp. 42–46; Roland Mousnier, *The Institutions of France under the Absolute Monarchy, 1598–1789*, vol. 2: *The Organs of State and Society* (Chicago: University of Chicago Press, 1979), pp. 502–27; William Beik, *Absolutism and Society in Seventeenth-Century France: State Power and Provincial Aristocracy in Languedoc* (Cambridge: Cambridge University Press, 1985), pp. 131–46.

Protests against the state's breach of custom and privilege were met by Séquier's justification based on the principle of reason of state. The intendants, he said in blunt contemporary French, "exécutent dans les provinces des edictz qui n'ont point esté enregistrée au Parlement, edictz que la necessité publique de l'estat rend necessaire."[10] The parlements' judicial duties were partially arrogated by the intendants, as cases stemming from laws against treason and tax evasion came under their purview. Town guilds, banks, tax collectors and other administrators came under the control of the intendant, who was also acquiring considerable influence in the outcomes of municipal elections. Intendants further penetrated French society by assuming control of the ante-diluvian military levies (ban, and arrière ban) as well as a new, more modern militia. They conscripted peasants, attached them to regular army units, and deployed them far from the unfortunate conscripts' villages. Intendants quartered troops in their areas of responsibility and supplied them upon their return from foreign campaigns. In times of need, of which there were many, they were empowered to appropriate means of transport as well as the labor of their owners.[11]

The need for war resources led to a program of economic development directed by one of Louis XIV's many brilliant ministers. What Vauban and LeTellier had been for the army, Jean Baptiste Colbert was for the economy and the navy. Prior to Colbert's appointment in 1661 the state had only a few programs of economic protection and regulation, though they increased somewhat during the early years of the Thirty Years' War. But with full involvement in wars against mighty coalitions, the economy had to be stimulated to support an army that reached 290,000 by the early eighteenth century. Colbert directed subsidies to industry, gave tax exemptions to others (especially those in backward provinces), and imported Dutch and Swedish engineers to boost French mineralogical production. He lured skilled foreign workers to add to France's human capital, and used colonies as closed markets to foster national industry. Centuries before a Japanese ministry enacted similar policies, Colbert's ministry regulated the quality of national products and exports.

The French state enacted ambitious legal and economic programs, often thought to be the creation of the bourgeoisie or the Revolution. Colbert

[10] The intendants "execute in the provinces edicts that have not at all been registered by Parlement, edicts that the public necessity of state make necessary" (my translation). Quoted in Bonney, *Political Change,* p. 246.

[11] Douglas Clark Baxter, *Servants of the Sword: French Intendants of the Army 1630–70* (Urbana: University of Illinois Press, 1976), pp. 68–71; Mousnier, *Institutions of France,* 1: 429–75; Mousnier, *Institutions of France,* 2: 512–38; Bonney, *Political Change,* pp. 244–58, 318–43; André Corvisier, *L'Armée Française de la fin du XVIIe siècle au ministère de Choiseul, Le Soldat,* Tome Premier (Paris: Presses Universitaires de France, 1964), pp. 109–231. Though considerable, the intendants' power was not unlimited. Local notables were consulted and often mollified to prevent the coalescence of local opposition into rebellion. Once again, absolutism was never absolute. See William Beik, *Absolutism and Society,* pp. 98–116.

restructured much of civil law until France had national laws on contract, trade policies, bankruptcy, and even bookkeeping. It was also the policy of the Colbert ministry to construct an integrated, national market by means of a system of roads, bridges, and canals that linked various parts of the nation together, especially those recently acquired through conquest. It is important to emphasize that this integration was not a consequence, intended or unintended, of economic programs and laws advocated by the middle classes, rather it was the result of the state's intention to develop an economy to support and expand the army. The centerpiece of Colbertian mercantilism was the stimulation of national trade. Growth in international commerce would benefit domestic industries, the state's revenues, and of course its war making capacity, the ultimate end never far from the ministry's helmsman. The links among trade, finance, and war-making are probably best expressed by Colbert himself: "Trade is the source of finance and finance is the vital nerve of war."[12]

The genesis and organization of the Prussian and French states bear similarities, but further comparisons reveal substantial differences affecting their long-run stability—French absolutism collapsed in 1789 while its Prussian rival endured in some form until 1918. What were the key fissures that made the French state fall apart in 1789?

First of all, there was fiscal insolvency. Louis's wars were costly, largely unsuccessful, and perhaps even foolhardy. It is wry commentary on his overreaching ambitions that after a century of internecine warfare, bitter enemies across Europe could settle differences and ally themselves against France. War left France a disastrous diplomatic legacy with almost all the European powers aligned against it; but its fiscal system, the sinews of war as the expression went, was serviceable at the time of Louis's death in 1715. Despite his deathbed lament of having waged war too much, his successors were only a little less bellicose: the national budget of 1752, a period of relative calm between wars, allocated 42 percent of expenditures to the military, and, ominously, another 21 percent to debt servicing. But it was the Seven Years' War (1756–63) that led to the loss of colonial revenue and to the penultimate debt crisis, which was soon followed by another crisis from financing the American colonial revolt. Its sinews diminishing, the French state atrophied and struggled to find new sources of revenue, only to find itself challenged by social classes and institutions emboldened by state weakness.

---

12 Quoted in Edward Mead Earle, "Adam Smith, Alexander Hamilton, Friedrich List: The Economic Foundations of Military Power," in Peter Paret, ed., *Makers of Modern Strategy from Machiavelli to the Nuclear Age* (Princeton: Princeton University Press, 1986), p. 217; see also Charles Woolsey Cole, *Colbert and a Century of French Mercantilism*, 2 vols. (Morningside Heights, N. Y.: Columbia University Press, 1939), 1:102–64, 312–83; 2:363–463. Cf. Perry Anderson's account of the western absolutist state's relation to legal and economic integration in *Lineages of the Absolutist State* (London: Verso, 1974), pp. 1–42.

First among these classes was the aristocracy whose political acquiescence had come at the price of the state's continuation of an anachronistic system of privileges. When new fiscal needs led to royal challenges of these anachronisms, the noblesse vociferously opposed reform and used its considerable presence in the state to block it, leading to further paralysis. The aristocracy's use of political institutions within the central state was followed by the resurrection of the old parlements and provincial estates. The French aristocracy was more than a powerful class, it was a class with considerable influence, if not control, over numerous, independent political institutions in virtually every corner of France. Kept well in check while monarchal power was strong, surviving components of constitutional government such as the provincial estates and parlements found new courage as Bourbon power declined.

A third difference between France and Prussia was the capacity for large-scale peasant rebellion. This capacity was extremely low in the the Prussian case owing to the destruction of autonomous village government in the course of agrarian commercialization, close administrative control by seigneurs and agents of the Kantonsystem, and internal stratifications dividing the peasantry. But in the French countryside neither intendants nor seigneurs undermined village government. Landed elites gave peasants leeway in their administration and agricultural production, preferring instead simply to squeeze out rents and dues. Intendants found village government an efficient tax-collection instrument: by utilizing peasant communal institutions, village defaults could be compensated by suing wealthy peasants, and the costs of determining tax obligations and prosecuting cheaters were shifted onto village elders. Intendant interaction with the peasants even served to weaken seigneurial control over their former fiefs and the villeins on them.[13] Thus, autonomous peasant organizations and a relative absence of outside administrative control contrasted markedly with the East Elbian serfs, whose village government had been utterly crushed in the course of the manorial reaction. Revolutionary capacity was furthered by the relatively unstratified nature of the French peasantry. When combined with the common experience of increasing seigneurial exploitation, a hostile, unified class was created.[14] As the state's repressive capacity decreased, peasant rebellions spread throughout France, shattering what remained of state coherence in the provinces. Thus, owing to fiscal overextension brought on by injudicious use of military resources, by the

[13] See Mousnier, *Institutions of France*, 1:559–61; Hilton R. Root, *Peasants and King in Burgundy: Agrarian Foundations of French Absolutism* (Berkeley and Los Angeles: University of California Press, 1987), pp. 28–33, 45–65.

[14] Albert Soboul, "The French Rural Community in the Eighteenth and Nineteenth Centuries," *Past and Present* 10 (1956): 84. On Prussian peasant stratification see Marion W. Gray, "Prussia in Transition: Society and Politics under the Stein Reform Ministry of 1808," *Transactions of the American Philosophical Society* 76, pt. 1 (1986): 19–21; Berdahl, *The Politics of the Prussian Nobility*, pp. 28–43.

survival of the political institutions of an independent noblesse, and by the peasantry's capacity for widespread revolt, French military-bureaucratic absolutism lacked the capacity for maintaining itself into the nineteenth century.

Military-bureaucratic absolutism had fallen and constitutional institutions reemerged, but new state forms had yet to develop. The events of the revolutionary period led to new divisions, exacerbated old ones, and created antagonisms across many levels—class, religion, and region—of French society. Peasant seized noble lands, destroyed chateaus, and murdered thousands of people. Regional revolts were repressed, often with the use of military force, leaving enduring hatred for central power, irrespective of whether the tricoleur or fleur-de-lis flew on its guidons. Thousands of nobles were executed on the orders of the Committee for Public Safety leading to lasting enmity between the aristocracy and the middle class, which composed the leadership of the Terror. Anticlericalism erupted as Church lands were seized, the feudal privileges of the ecclesiastical estate were abolished, and peasants vented their hatred on clerical seigneurs.

Animosities were assuaged only briefly and partially by the intoxicating unity engendered by Napoleon's spectacular victories. But with ultimate defeat in 1815, animosities resurfaced and became lasting parts of French political life, reinforced by many ensuing military debacles. All of this precluded fundamental trust, broad-based parties, and viable coalitions. French politics lurched from constitutions aimed at excluding all but one group, to those requiring coalitions between two or more social groups. Both in and out of the national assembly, consensus and trust eluded political institutions. Related to these social divisions was the rapid politicization of virtually all segments of French society. The retention of political power within the hands of the state ministries was swiftly followed by the broadening of political activity by not only the parlements, estates, and the Estates-General, but also by numerous other institutions and most of the general public. During the early phases of the Revolution, parlements and the Estates-General mobilized popular support to bolster their hand in the struggle against autocracy. In the heady days of 1789, when old processes of government had fallen and new ones had yet to take form, popular assemblies reemerged even below the provincial level in many villages.[15] In order to sustain the Revolution's more radical phases, the leadership mobilized the urban lower classes and used them to intimidate conservative elements who favored a more limited revolutionary agenda. Napoleon contributed to this widespread politicization of the masses

[15] Jean-Paul Bertaud, *The Army of the French Revolution*, trans. R. R. Palmer (Princeton: Princeton University Press, 1988); Richard Cobb, *The People's Armies:* The armées revolutionnaires: *Instrument of the Terror in the Departments, April 1793 to Floréal Year II,* trans. by Marianne Elliott (New Haven, Conn.: Yale University Press, 1987).

by using newspapers, architecture, and even the arts to impress political and military goals on the public.[16]

A further mechanism of mass mobilization of the period was the army itself. France's mass army, numbering 700,000 strong in 1794, could not be drilled and trained as methodically as prevailing military doctrines held. Instead, the army relied on political indoctrination—raising the soldier's political consciousness and convincing him that he, a citizen of the new Republic, had a stake in the war's outcome—in the hope that such indoctrination would compensate for the lack of drill. Efficacy in battle would be based on an inner sense of patriotic and moral duty, rather than on rote and fear.[17] Frenchmen were transformed from passive subjects to citizens with rights and political expectations with which they would not part easily. Hence, when settlements in 1815 and 1830 sought to impose a political system based on a narrow franchise, one that favored the aristocracy, slighted the middle classes, and completely ignored the lower classes, class antagonisms and popular restiveness could be held in check only temporarily, until these governments fell when faced by popular insurrection. The 1848 attempt at government based on universal suffrage led only to the inability to find a stable consensus, to military intervention, and to a form of authoritarian government that shrewdly discharged popular passions by means of military adventurism and plebiscitary spectacles.

The Revolution's significance for political developments was two-fold. It engendered popular mobilizations and hostilities that plagued French politics for generations to come, but perhaps more importantly, it also destroyed or at least partially dismantled military and bureaucratic organs that dominated politics and much of the economy. In so much as Bourbon absolutism's fall at least made an eventual liberal outcome a possibility, the Revolution's legacy, stripped of the mythology and sentimentality surrounding it, was a mixed one that entailed opportunities as well as millstones. Its significance for constitutional development, though, is clear: military-bureaucratic absolutism was gone, replaced by a state that, although intrusive and rather authoritarian, was nonetheless one unable to restore the monolithic edifice of Louis. France had to make do with stumbling along with its vociferous, unmanageable populace until a viable polity embracing principles of constitutionalism could be made.

---

[16] Alfred Cobban, *A History of Modern France*, vol. 2, *From the First Empire to the Second Empire 1799–1871* (Harmondsworth: Penguin Books, 1986), pp. 36–38; Maurice Agulhon, *Marianne into Battle: Republican Imagery and Symbolism in France, 1789–1880*, trans. Janet Lloyd (Cambridge: Cambridge University Press, 1979), pp. 1–37.

[17] Gunther E. Rothenberg, *The Art of Warfare in the Age of Napoleon* (Bloomington: Indiana University Press, 1981), pp. 94–114.

England

Protected somewhat by its insular position, England nonetheless took part in many European conflicts. War, or conflict just short of it, took place with France over the Huguenot affair, and with Spain as it sought to reassert control over the Netherlands. In addition, in the 1640s, England was involved in a civil war. Most of these struggles were, by European standards, rather brief, and did not require high levels of resource mobilization. Accordingly, state innovation was comparatively light. Constitutional government persisted to become the basis for modern democracy.

Henry VIII led armies onto the continent on several occasions: in 1513 he stood at the head of 31,000 soldiers, and on later campaigns (1544–46) 52,000. These levels are a bit larger than feudal levies, but much smaller than the armies Spain was beginning to field. Nor were they professional soldiers, or even knights or drilled militias. Henry's force was little more than a rapidly put together collection of freebooters and dregs augmented by a few thousand German mercenaries. Neither gunpowder nor even the pike made serious inroads into the English armories of the sixteenth century.

Elizabeth's wars with France and Spain had only slightly more political significance. Modern cavalry and infantry (pikemen) were introduced but did not become the standard. Expeditionary forces were rapidly assembled as war clouds loomed and then rapidly disbanded on war's end. Neither quantitative changes nor substantive state centralization are in evidence. Elizabeth had placed officials (Lord-Lieutenants) in the counties to supervise the militias, but, as was the case with the Justices of the Peace, they were appointed only after consultation with local notables. Other than this, the "Catholic threat" led only to the construction of a beacon system and the placing of batteries in coastal communities. At a time when the military revolution began to sweep Europe, Parliament enacted laws encouraging Englishmen to hone their martial skills with the longbow. Some militia units (trained bands) received a measure of modern training and weaponry, but military reform was only half-hearted, and would remain so for quite some time.[18]

It is well known to anyone familiar with swashbuckling adventure stories that much of English warfare was fought on the high seas. Again, however, we find no immense expenditure or state expansion. The basis of the Elizabethan fleets that defeated those of Spain and interdicted its colonial commerce lay not in an admiralty commanding state-financed ships of the line, rather it lay in independent privateers. During almost two decades of naval strife with Spain

---

[18] Gilbert John Millar, *Tudor Mercenaries and Auxiliaries, 1485–1547* (Charlottesville: University of Virginia Press, 1980), pp. 44–48; Sir Charles Oman, *A History of the Art of War in the Sixteenth Century* (New York: E. P. Dutton, 1937), pp. 320–48; Lindsay Boynton, *The Elizabethan Militia, 1558–1658* (Toronto: University of Toronto Press, 1967), pp. 145 ff.

(1585–1603) England spent only about £55,000 per annum on its naval forces, which, to provide perspective, would furnish only 18,000 footsoldiers with pike and armor, but not with food, clothing, and other necessities. Spain spent approximately 10 million ducats (4 ducats = £1) on the Armada alone, and over 2 million ducats per year fighting the rebellion in the Netherlands. Privateers proved quite successful in preventing French and Spanish land forces (whose superiority was above question) from swiftly and catastrophically demonstrating the backwardness of the English military. England made do with only a small army and navy. Military expenditures were not high and were paid for by routine means within the constitutional framework.[19]

Though England was able to remain largely uninvolved in the Thirty Years' War, constitutional conflicts nonetheless developed, foreshadowing those of the Civil War (1642–48). The breakdown of constitutional government from 1640 to 1642 led to open warfare between king and Parliament, and, perversely, to centralizing intrusions on the part of Parliament. Charles's army was cut off from traditional sources of revenue granted by Parliament. He arranged a daughter's marriage to the Prince of Orange's son in the hope that he could draw upon the Netherlands' considerable resources, but in this he was disappointed: the Dutch merchant elite would not risk disrupting commerce. He fielded an army funded by taxes levied in occupied counties, generous donations from supporters, and the sale of sequestered estates of Parliamentary supporters. Despite this, the royalist army remained small, poorly equipped, and infrequently paid; only unity of purpose and initial command superiority prevented a shorter war.[20] Owing to the nature of the war, king against Parliament, there were no constitutional disputes over resource mobilization, but rather the question became how would Parliament, unaccustomed to execu-

[19] H. W. Richmond, *Statesmen and Sea Power* (Oxford: Oxford University Press, 1946), cited in Paul M. Kennedy, *The Rise and Fall of British Naval Mastery* (London: The Ashfield Press, 1987), p. 26; Geoffrey Parker, *Philip II* (Boston: Little, Brown, 1978), p. 178; Parker, *The Army of Flanders and the Spanish Road, 1567–1659* (Cambridge: Cambridge University Press, 1972), pp. 48–49; Kenneth R. Andrews, *Elizabethan Privateering: English Privateering during the Spanish War, 1585–1603* (Cambridge: Cambridge University Press, 1964); idem., *Trade Plunder and Settlement: Maritime Enterprise and the Genesis of the British Empire, 1480–1630* (Cambridge: Cambridge University Press, 1984), pp. 223–55; Kennedy, *British Naval Mastery,* pp. 24–35; R. B. Wernham, *After the Armada: Elizabethan England and the Struggle for Western Europe 1588–1595* (Oxford: Clarendon Press, 1984), pp. 235–61.

[20] Ronald Hutton, *The Royalist War Effort, 1642–1646* (London: Longman, 1982), pp. 86–94; Peter Young, *The Cavalier Army: Its Organization and Everyday Life* (London: George Allen and Unwin, 1974); David Underdown, *Revel, Riot, and Rebellion: Popular Politics and Culture in England, 1603–1660* (Oxford: Oxford University Press, 1987), pp. 208–38. For a general military history of the conflict see J. P. Kenyon, *The Civil Wars of England* (New York: Knopf, 1988), pp. 48–157; J. F. C. Fuller, *A Military History of the Western World,* vol. 2, *From the Defeat of the Spanish Armada to the Battle of Waterloo* (New York: Da Capo, 1955), pp. 85–117.

tive leadership, handle even light mobilization, let alone day-to-day governmental affairs?

Despite four years of war with the king, Parliamentary forces underwent no military revolution as experienced by continental armies, especially in terms of size. Early failures led to the creation of the New Model Army, whose principal reforms were the dearistocratization of most military commands and the creation of well-organized tactical units patterned after Cromwell's regiment. The New Model, however, never reached the 21,000 men authorized by Parliament; its finances and logistics never attained any level of regularity or coherence. No extraparliamentary source of income or central command structure developed during the Civil War. Indeed, there were serious impediments to the development of a powerful organ like that of continental absolutisms. First, along with dearistocratization came Parliamentary politicking over commissions in the New Model; various constituencies, social classes, and religions had to be mollified by awarding them high posts. Owing to the tactical requirements of the war, forces were geographically dispersed and tactically independent, precluding the development of command structures at higher levels. The Council of War (comprising senior military persons) had only minor organizational growth in the course of the war. In any event, it was always beholden to Parliament, which maintained not only power of the purse, but also control of war strategy.[21]

It is one of the twists of the war that Parliament itself adopted unseemly, authoritarian measures to finance the war, measures often lost in the gradualist, unilinear sweeps of English history, but which fall short of absolutism. Parliamentary revenue was initially predicated on control of commercial centers in the south, including the customs collection offices that were the traditional sources of revenue, but as the war dragged on, commerce and revenue declined, requiring new sources of revenue. In 1642, quite early in the war, both Houses authorized the confiscation and sale of royalist property, as well as taxation to be collected forcibly if need be, which was the case. County Committees were set up in the country, where they interfered with elections, quartered troops, and otherwise meddled in local affairs, disaffecting both local notables and the populace as a whole. Parliament came to infringe upon the constitution more than any Stuart monarch dared. Thus, we have an agonizingly convoluted situation that recalls the words of an American officer in a different but no less convoluted war: in order to preserve the constitution, it was necessary to destroy it, or at least certain parts of it.

But English constitutionalism was not demolished; military-bureaucratic absolutism was not in the offing. Even during the 1650s, when England was at

---

[21] Mark A. Kishlansky, *The Rise of the New Model Army* (Cambridge: Cambridge University Press, 1983), pp. 41–69.

war with Scotland, the Dutch Republic, and Spain, and the army swelled to 70,000 men, we find on the Parliamentary side no autocrat reigning above the law. Local autonomy was not completely or even substantially eliminated; there was, on the other hand, an uncomfortable duality in the country. The rationale for these authoritarian measures lay not in a sustained external threat—Scotland was swiftly defeated by the New Model, and the other wars were naval duels—but from a transient internal threat and attendant unrest. Finally and most importantly, Parliament was still intact and in control. Seizures and privations had been done in its name, through constitutional means (save of course royal approval), and by men who had been elected.

With the war's end came loss of Parliamentary unity; dissension and factionalism erupted. Collapse was avoided only by Pride's Purge (1648), which dismissed many MPs, and ushered in the rule of Cromwell in conjunction with the purged Parliament (or Rump) and later nominated Parliaments.[22] Conflict between Parliament and the country was aggravated, as the Rump, whose linkage to the counties and towns was weaker following the purge, sought to return order to a land wracked by depression, unemployment, inflation, and near famine. The only answer seemed to lie in central control. Many recalcitrant sheriffs, JPs, and even County Committees were replaced on order of the Rump, which was dominated by radical Puritans. Local militias as well as other aspects of traditional local life came under the watch of Cromwell's major generals, who the normally egalitarian Christopher Hill says were "lowborn upstarts, many [of whom] came from outside the county: all had troops of horse behind them to make their commands effective."[23]

Was this, then, military-bureaucratic absolutism? Again, the policies and institutions of Cromwell and the purged Parliaments fall short. First of all, the Rump, Barebones (1653), and later Protectorate Parliaments (1653–60) were nonetheless Parliaments, and Cromwell never ruled or taxed without them. They were not ideally representative bodies—what early modern estates was? But neither were they autocratical bureaucracies or rubber stamps. Interest articulation and regional voice were still proffered: the intrusiveness of the major generals was reined in after Parliamentary opposition became clear. Perhaps the clearest evidence of the independence of the Protectorate Parliaments is the fact that Cromwell had alternately to dissolve and convoke so many. The political history of the Protectorate is one of continuous conflict between the Lord Protector and Parliament over a constitutional settlement,

---

[22] Kishlansky, *New Model Army*, pp. 105–38; David Underdown, *Pride's Purge: Politics in the Puritan Revolution* (Oxford: Clarendon Press, 1971), pp. 258–59.

[23] Christopher Hill, *God's Englishman: Oliver Cromwell and the English Revolution* (New York: Harper & Row, 1972), p. 175. See also Underdown, *Pride's Purge,* pp. 292–303; Derek Hirst, *Authority and Conflict: England, 1603–1658* (Cambridge, Mass.: Harvard University Press), pp. 337–39.

with Cromwell relenting on many points. War needs were met by Parliamentary subsidy, loans, and naval booty and a little arm-twisting of local committees. Cromwell never resorted to abolishing representative government and local autonomy. Second, while many local officials had been replaced by Whitehall, many more remained in place, either silently acquiescing, or dragging their feet. Local autonomy had been damaged in some areas, compromised in others, but it survived the upheavals of the war and its aftermath. The extent of penetration does not compare with that of Brandenburg-Prussia or Bourbon France. Third, it is important to remember that intrusions stemmed not from the needs of protracted war that required a permanent local presence, but from the short-lived need for order after a decade of havoc. Finally, and perhaps most importantly, the government of the 1650s never built self-generating bureaucratic machinery. Nor did it have a stable autocratic center to provide an element of continuity, only the increasingly chaotic House of Commons. The Lord Protector's death in 1658 led to a succession of directionless Parliaments and ultimately to a Stuart Restoration two years later, which essentially restored the constitutional order of king and parliament.[24]

England was spared the heavy warfare that raged on the continent and its state experienced no Prussian-style expansion, only transient agencies charged with quelling disorder and maintaining some central authority, all of which were soon dismantled. At the end of the civil war period the state remained rather archaic by the standards of the day, but a constitutional form of government remained.

Sweden

The Swedish case illustrates that the linkage between modern warfare and the destruction of medieval constitutionalism is not a direct one. Domestic resource mobilization has been decisive. Brandenburg-Prussia and France mobilized their own resources for war and replaced constitutional government with absolutist bureaucracies. Spared protracted war for most of the seventeenth century, England maintained a constitutional trajectory. During the Thirty Years' War, Sweden was able to avail itself of sufficient resources in Germany to obviate the need to mobilize its own army, also obviating pressures to build extractive state machinery. But Sweden's constitutional state encountered another threat from a Caesarist form of absolutism mixing mili-

[24] Hirst, *Authority and Conflict*, pp. 343–56; G. E. Aylmer, *The State's Servants: The Civil Service of the English Republic, 1649–1660* (London: Routledge & Kegan Paul, 1973), pp. 48–49, 305–17; Russell, *Crisis of Parliaments*, pp. 390–96. Aylmer, no Cromwell sympathizer, states that the 1654 elections were as free as any in the century; see *Rebellion or Revolution? England, 1640–1660* (New York: Oxford University Press), pp. 161–89.

tarism and populism. Thus, a second period, that of Caroline absolutism, will be examined here. Like Cromwell's rule in England, this period featured some trappings of autocracy, but it was by no means a military-bureaucratic absolutism. Constitutional institutions existed alongside the monarchy and were critical in supporting the crown. When Charles XII attempted to move towards firmer control, that is, in the direction of military-bureaucratic absolutism, constitutional forces humbled the monarch, and redirected the nation back in the direction of constitutionalism.

In the seventeenth century, Sweden entered the struggles for continental mastery and became one of the principals in the Thirty Years' War. It fielded huge armies and defeated or deadlocked the great military powers of the day without mobilizing its own resources. Instead, the Hammer of Europe, as it was fearfully called, relied mainly on mobilizing the resources of foreign territories and, to a lesser extent, on alliances with and subsidies from common Habsburg foes.[25] Sweden fielded armies as large as 175,000 troops for eighteen years of war against the combined might of Austria, Spain, and the Catholic League, yet domestic resource mobilization was light. The crown sold substantial amounts of its land holdings, but these revenues were inadequate. Swedish military success was based on availing itself of resources in foreign lands.

A major source of revenue came from Sweden's control of the Baltic ports, through which the West's grain was shipped. A truce worked out between Sweden and Poland enabled the former to levy tolls on ships engaged in the lucrative Baltic grain trade. The income derived was formidable and collected with little effort. But Germany would pay in other ways as well. Swedish quartermasters were highly skilled at determining the wealth of a region, then systematically organizing and appropriating it. Such were the extractions of the army in Germany that Swedish domestic taxation declined during the Thirty Years' War.

The impact of war on the Swedish state was light but nonetheless deserves some description, for the military campaigns did leave some mark. There were pressures but they were not strong, and they encountered stiff opposition from constitutional organs. The state apparatus wielded by Gustavus Adolphus at the outset of his reign in 1611 was anything but impressive; there had been no organizational innovation in the executive since the 1540s. There were neither clear procedures nor differentiated ministries. The Swedish state at the beginning of the Thirty Years' War was a "mass of unborn departments, incapable itself of generating the energy to keep its own business in plausible vibra-

---

[25] On Sweden's remarkable military campaigns see C. V. Wedgwood, *The Thirty Years War* (Garden City, N. Y.: Anchor, 1961), pp. 259ff; Parker, *The Thirty Years War*, pp. 121ff; Günter Barudio, *Der Teutsche Krieg, 1618–1648* (Franfurt am Main: S. Fischer, 1985), pp. 356–415.

tion."[26] The continental wars proved to be the midwife for the mass of unborn departments. At the time of the intervention in the Thirty Years' War, a war council was created and charged with recruiting and outfitting the military. It operated within the confines of the chancery and never attained institutional predominance there, nor did it become autonomous of the parliamentary committees. The *krigsrätt*, like the exchequer and other newly solidifying ministries, was being staffed not from a military elite or subaltern middle classes, but principally from the ranks of the nobility and clergy, whose close ties to the riksdag precluded militarization of state and society.[27]

The war's most significant impact was in the localities, but even here it was rather light due to the strength of popular government and to the limited nature of domestic resource mobilization. The weak bailiff system was overhauled and systematized as national taxation and recruitment required greater efficiency in local administration. But whereas the French intendants and the Prussian kommissariats wrested local control from traditional systems and subordinated them, Sweden had no need for coercive extraction, and a modus vivendi emerged between the crown's agents and local figures, who determined assessments, exemptions, and various procedures. Thus, light resource mobilization led to a smoother working relationship between the central government and the localities, thereby strengthening constitutionalism and adapting it to a modernizing world. The real administrative acceleration took place not in Sweden but with the armies in Germany. Here is where administrative, logistical, and command structures were needed, close to the fronts and the resources, not the homeland. A chancery and exchequer were built in Mainz to manage the armies, and magazines were constructed throughout Germany. Like the rank and file of the troops, the staff of these offices was mainly German, and when peace finally came, they, like their kin in the regiments, were demobilized. Neither could be afforded in Sweden, neither was needed.[28]

Sweden's withdrawal from Germany at the end of the Thirty Years' War deprived it of much of the financial base upon which its armies relied, and set the stage for the state-making program of the Caroline monarchs (1672–1718). Without the verdant resources of Germany or some other country, Swedish finances could not hold up. War with Poland and Brandenburg-Prussia (1655–60) proved disastrous. Attempts to mulct the Vistula valley failed. At war's close Sweden had nothing to show but a burdensome debt

---

[26] Michael Roberts, *Gustavus Adolphus: A History of Sweden, 1611–1632*, vol. 1 (London: Longmans, 1953), p. 273.

[27] Michael Roberts, *The Swedish Imperial Experience, 1560–1718* (Cambridge: Cambridge University Press, 1979), pp. 61–64; idem, *Gustavus Adolphus* 1:276–78. This early link between the state civil service and the riksdag is critical to understanding the nature of Caroline absolutism and its collapse and transition to parliamentarism.

[28] Roberts, *Gustavus Adolphus* 2:620–23. Cf. Jan Lindegren, "The Swedish 'Military' State, 1560–1720," *Scandinavian Journal of History* 10 (1985): 305–36.

weighing heavily on the backward country, pointing out the inadequacies of its military.[29] Second, the sale of crown lands during the Thirty Years' War continued under periods of magnate regencies. The rapid accumulation of land in magnate hands spread fear among the peasantry that the process of enserfment rolling across eastern Europe would soon creep northward. Third, the magnates also incurred the wrath of the lesser aristocracy, who felt their opportunities for advancement were stymied by the magnate stranglehold over high offices in the state. The nation as a whole was hostile to the magnate class for their perceived misrule during regencies and for their immunities that foisted war debt onto lower classes.

Facing war with Denmark and Brandenburg without prospects of adequate finance, Charles XI took full advantage of these class tensions and forcibly took control of alienated crown properties. (The *reduktion*, as it was called, itself was at least quasi constitutional: the Land Law of 1350 forbade the sale of crown lands, thus the crown's resumption without compensation was not as arbitrary as it might initially seem.) Lower classes saw the reduktion as forcing the privileged elites to assume a fair share of the tax burden; the peasants also saw it as preventing serfdom from spreading into their villages. The aristocracy, which in 1655 had controlled 72 percent of the farmland, possessed less than 33 percent by the end of the century. During the same period the numbers of the yeomanry doubled.[30]

The reduktion gave the crown sufficient revenues to manage government without support from parliament, while it relied on a quasi feudal military system that supported soldiers with resumed lands and not with parliamentary subsidies. This independence from the estates has often been the death knell of constitutionalism, as monarchs had no need for subsidies from parliament and had the military apparatus to destroy it. But Charles's bold stroke could only have been undertaken by rallying support from the riksdag and other quarters of Swedish society. Politics under Caroline absolutism differs markedly from Prussian or French absolutism. The crown, it is true, rode roughshod over the riksdag. It forced loans, intimidated on other issues, and successfully invoked necessity over strict constitutional propriety. In later years, Charles XII arrogated control over war and taxation, and was effectively ruling without the council of the riksdag. Furthermore, royal influence over elections and administration of the towns and villages was on the rise.[31]

---

[29] Roberts, *The Swedish Imperial Experience*, pp. 54–55; Sven-Erik Åström, "The Swedish Economy and Sweden's Role as a Great Power, 1632–1697," in Michael Roberts ed., *Sweden's Age of Greatness, 1632–1718* (New York: St. Martin's Press, 1973), p. 88.

[30] Ingvar Andersson, *A History of Sweden* (Stockholm: Natur och Kultur, 1962), p. 216; Michael Roberts, *Essays in Swedish History* (Minneapolis: University of Minnesota Press, 1967), p. 248; Claude Nordmann, *Grandeur et liberté de la Suède (1660–1792)* (Paris: Béatrice-Nauwelaerts, 1971), pp. 73–80.

[31] Roberts, *The Swedish Imperial Experience*, pp. 79–82; Günter Barudio, *Absolutismus, Zerstörung der "Libertären Verfassung": Studien zur "Karolinischen Eingewalt" in Schweden*

Local government, however, was never demolished or circumvented as in Brandenburg-Prussia and France respectively. Provincial and village institutions persisted, despite encroachments by the king. Nor were personal rights and the rule of law suspended. We find no systematic use of torture or arbitrary justice; it would have been most unwise for a populist monarch to do so. In fact, the crown remained scrupulously respectful of the law especially in regard to the rights of his popular base: "The crown was the common man's refuge, his ally, his safeguard against injustice and oppression."[32] The riksdag was initially strengthened by the anti-magnate program of Charles XI; it was charged with conducting an inquiry into magnate misrule, and its purview was expanded to include national economic policy and increased judicial functions. Though it was largely circumvented during the rule of Charles XII, the riksdag was not dismantled, and it had substantial influence in the state bureaucracy.[33]

The state itself was never particularly extensive, at least by the standards of the day. But of more significance is the state's relation to Swedish society. The bureaucracy never attained an identity distinct from the social classes, indeed it was closely linked to them. The civil service was drawn from the ranks of the lower aristocracy, who had been irritated by the magnate's monopoly of office. As part of his anti-magnate/popular mobilization program, Charles XI brought into the civil service members of the riksdag itself, thereby fusing the state with parliament. Participation of riksdag members in the state provided the opportunity for civil society itself to have its voice heard in the corporatist ministries of the Caroline period.[34] And as Charles XII would learn, it also provided an important obstacle to any movement away from Caesarism in the direction of military-bureaucratic absolutism.

Perhaps the most important difference between Swedish Caesarism and military-bureaucratic absolutism is the popular base. Its origin was in popular mobilization that augmented royal power without providing it an army and state to suppress or rule without popular support. But, the king walked a thin line: he was given wide latitude on domestic and foreign matters, but his field of opportunity was always restricted by the necessity of maintaining rapport with the populace. Abolishing the estates, sweeping away local assemblies and privileges, and open abuse of the law would have eroded the crown's basis of

zwischen 1680 und 1693 (Wiesbaden: Franz Steiner, 1976), pp. 121–60; Barudio, Absolutismus, pp. 95–96; Nordmann, Grandeur et liberté, pp. 96–97.

[32] Roberts, Essays in Swedish History, p. 37.

[33] Ibid. p. 255. This expansion of riksdag power provided unintended movement in the direction of parliamentary government. See Michael Roberts, Sweden's Age of Liberty (Cambridge: Cambridge University Press, 1986), pp. 4–5.

[34] Roberts, Essays in Swedish History, pp. 249–58; Nordmann, Grandeur et liberté, pp. 94–95; Werner Buchholz, Staat und Ständegesellschaft in Schweden zur Zeit des Überganges vom Absolutismus zum Ständeparliamentismus, 1718–1770 (Stockholm: Almquist & Wiksell, 1979), passim.

support. Popular support is a decidedly untrustworthy pillar upon which to build absolutism; a strong state and a powerful army are much better. Transient political fortunes and malaise from military defeat could erode popular support and lead to collapse.

In 1709 Sweden suffered one the most catastrophic defeats in military history, where the bulk of the army was annihilated by Peter the Great who patiently waited for his enemy to run out of supplies and strike desperately at his logistical center at Poltava. This confronted the monarch with the double problems of maintaining his image as military hero as well as raising a new army to face powerful opponents now pressing into the homeland. For the first time Sweden had to attempt to mobilize domestic resources—a move that would have political ramifications—or face almost certain conquest by Russia. These demands were met with resistance from a war-weary peasantry, the bureaucracy, and the riksdag. Peasant opposition manifested itself not in overt rebellion but critical withdrawal of support for populist absolutism. The absence of a massive peasant revolt was not for want of the institutional network at the village level as existed in France and Russia at the time of their social revolutions. Peasant institutions were probably more coherent and capable of strong opposition in Scandinavia than anywhere else in Europe. But the source of rebellion in France and Russia lay not in broad constitutional questions but in the more practical ones of land, and here the Swedish peasantry had little complaint; they were perhaps the freest cultivating class in Europe—the reduktion had seen to that. Thus, when taxes were raised and new levies called for, the result was not class-based upheaval, only widespread unrest and disapproval of the crown's interminable and burdensome wars.[35] Without the peasantry to call upon to counter opposition from other quarters, as his predecessors had had in their domestic conflicts, the crown faced an increasingly unified opposition in the riksdag and state.

The debacle at Poltava was followed by another decade of inconclusive war that led to fiscal strain and disaffection in the riksdag, the state, and the officer corps—three groups with substantial overlap and close ties. By 1718 calls for new taxes and increased economic controls precipitated open conflict between state ministries and the crown. The nation, they reasoned, had endured enough. Even the magnates were reemerging in a united front against absolutism. Disaffection spread and bordered on open revolt when the exchequer was unable to meet the payroll of the civil service and military. A coup for which the riksdag had been planning was obviated by the death, some say assassination, of Charles. Elements of the constitution that had been in the background

[35] Nordmann, *Grandeur et liberté*, pp. 179–81. Reliance on foreign resources became increasingly rare as field marshals realized the importance of rational supply systems. Bonaparte is the obvious exception, but of course his army disintegrated for want of supply during the 1812 campaign in Russia.

throughout the Caesarist period came to the fore and coalesced into a practical parliamentary democracy. The riksdag reasserted itself and invited a foreigner to become its constitutional monarch. Linkages between the civil service and the riksdag that began with Charles XI in his anti-magnate program and continued throughout his son's rule proved, through some cunning passage, to be the foundation for a parliamentary/ministerial government.[36] The riksdag dismantled the array of Caroline economic controls and removed state organs in the localities. Factions in the riksdag developed into fairly coherent political parties, which alternated political power in the eighteenth century.[37]

War led to two changes in the Swedish state. During the Thirty Years' War the chaotic household government was reformed: trained personnel replaced the generalist, and specialized departments emerged where little differentiation had been before. This was essential in order to streamline the decision-making process in the state and to ensure a more efficient collection and allocation of the light but, nevertheless, important resources mobilized in Sweden itself. The militarist-populist absolutism of Charles XII engineered an expansion of the state, and in a direction with mixed constitutional significance. State managerialism grew, but through a bureaucracy recruited from the ranks of the national parliament, a move necessitated by the monarch's anti-magnate program upon which his populism was based. When military catastrophe pressured Charles to move in the direction of military-bureaucratic absolutism, popular support collapsed, and the aristocracy in the state blocked reform. The result of the populist-inspired fusion of the riksdag with the state, and of the continuing mistrust of the monarchy even after Charles's death, was the emergence of a parliamentary-executive form of government, that is, increased parliamentary control of finances, the army, and diplomacy, indeed, increased parliamentary control over the state as a whole. Thus, military dynamics modernized the Swedish state and propelled it in the direction of a modern parliamentary form.

The Netherlands

In the mid-sixteenth century the Dutch repulsed Spanish efforts to impose military-bureaucratic absolutism on the northern provinces of the Low Countries, thereby preserving constitutional government. But the question remains

---

[36] Buchholz, *Staat und Ständegesellschaft*, pp. 38–88; Roberts, The Age of Liberty, pp. 6, 75–82; Nordmann, *Grandeur et liberté*, pp. 203–4.

[37] Buchholz, *Staat und Ständegesellschaft*, pp. 123–69; Roberts, *The Age of Liberty*, pp. 111–75; Michael F. Metcalf, "The First 'Modern' Party System? Political Parties, Sweden's Age of Liberty and the Historians," *Scandinavian Journal of History* 2 (1977): 265–87; idem, "Structuring Parliamentary Politics: Party Organization in Eighteenth-Century Sweden," *Parliaments, Estates, and Representation* 1 (1981): 35–49.

why didn't the Dutch themselves adopt autocratic measures in the next 150
years of warfare against the greatest military powers of the time? Why didn't
forcible extraction of war resources lead to the construction of a powerful
autocratic state by an indigenous figure?

Absolutism was unlikely in the Netherlands owing to a shift in the political
structure at the outset of the revolt against Spain. Military-bureaucratic states
have developd only in lands with a constitutional dualism at the heart of the
political system, that is, with a monarch of some sort and a parliament, who
together managed the country's affairs. In Brandenburg-Prussia and France
the crown was able to overwhelm constitutional institutions. With the ouster
of Spanish officials, this autocratic trajectory was not possible in the Netherlands: there was no central figure at the head of a state machinery sufficient to
overwhelm the estates and move the country toward military-bureaucratic
absolutism.

The young republic faced war with many of the major powers, and there
must have been some pressure to adopt an authoritarian governmental structure. Three factors, however, reduced the need to mobilize domestic resources: state-system dynamics, geographic obstacles to invaders, and the republic's extraordinary level of economic development. From the Dutch
Republic's earliest days to its triumph over France in the War of the Spanish
Succession, it benefited enormously from communities of interest in battling a
common foe. The import of this for resource mobilization is obvious: alliances
bring foreign armies and/or subsidies, which mean fewer domestic resources
will have to be mobilized. Alliances deploy other countries' resources against
the enemy. Even in the earliest days of the revolt against Spain, the Dutch
benefited from alliances and common enemies. This should hardly be surprising given the bellicosity of the Spanish Habsburgs; common enemies were in
no short supply: "Spain always fought in the Netherlands with only one hand;
at the same time she sought to defend the Mediterranean (until 1578), con-
quer Portugal (1579–83), invade England (1587–8), set a Habsburg on
the French throne (1589–98) or secure the duchy of Mantua for a Spanish
claimant."[38]

Geography, too, favored the Dutch in a manner limiting domestic resource
mobilization. Natural obstacles and man-made bastions gave tremendous advantages to the army on the defensive, as were the Dutch throughout most of
their wars. Behind numerous rivers, marshes, and bastions, the Dutch army
could defend the nation against numerically superior invaders, often using
relatively poorly trained town militias in the garrisons, where they could tie
down even the most seasoned Spanish troops. These defensive advantages
meant that the Spanish army would have to be much larger than its opponent's

---

[38] Geoffrey Parker, *The Army of Flanders and the Spanish Road, 1567–1659* (Cambridge:
Cambridge University Press, 1972), p. 146.

and better supplied to avoid desertions and mutinies in the course of long, miserable sieges. But, as already noted, Spain was hopelessly overcommitted.

Thus far in the study, countries have had what might be called agrarian economies, relatively undeveloped systems of production that were hard-pressed to support modern armies without centralized means of extraction. But a more highly developed economy, especially a commercial one, can undergo periods of protracted modern warfare without building extractive states. The Dutch Republic by no means had an agrarian economy. Its rural sector produced only the simplest foodstuffs for local consumption. The Republic was an immensely wealthy trading center that by 1600 had attained global commercial ascendency over Venice.[39] Its astounding wealth was channeled into the war effort without building an extractive state. As long as the Dutch navy maintained mastery of the sea, the economy and war finance were secure.

The Dutch ousted the centralized executive authority of Spain, and replaced it with the Union of Utrecht (1579). Although it was the formal constitution of the United Provinces, it reads more like a mutual defense pact than a binding set of national principles of government. It called for no central executive, not even for central finance; it only recognized an ill-defined sovereignty of the seven provincial states, which themselves were tied to town councils throughout the land.[40] Given this confusing state of affairs, one might ask, "L'état c'est qui?" How could such a congeries of provincial assemblies, even with the blessings of foreign alliances, spectacular wealth, and geographic barriers, sustain itself during peace let alone during years and even decades of war?

One of the recurring themes of this period's history is that cumbersome, particularist estates were serious obstacles to military modernization and decisive conduct of early modern warfare. The record of parliaments ruling on their own, in war or peace, is not good. The House of Commons tore itself apart during the Civil War period, alienated much of the population, and maintained control only after a couple of purges. The Polish diet was paralyzed by foreign intrigues, and the country was partitioned. The states of Catalonia fared no better during the long revolt against Spain, nor did the Parisian parlement during the Fronde. Internal conflicts, regionalism, and unwieldy numbers tore these assemblies apart. What, we must ask, was distinctive about the Dutch states that allowed them to manage affairs efficiently even in dire straits?

---

[39] C. R. Boxer, *The Dutch Seaborne Empire, 1600–1800* (London: Penguin, 1988), passim; Simon Schama, *The Embarrassment of Riches: An Interpretation of Dutch Culture in the Golden Ages* (Berkeley and Los Angeles: University of California Press, 1988), passim; Peter Kriedte, *Peasants, Landlords and Merchant Capitalists: Europe and the World Economy, 1500–1800* (Cambridge: Cambridge University Press, 1983), pp. 78–91.

[40] Herbert H. Rowen, ed., *The Low Countries in Early Modern Times* (New York: Walker, 1972), pp. 67–74; Pieter Geyl, *The Revolt of the Netherlands, 1555–1609* (London: Ernest Benn, 1980), pp. 139–41, 186–87; *The New Cambridge Modern History* 4:361–62.

The Netherlands was also divided along class, regional, and religious lines: anti-oligarchic sentiment smoldered, Hollanders were resented, and religious strife was prevalent. But at the level of political elites, especially at the level of the states of the province Holland, there were far fewer cleavages. Here, a merchant oligarchy, closely tied by maritime trade and based in a compact region, controlled government for the province, and more often than not for the entire Republic. It was a closed clique, a sort of mercantile *cosa nostra*, that could deliberate and form policy without the delays of convoking far-flung delegates, and without the potentially paralyzing divisions of regionalism and class. In the Republic, economic and political power were concentrated in the province of Holland, to such an extent that many confuse this provincial part for the national whole. Holland built political supremacy on its contribution of almost 60 percent of the country's budget, with half of that coming from the Amsterdam regents.[41] Perhaps only in Holland does Marx's observation about the state being but the board of directors for the bourgeoisie really square with political realities.

The Dutch Republic faced the same Caesarist dynamics that helped Charles XII build his state in Sweden. Lower-class hostility to oligarchic rule, national resentment to Holland's supremacy, and popular elation over the victories of military leaders or stadholders all combined to provide a basis for a Caesarist state. Stadholder power was limited in two ways significant for constitutional questions. First, mobilization of institutional support lay in politicking and building coalitions in the provincial states and town governments outside Holland. In this respect, the political system was invigorated to some extent and the hegemony of Holland, itself probably a long-term obstacle to democracy, was checked. Even when Orange-Holland tensions ran high (at least twice to the brink of civil war) the stadholder was not acting on his own, rather as an agent with the full authority of the States-General. Second, the impact of popular mobilization was attenuated by the concrete issues that pitted the stadholders against Holland, namely war and peace. The burghers of Holland successfully countered Orangist support for continued war by pointing out to the lower classes that war was generally detrimental to prosperity and their own material interests.[42]

Furthermore, stadholders never obtained independent sources of revenue, nor did they acquire an overpowering amount of political power in the states—there was always the counterpoise of Holland's political and economic power. Neither finance nor war policy was in Orange control; Holland controlled both. In 1631 Holland ordered Frederick Henry to break off a very

---

[41] Herbert H. Rowen, *The Princes of Orange: The Stadholders in the Dutch Republic* (Cambridge: Cambridge University Press, 1988), p. 84; Parker, "Why Did the Dutch Revolt Last So Long?" in *Spain and the Netherlands*, p. 58.

[42] Rowen, *Princes of Orange*, pp. 39–50, 84–94; Jonathan I. Israel, *The Dutch Republic and the Hispanic World 1606–1661* (Oxford: Clarendon Press, 1986), pp. 262–63.

promising offensive in the Spanish Netherlands and respond to a threat from another quarter. Fourteen years later, Holland ignored Frederick Henry's strategy for a land offensive in favor of a naval attack against Denmark, which was then threatening the Baltic trade. The same stadholder's efforts to continue the Thirty Years' War came to nought as Holland adamantly withheld finances for two years prior to the Peace of Westphalia.[43]

Holland and the other provinces also had numerous institutional checks on the military. After all, a highly corporate military loyal to its commander might easily overpower its civilian paymasters. The command structure of the Dutch army, the States army as it was called, was highly convoluted. Individual regiments were paid for by single provinces and were administratively under that province's preeminence—owing to Holland's share of the budget, a device that served to maintain that province's control. Troop movements could not be made without prior approval from the provincial states. Officers had to be approved by the States-General. Furthermore, the States-General assigned "field deputies" to each unit to monitor movements and plan tactics, just as the Venetian Senate assigned *provveditores* to the commands of its military enterprisers. Nor was the navy more unified: there were five admiralties to contend with in planning naval strategy. Much of the fleet was in the hands of the Dutch East India Company.[44]

Domestic resource mobilization was limited due to numerous alliances, geographic benefits, and to the inflow of commercial wealth that was easily channeled to the war effort. A small but effective state developed among the oligarchy of Holland's parliament, which managed national affairs and thwarted pressures in the direction of a caesarist state, while preserving the country's medieval basis for democracy.

Poland

Prussia and France responded to the challenge of the military revolution by building autocratic states to mobilize domestic resources. Other countries in this study either faced relatively light military threats or avoided domestic resource mobilization by various specific means: by mobilizing foreign resources, by benefit of geographical advantages, by international alliances, or by virtue of a markedly advanced economy. The political history of Poland demonstrates the tragic consequences of failing to build an effective response to the challenges of modern warfare. Polish constitutionalism was the privilege of a large, powerful aristocratic class, whose size, paralyzing institutions, and

[43] Israel, *The Dutch Republic*, pp. 319–23; Rowen, *Princes of Orange*, p. 63.
[44] Rowen, *Princes of Orange*, pp. 60–84; Geoffrey Parker, *The Dutch Revolt* (Ithaca, N. Y.: Cornell University Press, 1980), pp. 122–25.

simple incompetence prevented any substantial measure of state centralization and military reform until it was too late.

Poland was unable to follow the military-bureaucratic pattern of France and Prussia for two principal reasons. First, the demise of the Jagiellonian dynasty, combined with the rise of a wealthy, independent, and politically powerful gentry, effectively precluded a military-bureaucratic outcome, just as the ouster of Spanish authority had in the Netherlands. The gentry (*szlachta*) had taken virtually complete control of government. After the late sixteenth century, the Polish monarchy was little more than the subordinate steward of gentry interests. The second model, parliamentary control, as exemplified by the states of Holland, could not be followed since the Polish parliament was so big and was paralyzed by the construction of its constitution. Most European estates consisted of several hundred members but, because each member of the gentry was allowed representation, the Polish parliament was substantially larger than its counterparts. Its huge size, then, made effective decision making impossible. Debates were often interminable, directionless, and inconclusive. Moreover, a constitutional provision called the Liberum Veto was an insurmountable obstacle to state centralization. The work of an entire diet could be undone by a single, unexplained shout of "Nie pozwalam" (I do not allow it). Reform aimed at streamlining this absurd form of representative government could itself be thwarted by a single veto. A Russian minister ominously observed: "Poland is constantly plunged into disorder; as long as she keeps her present constitution, she does not deserve to be considered among the European powers."[45]

The gentry consistently opposed military modernization that would require a more powerful state to support it. Gentry opposition stemmed from three main sources. First, the gentry saw its preeminence in the military as a basis for its cherished privileges and rights; they were reluctant to endanger that basis by restructuring the military in a manner that elevated commoners to importance. Second, they adamantly refused to pay for a standing army. Instead, parsimonious nobles held fast to the principle—long since obsolete in the West—that the king must finance the state and the army from his personal demesne, a burden not even the expansive latifundia of the Radziwills could assume. Even during the disastrous Swedish War (1655–60), which came close to extinguishing national independence, the crown's triumph in getting an infantry conscription system was thwarted by the gentry's refusal to allocate money to equip the soldiers. Finally, opposition to military reform came from the gentry's reluctance to share its servile labor with the army.[46]

---

[45] Quoted in Norman Davies, *God's Playground: A History of Poland in Two Volumes*, vol. 1 *The Origins to 1795* (New York: Columbia University Press, 1982), p. 511.

[46] Jan Wimmer, "L'infantérie dans l'armée polonaise aux XV-XVIIIe siècles," in Witold Bieganski, Piotr Stawecki, and Janusz Wojtasik, eds., *Histoire militaire de Pologne: Problèmes choisis* (Varsovie: Édition du Ministère de la Défense Nationale, 1970), pp. 89–92; Stanisław

Aside from assorted anxieties over military reform and state expansion, two other considerations help to account for retention of antiquated feudal levies. First, a substantial external threat was presented not by modern armies, but rather by Cossack and Tatar raiding parties. The light cavalry of the Polish gentry was at least as useful as a centrally-directed army in this form of irregular, frontier warfare, which prized reconnaissance and pursuit along lengthy frontiers.[47] Second, in the seventeenth century, the Polish military won impressive victories over large modern armies, despite its increasing decrepitude. It is not possible here to recount each conflict in which Poland found itself during this century, but we may elucidate important reasons for these initially puzzling successes by focusing on three principal ones. Poland won great victories over Russia, had a protegé temporarily installed as tsar, and expanded far into the east. But these were effected during a time of internal chaos in Russia (the Time of Troubles), during which it was wracked by civil wars, boyar treachery, and jarring peasant rebellions. Poland could attack without encountering coherent resistance.

In the mid-seventeenth century, Poland found itself warring with Russia, Sweden, and Brandenburg. The battles with the latter two foes were unmitigated disasters for Poland. The military performed miserably; many provinces as well as Warsaw itself capitulated to the invaders. Here, when sizeable annexations seemed inescapable, alliances came to Poland's aid. Fearing a disadvantageous shift of power to its old nemesis from the Thirty Years' War, Austria prevailed upon the Romanovs to cease hostilities thereby freeing Poland's eastern forces. Polish diplomacy triumphed where its army had failed when it ceded East Prussia to the newly modernized Brandenburg-Prussia in exchange for a Polish *volte-face*. Fortuitous, short-lived alliances, not military might, won this round in the struggle for sovereignty. It is important to note that this respite granted by the international order did not stem from long-term Polish diplomacy—the chaotic Polish state was incapable of that; its reprieve came mainly from external actors in Vienna and Berlin who feared a more powerful predator in the region.

Finally, in the late seventeenth century, Poland engaged in wars against Austria and Prussia, and then allied with Austria against the Ottoman Empire. This, of course, was the period of Poland's greatest military hero, Jan Sobieski, who fought lengthy wars against large modern armies including that of the Porte. But once again, alliances and foreign subsidies, not internal military machinery, account for Poland's successes of this period. It will not, I hope,

Herbst, "L'armée polonaise et l'art militaire au XVIIIe siécle," *Acta Poloniae Historica* 3 (1960): 33–48.
    [47] Jerzy Teodorczyk, "L'armée polonaise aux XVe–XVIIIe siècles," in Biegnaski, Stawecki, and Wojtasik, *Histoire militaire de Pologne,* pp. 102–3; Geoffrey Parker, *The Military Revolution,* p. 37.

tarnish Sobieski's great military reputation to note that he commanded scarcely 25,000 Polish soldiers and received 200,000 livres annually from France; or that Sobieski's legendary relief of Vienna (1683) was undertaken by the same number of Polish troops augmented by imperial and mercenary troops recruited, paid, and supplied by a subsidy from Austria.[48] Foreign subsidies and alliances, not modern military organization, were the keys to Polish success on the battlefield. By fostering the illusion that the levies could still hold their own against modern armies, subsidies and alliances served to postpone badly needed military reforms.

By the outset of the eighteenth century, the protective factors upon which Polish sovereignty depended had disappeared. Political turmoil in Russia had been settled with the accession of the Romanov dynasty (1613). Peter the Great's governmental and military reforms in the early eighteenth century made the Russian army among the most formidable in Europe. Poland's other neighbors also modernized their armed forces. Brandenburg-Prussia's military developed from the Great Elector's small force to Frederick the Great's juggernaut. Austria, too, had modernized during protracted wars with the Turks and Bourbons. Surrounded by such military might, Poland could not rely on foreign resource mobilization, as had the Swedes. Even an initial penetration of foreign soil would have resulted in a swift and crushing counterstroke, the likes of which the weak German principalities or the distant and partially demobilized Catholic armies could not have delivered against the Swedes.

International alliances provided the basis for national survival in the seventeenth century but became the basis for its demise in the eighteenth. To a certain extent alliances stem from the logic of the international order, but they nonetheless must be made, continued, and remade when need be. Unfortunately, there was no coherent state to pursue a sustained diplomatic policy preventing an alliance of surrounding countries. The Great Northern War shattered Poland's illusions. Poland came under Russian hegemony: its army was limited to 24,000; Russian and Prussian armies entered and plundered the land with impunity; and, as if to ensure no military reform, Prussian officials were barred from state service. The next half century was one of intense foreign manipulation of gentry cliques, which prevented badly needed reform, thus maintaining a feckless neighbor.[49]

Hegemonized and manipulated by foreign powers, Poland was unable to mount effective reform. This situation preserved a measure of sovereignty until

[48] *The Cambridge History of Poland* 1:547–48.
[49] Michael G. Müller, *Polen zwischen Preussen und Russland: Souveränitätskrise und Reformpolitik 1736–1752* (Berlin: Colloquium Verlag, 1983); Jerzy T. Lukowski, "Towards Partition: Polish Magnates and Russian Intervention in Poland during the Early Reign of Stanislaw August Poniotowski," *Historical Journal* 28 (1985): 557–74; Daniel Stone, *Polish Politics and National Reform 1775–1788* (New York: Eastern European Quarterly, 1976), pp. 44–46; Davies, *God's Playground*, 1:347–48.

the surrounding powers could agree on dividing the estate and then arranging the death of this eastern European nation. But perhaps Frederick the Great's metaphor is better: he viewed Poland as, "an artichoke, ready to be consumed leaf by leaf."[50] Though hardly favored by natural barriers, Poland's demise must be attributed to its failure to emulate neighboring powers and modernize. Had it done so, Russia, Prussia, or Austria might well have found Poland a desirable ally against the others, and thus the partitioning alliance might have been prevented. As it was, Poland was only a weak and tempting target for the powerful surrounding states, a source of regional instability and international tension that the major powers only too willingly and decisively removed.

War has indeed shaped the modern state in Europe, but hardly in a uniform way. Some states became powerful military-centered absolutisms, others remained constitutional ones enduring either a modicum off administrative streamlining or a limited Caesarist period, while still other states became targets for annexation and ceased to exist. Theoretical models, Barrington Moore once observed, act as searchlights, illuminating large amounts of information. But he also cautioned that searchlights can be blinding, preventing our seeing crucial forces. I would suggest that social history has both enlightened and blinded, and that, unpleasant as it may be, war has played an important role in the making of the modern world. War is not an agreeable thing to study; it does not fit with most academic research; we have in our day welcomed the decline of large-scale war. All these factors combine to make the study of war less prominent than it might be.

The broad theoretic message here is that military organization has had immensely important consequences for state and society. Class-based arguments about the origins of dictatorship and democracy need to be complemented with ones recognizing the importance of military organization, geopolitics, and resource mobilization. Weber knew well the importance of both economic and military structures: "Whether the military organization is based on the principle of self-equipment or that of equipment by a military warlord who furnishes horses, arms and provisions, is a distinction quite as fundamental for social history as is the question whether the means of economic production are the property of the worker or of a capitalistic entrepreneur."[51] Students of political history need to recognize the importance of economic and military forces alike—and remain open to the possibility of other, equally portentous causal factors. Along with Barrington Moore, we should also show magnaninity toward the arguments of those who follow after us in scholarly quests.

50 Quoted in Davies, *God's Playground*, 1:515.
51 Max Weber, *General Economic History*, trans. Frank H. Knight (New Brunswick, N. J.: Transaction Books, 1982), p. 320.

CHAPTER 3

Where Do Rights
Come From?

CHARLES TILLY

Where do rights come from? We could ground this grand question in
analytic philosophy à la Rawls, metaphysics à la Rousseau, or rational action à
la Riker. I want instead to ground it in European political history.[1] In this, I
take my lead from Barrington Moore's *Social Origins of Dictatorship and
Democracy,* which repeatedly treats rights as historical products, outcomes of
struggle. In particular, *Social Origins* argues that the creation of democracy—
checking of arbitrary rulers, establishment of just, rational political rules, and
influence of the "underlying population" in the making of such rules[2]—
entailed the making of rights.

In that book, Moore grounded the crucial rights in Western European
feudalism. "For our purposes," he argued, "the most important aspect was the

[1] This paper owes its existence to a question Mayer Zald asked over coffee in the basement of
the Michigan Union. Readers may blame him for the question, but not for the answer. The
Vilhelm Aubert Memorial Symposium, University of Oslo, August 1990, heard a premature
version, and circulated that version slightly modified in Lars Mjøset, ed., *Contributions to the
Comparative Study of Development* (Oslo: Institute for Social Research, 1992). I am grateful for
criticism to Thomas Janoski, Lars Mjøset, Sidney Tarrow, Viviana Zelizer, and members of the
New School's proseminar on state formation and collective action. Although I have updated
references, the essay records my understanding of its subject in 1990, when I wrote it. For later
versions see *European Revolutions, 1492–1992* (Oxford: Blackwell, 1993), "Entanglements of
European Cities and States," in Charles Tilly and Wim Blockmans, eds., *Cities and the Rise of
States in Europe, AD 1000–1800* (Boulder: Westview, 1994), and "The Emergence of Citizen-
ship in France and Elsewhere," in Charles Tilly, ed., *Citizenship, Identity, and Social History*
(Cambridge: Cambridge University Press, 1995).

[2] Barrington Moore, Jr., *Social Origins of Dictatorship and Democracy* (Boston: Beacon
Press, 1966), p. 414.

growth of the notion of the immunity of certain groups and persons from the power of the ruler, along with the conception of the right of resistance to unjust authority. Together with the conception of contract as a mutual engagement freely undertaken by free persons, derived from the feudal relation of vassalage, this complex of ideas and practices constitutes a crucial legacy from European medieval society to modern Western conceptions of a free society."[3] Despite this passage's whiff of idealism, Moore's comparative history portrayed those crucial rights as coming to fruition by means of revolution and class struggle; he gave his opening chapter, after all, the title "England and the Contributions of Violence to Gradualism." My argument will diverge from Moore's in three directions: doubting the centrality of feudalism, downgrading the relative importance of ideas, and considering the crucial events to have occurred after the general dissolution of feudalism. It will nevertheless agree with Moore in two fundamental ways: by emphasizing resistance and struggle, by grounding rights in the specific histories of different European regions.

Grounded historically, the question about origins of rights becomes a naturalistic one: How have European people acquired enforceable claims on the states to which they were subject? More narrowly, how have rights of citizenship come into being? How did authorities come to owe goods, services, and protections to people merely on the ground of their belonging to a category, the category of people in the political community attached to a state? How did that political community expand to include most people, or at least most households, in the population at large?

Even more surprising, how did ordinary people get the power to enforce such weighty obligations? Vying in vain in a national arena, did Europeans instead wrest rights from local authorities and then see them eventually extended to a national scale? Or did benevolent despots first grant these rights to a small number of companions, and then, as enlightenment spread among rulers and ruled, extend them gradually to the rest of the population? Or did they emerge from struggle at a national scale? My answer hews to the third alternative: struggle at a national scale. Rights, in this formulation, resemble what Amartya Sen calls entitlements, enforceable claims on the delivery of goods, services, or protections by specific others.[4] Rights exist when one party can effectively insist that another deliver goods, services, or protections, and third parties will act to reinforce (or at least not to hinder) their delivery. Such entitlements become *citizenship* rights when the object of claims is a state or its agent and the successful claimant qualifies by simple membership in a broad

---

[3] Ibid., p. 415.
[4] Amartya Sen, *Poverty and Famines: An Essay on Entitlement and Deprivation* (Oxford: Clarendon Press, 1981).

category of persons subject to the state's jurisdiction. Citizenship rights came into being because relatively organized members of the general population bargained with state authorities for several centuries, bargained first over the means of war, then over enforceable claims that would serve their interests outside of war. This bargaining enlarged the obligations of states to their citizens, broadening the range of enforceable claims citizens could make on states even more than it expanded the population who held rights of citizenship.

This view of the origin of rights emerges from the confluence of work on state transformation and work on collective action, two largely separate streams that, once joined, refresh our understanding.[5] They clarify the paradoxical processes by which greatly unequal struggles produced mutually recognized/rights: rights of citizens and groups of citizens with respect to states, as well as rights of state officials (and even of states as corporate entities) with

[5] Recent surveys and syntheses of relevant literatures include George Reid Andrews and Herrick Chapman, eds., *The Social Construction of Democracy, 1870–1990* (New York: New York University Press, 1995), Karen Barkey and Sunita Parikh, "Comparative Perspectives on the State," *Annual Review of Sociology* 17 (1991): 523–49; Rogers Brubaker, *Citizenship and Nationhood in France and Germany* (Cambridge: Harvard University Press, 1992), John L. Campbell, "The State and Fiscal Sociology," *Annual Review of Sociology* 19 (1993): 163–85; Simona Cerutti, Robert Descimon, and Maarten Prak, eds., "Cittadinanze," *Quaderni Storici* 30 (1995): 281–514; Erik Örjan Emilsson, *Sweden and the European Miracles: Conquest, Growth and Voice: A Survey of Problems and Theories* (Gothenburg: Ekonomisk-Historiska Institutionen vid Göteborgs Universitet, 1996); Olivier Fillieule, ed., *Sociologie de la protestation: Les Formes de l'action collective dans la France contemporaine* (Paris: L'Harmattan, 1993); Stefan Immerfall, "Macrohistorical Models in Historical-Electoral Research: A Fresh Look at the Stein-Rokkan-Tradition," *Historical Social Research* 17 (1992); 103–16; Andrew Kirby, *Power/Resistance: Local Politics and the Chaotic State* (Bloomington: Indiana University Press, 1993); Kuen Koch, *Over Staat en Statenvorming* (Leiden: DSWO Press, 1993); John Lynn, "How War Fed War: The Tax of Violence and Contributions during the *Grand Siècle*," *Journal of Modern History* 65 (1993): 286–310; Michael Mann, *The Sources of Social Power*, 2 vols. (Cambridge: Cambridge University Press, 1986 and 1993); John Markoff, *Waves of Democracy: Social Movements and Political Change* (Thousand Oaks, Calif.: Pine Grove Press, 1996); Gloria Martínez Dorado, "La formación del Estado y la acción colectiva en España, 1808–1845," *Historia Social* 15 (1993): 101–18; Doug McAdam, John D. McCarthy and Mayer N. Zald, eds., *Comparative Perspectives on Social Movements: Political Opportunities, Mobilizing Structures, and Cultural Framings* (Cambridge: Cambridge University Press, 1996), Gérard Noiriel, "L'Identification des citoyens: Naissance de l'état civil républicain," *Genèses* 13 (1993): 3–28; Juan Pro Ruiz, *Estado, geometría y propriedad. Les orígenes del catastro en España, 1715–1941* (Madrid: Ministerio de Economia y Hacienda, 1992); Dietrich Rueschemeyer, Evelyne Huber Stephens, and John D. Stephens, *Capitalist Development and Democracy* (Chicago: University of Chicago Press, 1992); Bernard S. Silberman, *Cages of Reason: The Rise of the Rational State in France, Japan, the United States, and Great Britain* (Chicago: University of Chicago Press, 1993); Sidney Tarrow, *Power in Movement* (Cambridge: Cambridge University Press, 1994), Christian Topalov, "Patriotismes et citoyennetés," *Genèses* 3 (1991): 162–76; Mark Traugott, ed., *Repertoires and Cycles of Collective Action* (Durham, N.C.: Duke University Press, 1995); Patrick Weil, "Immigration, nation et nationalité: Regards comparatifs et croisés," *Revue francaise de science politique* 44 (1994): 308–26.

respect to citizens. From previous work on state transformation comes recognition of the extractive, repressive relationship of states to subject populations through most of history, leaving us to wonder that they should ever concede extensive citizens' claims. From previous work on collective action comes a twofold model of struggle: (1) struggle over demands made by states on their subjects, by subjects on states, or by subjects on each other; and (2) struggle by specific groups of subjects to enter the polity (the set of persons and groups having routine, enforceable claims on the state), to help others enter the polity, to defend certain polity memberships, or to exclude others from the polity. In caricature, the argument says that rights of citizenship formed as the bargains struck in the course of both sorts of struggle, first chiefly in defense against invasive state demands for the means of war, later in the pursuit of a much wider range of collective action and state intervention.

This way of explaining rights is at once empiricist, speculative, and cynical. It is empiricist because it infers regularities from diverse experiences of Europeans over the last thousand years of state formation and transformation. It is speculative because no one has assembled the mass of comparative evidence required for definitive verification or falsification. It is cynical because it assumes that whatever enforceable claims on states people acquired, however wrong they may now appear to be, constituted rights. It does not label as "rights" only those obligations of which I personally approve. In self-righteous retrospect, I do not like the legal support Prussian Junkers received from their state in making serfs out of free peasants, but for me the Junkers' enforceable claim to state assistance in apprehending rebels and runaways qualifies as rights.

The Junker right to discipline rebels and runaways did not, however, constitute a right of citizenship. Citizenship rights belong in principle (if not always in practice) to everyone who qualifies as a full-fledged member of a given state; membership in the category suffices to qualify a person for the enforceable claims. Although all systems of citizenship establish more than one category of eligibility (even today's democratic states exclude children, prisoners, and certified incompetents from some citizenship rights), the major dividing line separates noncitizens from native-born and naturalized citizens. These days, citizens of European states typically have rights to vote in national and local elections, to engage in a wide range of collective action outside of elections, to receive a considerable number of governmental benefits and services, to move freely within the frontiers of their states, and even to receive the protection of their states when they travel or reside outside their frontiers; citizens can lose these rights only through a formal process of degradation, such as a criminal sentence or commitment to a psychiatric hospital; with respect to the same states, otherwise identical noncitizen neighbors do not generally share these rights.

Expansion of Rights, Creation of Citizenship

T. H. Marshall's classic formulation distinguished three elements of citizenship: civil, political, and social.[6] Civil rights comprised those elements protecting individual freedom; political rights, those elements guaranteeing participation in the exercise of political power; and social rights, those providing access to material and cultural satisfactions.[7] Thinking of England, Marshall assigned the definitive acquisition of civil rights to the eighteenth century, of political rights to the nineteenth, and of social rights to the twentieth. By the 1830s, he argued, "the civil rights attached to the status of freedom had already acquired sufficient substance to justify us in speaking of a general status of citizenship."[8] In each case, Marshall conceived of the rights' extension as the almost-Hegelian realization of a principle in history. Characteristic common sense and fair play, it is true, infused the English version of the Geist.

Although at times he recognized that labor fought capital and the state for its social rights, Marshall explicitly rejected the line of argument I have taken: "Rights are not," he declared, "a proper matter for bargaining."[9] Despite recognizing that civil rights (protections of individual freedom) provided the frame for political and social rights, he did not see how the struggle for one kind of right prepared claimants to struggle for the next kind. No doubt he resisted that line of argument because in 1946, when he wrote, it would have made the struggle for social rights a matter of *rapport des forces* at a time when he sought to prepare his audience for intervention in the order of social classes and to justify that intervention as a matter of unavoidable principle. However that may be, his otherwise perceptive analysis suffered acutely from historical foreshortening. We can place it in more adequate perspective by attempting to place the gain and loss of rights more firmly into history than Marshall did.

Citizens of European states now enjoy *ipso facto* rights to education, housing, health care, income, and a wide variety of political participation. Some resident noncitizens also have legal access to many of these benefits, but the enforceability of their claims remains limited and contested. If France and other EU members grant the local vote to *ressortissants* of other states, the distinction will start to blur. When distinctions of this sort disappear, we have two linguistic choices: we can say that the rights attached to citizenship have

[6] For explications and critiques of Marshall's analysis, see J. M. Barbalet, *Citizenship* (Minneapolis: University of Minnesota Press, 1988); Margaret R. Somers, "Citizenship and the Place of the Public Sphere: Law, Community, and Political Culture in the Transition to Democracy," *American Sociological Review* 58 (1993): 587–620; Bryan S. Turner, ed., *Citizenship and Social Theory* (Newbury Park: Sage, 1993).

[7] T. H. Marshall, *Class, Citizenship, and Social Development* (Garden City: Doubleday, 1965), p. 78.

[8] Ibid., p. 84.

[9] Ibid., p. 122.

diminished, or we can say that states have begun to equate citizenship with authorized long-term residence. In the case of Europe, a third choice may also apply: that citizenship rights have devolved to the European Community. The test will come with the treatment of nationals from outside the Community. In the meantime, citizenship makes a significant difference to the claims on a state that any individual can enforce.

As the European Community's scope expands, one of the thorniest issues its members face grows on precisely that flowering bush: to what extent, in what ways, and with what sort of enforcement will citizenship rights become vested in the Community as a whole rather than in any particular state? To what extent will they become uniform and transferable among states? Instead of rebels and runaways, what about refugees?[10] If one European state recognizes a set of people as political refugees who have high priority for citizenship, must all other members of the Community recognize those rights? Will the right of a newly unemployed worker to income, job placement, and retraining apply in the state to which he has migrated? Who will pay the benefits? When rights vary from state to state, will the lowest common denominator prevail throughout Europe? The average? The highest value anywhere? Similar questions face the rebuilders of political life in Latin America and Eastern Europe, as the decline of authoritarian regimes brings a new era of constitution making. The question of citizenship has become newly salient.

It has, in fact, remained prominent in Europe for about three hundred years, since the time when larger European states began building big standing armies drawn largely from their own populations—armies (and often navies) supported by regular taxation and state-funded debt. To be sure, long before the seventeenth century, expatriate European merchants formed "nations" in metropolises such as Constantinople and Rome, gaining a measure of self-government and of protection from their home states in return for policing their own members, assuring their own food supplies in times of subsistence crisis, and bearing negotiated shares of citywide expenses. No doubt the generalization of resident diplomatic missions in later fifteenth-century Europe entailed a certain mutual recognition of citizenship. For the burghers of city-states such as Florence and federations of city-states such as the Dutch Republic, membership in the financial elites and political councils of their own cities qualified them for claims on their states as well, long before the seventeenth century; in that limited sense, as Max Weber half-understood, Bürgerschaft anticipated citizenship.

Most European states and their subjects, however, did not begin bargaining

---

[10] See Gérard Noiriel, *La Tyrannie du national: Le Droit d'asile en Europe 1793–1993*, Aristide Zolberg, Astri Suhrke, and Sergio Aguayo, *Escape from Violence: Conflict and the Refugee Crisis in the Developing World* (New York: Oxford, 1989).

out the rights and obligations of citizenship on a relatively large scale until the seventeenth and eighteenth centuries. Before then, unwritten constitutions frequently bound rulers to members of their ruling classes, but not to the ordinary population. Then rulers turned away from the episodic use of militias and mercenary forces for warfare, trying instead to staff standing armies from their own populations and to force the civilians in their own populations to pay for the armies routinely and well. Large populous states thus gained the advantage over small rich states, as a Venice or a Dutch Republic lost the ability simply to rent an army of poor foreigners and thereby to vanquish its neighbors.

From Indirect to Direct Rule

The attempts to establish standing armies raised a critical problem: the transition from indirect to direct rule. Until the creation of mass national armies, all larger European states ruled indirectly, counting on the cooptation of various sorts of magnates who acted for the state and guaranteed the delivery of resources to it, but who also retained a large measure of autonomy within their own reserved zones. Even France, that Tocquevillian model of centralization, relied heavily on hereditary governors, provincial estates, and privileged municipalities until Richelieu (pressed for funds to join the widening European wars of the 1620s) improvised intendants to bypass stubborn regional magnates. Mazarin and Colbert regularized intendants into direct and more or less subordinated regional executors of royal will. Even then the intendants spent much of their time negotiating with estates, *parlements*, military governors, and other regional power holders who had the power to block the crown's demands and sometimes to incite massive resistance against royal policy.

The dilemma bore sharp horns. Reliance on coopted power holders guaranteed a certain level of compliance so long as the crown limited its demands and respected the power holders' privileges, but it reinforced the central authority's chief domestic rivals and most dangerous enemies. The installation of direct, centralized rule, however, was a costly, risky, time-consuming operation that often exploded in rebellion.

The expansion of armed forces impelled high officials of European states to undertake the cost, the risk, and the effort. In large states such as Prussia and Russia, reliance on powerful, partly autonomous intermediaries set a severe limit on the portion of national resources to which the central state could gain access, even if up to that limit it made the amassing of resources easier. Two of war's many unfortunate features are that (1) it really is a zero-sum game at best, and a negative-sum game much of the time—if one party wins, another definitely loses, often incurring penalties greater than the putative winner's gains, (2) within the limits imposed by declining efficacy as a function of the time and space separating antagonists, the party with the most effective armed force sets the terms—a state having small, very efficient armed forces sometimes loses wars against a state having large, inefficient ones, and usually loses to a state having large, fairly efficient ones. As a consequence of these principles, the most effectively armed European states set the military terms for all the rest.

For several centuries before about 1750, the most effectively armed European states were those that could rent the most mercenary troops. Mercenaries—drawn especially from militarized and land-poor peasant regions such as Ireland, Scotland, Switzerland, Hesse, and Croatia—reached their European heyday in the sixteenth and seventeenth centuries, then began to lose ground in the eighteenth century, and became insignificant with the Napoleonic Wars. Mercenaries had the great advantage of being available rapidly for whoever had the necessary funds or credit. But they had dramatic disadvantages: they were expensive, unruly, unreliable if not paid, and a great nuisance if not deported once a war had ended; unemployed mercenaries often became bandits, pirates, or the equivalent on a larger scale: warlords.

The old European alternatives to nationally recruited mercenaries had been urban militias, private armies of great lords, and various sorts of feudal levies—the three overlapped. From the perspective of rulers, these forces had the advantages of being cheap and disposable. But they were available only in limited numbers, for limited terms, in service whose conditions themselves generally had well-specified limits; what is more, their leaders and patrons had minds, interests, and ambitions of their own. Only the invention of mass national armies recruited directly from the subject population by the state and operated under control of the state's own officers overcame the clear disadvantages of mercenaries and of the older levies.

The creation of a large, durable national army recruited from the domestic population, however, posed one of those problems of consent beloved of political philosophers. Supporting any army required large resources continuously over long periods: food, uniforms, weapons, transport, wages, and more. In the seventeenth century, most states that hired mercenaries borrowed money from local capitalists in the short run, bought the requisites on well-organized markets in which state functionaries and capitalists collaborated, then taxed the general population in various ways to repay their capitalist creditors. A national army had the added disadvantage of withdrawing able-bodied workers from households that relied on them for support. These workers would disappear from their households for years, possibly returning useless or not at all, and remitting no income in the meantime. Entrepreneurs who knew how to deliver freely hired mercenaries did not necessarily know how to pry unwilling recruits from reluctant households. Furthermore, standing armies required substantial increases in taxation.

How to gain consent? All army-building states turned to some combination of reliance on coopted entrepreneurs, aggressive recruitment, impressment, and conscription. Even so, they faced widespread resistance to the increased burden of taxation and to the seizure of young men for the military. They bargained. They bargained in different ways: by sending in troops to recruit troops and collect taxes, by negotiating quotas for troops and taxes with the headmen of regions and local communities, by confirming the rights of existing assemblies (Parliament in England, Estates in France, Cortes in Castile, Corts in Catalonia, States-General in the Dutch Republic) to legislate contributions to military budgets. Even bloody repression of rebellions typically involved bargaining. Authorities punished a few offenders spectacularly while pardoning others who agreed to comply with the state's demands. Furthermore, the settlement of a rebellion would generally state the grounds and procedures for legitimate future remonstrance. White-hot bargaining forged rights and obligations of citizenship.

Attention! These days the notion of citizenship brooks few levels and exceptions; an economically unequal but politically egalitarian world abhors the maintenance of formal distinctions among classes of citizens. Old-regime European states took a much more differentiated and pragmatic approach. The partial truth in the old idea (promulgated more effectively by T. H. Marshall and Reinhard Bendix than by anyone else) of citizenship as episodic enlargement of participation in national politics lies precisely there: nobles and clergy generally acquired the right of direct access to the sovereign long before bourgeois or, even more so, workers and peasants did. The error lies in conceiving of the process as one of gradual enlightenment rather than continuous struggle, and in imagining that the same sequence of inclusion appeared everywhere that enlightenment spread. The implicit strategy of rulers was to grant national rights to the minimum set of persons that would guarantee the delivery of militarily essential resources to the state, and to collaborate with citizens so privileged in exploiting and repressing the rest. Women and male servants, for example, only escaped from that collusion very recently. Indirect rule operated reasonably well with a small number of people having rights of citizenship—so few that in some cases the phrase "indirect rule" is more misleading than helpful.

Contrasting Experiences

The shift to direct rule did not immediately eliminate such distinctions. With whom rulers bargained varied according to their strategies for enlarging military force, which in turn depended on the social structures of the regions in which they based their states. Where rulers could coopt well-established regional power holders such as landlords who would guarantee a supply of troops and taxes to the state, nobilities and gentries flourished, distinctions actually increased, and citizenship in relation to the national state was slow to expand. Russia and Prussia followed that path, but not to a point that we could reasonably call direct rule, at least not until the twentieth century.

England came closer. There the state relied heavily on its squires and parsons to represent the state at the local level, but it also tolerated, however uneasily, considerable direct representation of parishioners, ratepayers, and freeholders vis-à-vis monarch and Parliament. Other states went even farther in the seventeenth and eighteenth centuries. Where rulers' agents bargained directly for resources with commercially active burghers or village elders, they had little choice but to concede claims on the state to large numbers of people, even if the consequence of those concessions was to reinforce the positions of those local elites within their own communities. Holland and Sweden followed different variants of that path.

In the process of building nationally based military forces and citizenship, indeed, Sweden was precocious. Sweden, poor in funds but rich in peasants, had recruited relatively large armies from its own population during its warlike sixteenth-century expansion; Gustav Vasa (1521–60) and his successors had managed that only through a dramatic series of internal struggles and the steadfast collaboration of their now-Protestant and national clergy. Even Sweden, however, relied heavily on mercenaries during the Thirty Years' War. Having discovered the limits of conquest by a small state, Sweden then became a pioneer in the creation of mass national armies.

Charles XI (1672–97) took back crown lands his predecessors had been selling to pay for mercenaries and distributed much of the land to soldier-peasants who owed national military service in payment for their farms. The clergy and state bureaucrats, who created a system of local surveillance and control that rivaled the Chinese and Japanese systems of their time, became guarantors of state claims and peasant rights. Under that system, Sweden became one of Europe's most militarized states; in 1708, for example, something like 5.5 percent of its entire population was under arms. (In the world of 1987 as a whole, by comparison, only about 0.5 percent of the population was in military service; in Sweden itself, the 1987 figure was about 0.8 percent. By contrast, among the world's most militarized states Israel then had 3.2 percent of its population actively under arms, Syria 3.6 percent, and Iraq on the order of 6 percent.) A military population of 5 or 6 percent lays enormous burdens on a population. Sweden created an extraordinary state bureaucracy to distribute that burden.

Despite its deserved reputation as a sea power, the Dutch Republic built substantial armies in the seventeenth century, and maintained about 5.3 percent of its population under arms in 1700. Holland and its neighbors built their great seventeenth-century military force by means of a peculiar federal state in which mercantile municipalities held decisive power and the *stadhouder*, when he wielded power at all, did so by means of patronage and canny bargaining among the cities. Indeed, stadhouders actually received their appointments from individual provinces (which means, in effect, from the provinces' leading cities); provinces did not all necessarily name the same stadhouder, and sometimes they named none at all. On the whole the state's armed forces actually consisted of troops and navies raised by the individual provinces, especially the disproportionately rich province of Holland. Provincial military forces were perpetually subject to withdrawal. The (contingently) United Provinces created very little central bureaucracy.

Prussia and Russia likewise turned toward their own populations for troops in the seventeenth century. Unlike Sweden, however, both states relied for recruitment and command on state-serving landlords who exercised great discretion within their own fiefs. Those great lords held the power to block excessive demands from the state. Thus Prussia and Russia rebuilt indirect rule and the obstacles it set to centralized control.

The contrast between Sweden and Holland, on the one hand, and Prussia and Russia, on the other, is instructive. In Sweden, peasants acquired direct political representation on a national scale, even to the extent of having their own formally constituted estates. In Holland and the other Dutch provinces, citizenship remained vested in municipal ruling classes until a series of struggles in the eighteenth century and the French conquest of 1798. In Prussia and Russia, peasants had practically no access to the national state except through the same landlords whose short-run interests lay in oppressing and exploiting them. Although no one should exaggerate the power of Swedish peasants or forget their subjection to clergy and bureaucrats, seventeenth-century Sweden had conceded a minimum set of citizenship rights to the population at large—or at least to the propertied classes—while its neighbors had granted none. On the contrary, as they built military power Prussia and Russia abridged the autonomies of merchants and villagers alike. The manner of recruiting soldiers made a large difference.

The French Revolution and Its Aftermath

Nevertheless, the decisive move to a model of mass national armies, direct rule, and extensive citizens' rights on a national scale came with the French

Revolution. Historians have the habit of thinking that revolutionary military activity was at first a by-product of revolutionary enthusiasm, with the implication that the new forms of rule created the military transformation rather than vice versa. There is some truth in this sense of causal priority, since the political mobilization of 1789 to 1794 produced military forces of a tenacity and patriotism Europe had rarely seen, since revolutionary action against the Catholic Church, the nobility, and royalty surely brought France into conflict with its European neighbors faster and more generally than prudent temporization would have, and since the first steps French people recognized as revolutionary—notably the establishment of a National Assembly centered on the Third Estate—implied a considerable movement away from the old intermediaries and toward direct rule mediated by elected representatives of the population at large.

Yet consider the importance of military changes in their own right: the crucial defection of French Guards in the Parisian revolution; the institution of citizen militias, a nearly universal feature of the local revolutionary activity of 1789; the search for weapons to arm the new Parisian militia, which was the immediate incentive for breaking into the Bastille; the strong ties between the military recruitment of 1791 or 1792 and the support for the Revolution in general; the sale of church and émigré property to finance the state's military efforts; the crucial place of military conscription in the widespread counter-revolutionary movements of 1793; the enactment of most instruments of the Terror in reaction to the double military threat from external enemies and domestic rebels; and the organization in the larger cities of so-called Revolutionary Armies whose chief business was bending the people of their hinterlands (including peasants who were reluctant to deliver food) to patriotic action.

Consider furthermore that it was precisely the fiscal crisis stemming from the American war—a crisis set in motion, not by the general inability of the French economy to absorb the cost, but by the fiscal limits intrinsic to the French system of indirect rule—that led to the momentous convocation of the Estates General in 1789. In 1787, the state (guided by Calonne) attempted to bypass the limits of indirect rule in the *pays d'élection*—those regions lacking their own estates to speak for regional privilege—by setting up representative assemblies and executive committees, but neither side invested enough power in its agents to produce effective bargaining of rights for fiscal cooperation.

Repeatedly, nevertheless, the effort to reorganize, enlarge, and finance the state's military activity led to bargaining with major sectors of the population, and thereby to the establishment or confirmation of enforceable claims such as the right to elected representation. Complaints about taxation—less its sheer bulk than the equity of its distribution—dominated parish, Third Estate, and noble *cahiers de doléances* prepared for the Estates General of 1789. What is more, the *cahiers* often linked citizenship directly to the payment of taxes.[11]

During the French Revolution, from the Declaration of the Rights of Man (August 26, 1789) onward, bargaining that established citizenship rights took place right out in the open. The first revolutionary constitution (1790) installed a sharp distinction between active citizens (who paid the equivalent of three or more days' wages in taxes, and had the right to vote) and passive citizens (who paid fewer taxes or none at all and could not vote). It also set up a secondary distinction of second-degree active citizens (who paid ten or more days' wages in taxes and could not only vote but also serve as electors and hold office). This latter group was a reasonable representation of the independent and propertied population who had dominated the Third Estate of 1789. But before the elections of fall 1792, in the shadow of general war, the National Assembly decreed that almost all males twenty-five and over could vote, with the exception of servants and other presumed dependents. Advocates of the expanded electorate argued specifically that men who could fight for the *patrie* should also be able to vote for its governors. Unwilling conscripts of March 1793 often turned the argument around, declaring that they would be ready to serve if the government also drafted the officeholders who were receiving military exemptions.

On June 23, 1793—in the midst of war, insurrection, and bitter struggles over the food supply—the Convention abrogated martial law (including the Le Chapelier law forbidding private associations such as guilds) yet authorized severe price controls. The next day it voted on a new constitution as well as on the recently drafted Declaration of the Rights of Man and the Citizen. While outlawing slavery (black insurgents of Saint-Domingue had finally received a hearing), they guaranteed not only manhood suffrage, but also rights to rebellion, to education, to public welfare, to property, and to subsistence. True, legislatures of Thermidor and thereafter abridged citizens' rights dramatically; manhood suffrage did not reappear in France until the Revolution of 1848. But by 1793 the French had clearly established the category of citizen as well as the principle and practice of negotiating the rights and obligations attached to that category in elected national assemblies. Their military conquests and their example spread category, principle, and practice to much of Europe.

The citizenship that emerged from the French Revolution and Napoleonic Wars remained exiguous by today's standards, although from an eighteenth-century perspective it was thick indeed. It consisted of property-restricted rights to vote for legislative assemblies, veterans' benefits, limited protection

---

[11] John Markoff, "Peasants Protest: The Claims of Lord, Church, and State in the *Cahiers de doléances* of 1789," *Comparative Studies in Society and History* 32 (1990): 413–54.

for political associations, relative freedom of movement within national boundaries, a measure of religious toleration, and little more. The array obviously varied from country to country within Europe; Russia in 1815 was far from granting anything resembling national citizenship, while in Great Britain even ambitious rulers did not dare to abridge the prerogatives of a Parliament chosen by an amalgam of electors, the general right of religious association (political and economic association remained much more fragile but never nonexistent), freedom to assemble for peaceful purposes (although which purposes were peaceful likewise remained open to negotiation and official interpretation), or the right to petition national authorities. Nevertheless through much of Europe it meant that the capitalists who were so crucial to state finance, had obtained political positions and freedom of action they had not enjoyed in most places during the eighteenth century.

What Happened, Again?

In a long, uneven first phase, the creation of mass national armies created the rudiments of national citizenship in European states. Then between the eighteenth century and the recent past, the rights attached to membership in the national category of citizen expanded dramatically. Why and how? It happened in two further phases: the second, a bourgeois-led drive for civil and political rights, and the third, a phase in which workers, petits bourgeois, and peasants bargained more autonomously with the state.

In the second phase, negotiation over the making of war continued to play a central role. General war among European powers diminished for a century after 1815, but Europeans maintained nationally recruited standing armies and exported war to the rest of the world in the form of imperial conquest. Greatly increased military budgets empowered the bourgeois- and landlord-dominated legislatures that had taken shape during the French wars and never quite disappeared after they had ended; they now became the loci of struggle over government expenditure, the gateways through which ministers and kings had to pass on their way to military expansion. But to balance their aristocratic counterparts in the legislature, fragments of the national bourgeoisie commonly formed coalitions, implicit or explicit, with unenfranchised but increasingly organized workers and petty bourgeois. Within limits, the same civil rights that advanced the bourgeois position supported the organization of workers and petty bourgeois. As they pushed for freedom of association, freedom of assembly, freedom of the press, and related liberties, they willy-nilly promoted the mobilization of poorer, less powerful members of their commercial world.

No exaggeration, please! The British Reform Act of 1832 slammed shut in the faces of organized workers a door they and the bourgeois who benefited from the Act had battered open together. Workers' consequent sense of betrayal helped motivate the great Chartist Movement that followed almost immediately. Its relation to the coalition-breaking of 1832, and the recognition of political advantages that industrial masters drew from it, explains to a considerable degree the surprisingly political program of Chartism. One might have expected impoverished and browbeaten workers to emphasize wages, employment, and working conditions rather than annual meetings of Parliament, but not until 1867 did substantial numbers of British workers begin to vote in national elections. European bourgeois of the post-Napoleonic period found themselves in an ambivalent position, enjoying the sharp political distinction between themselves and workers or shopkeepers, and yet wanting those workers and shopkeepers to act as counterweights against their powerful political rivals. Nevertheless, the net effect of their action was to enlarge the zone of civil rights and to make the state more vulnerable to workers', shopkeepers', and peasants' demands for political rights.

In the third phase, promoted by the bourgeois-worker-peasant coalitions of 1848 revolutions, the chief beneficiaries of expanded civil, political, and social rights began to mobilize and act more autonomously than before. If Marshall was right to name the twentieth century as the great age for social rights, the nineteenth century laid the foundations in two important ways: by providing workers, shopkeepers, and peasants with the space to organize legally and state their demands forcefully, and by initiating a three-way process of negotiation among workers, capitalists, and the state over state-enforced limits on exploitation and over the minimum material benefits to which all citizens were entitled. Under Bismarck, the newly formed German state preempted the negotiation by installing a remarkable social contract top down.[12] But to some degree most European states found themselves intervening in the organization of production and distribution under pressure from increasingly organized workers and consumers.

With the later nineteenth century came an age in which military expenditure and debt service for past military expenditure no longer dominated European state budgets, as they had ever since distinct budgets had started to form in the sixteenth century. Wars began to matter chiefly as times when state powers and budgets expanded, and ends of wars began to matter as crucial times of political mobilization; the widespread adoption of female suffrage after World War I illustrates those effects. But much more than suffrage was at stake. Social rights to public services—education, health, and welfare—became

---

[12] George Steinmetz, *Regulating the Social: The Welfare State and Local Politics in Imperial Germany* (Princeton: Princeton University Press, 1993).

Figure 3–1. Hypothetical trajectory of national citizenship in Europe

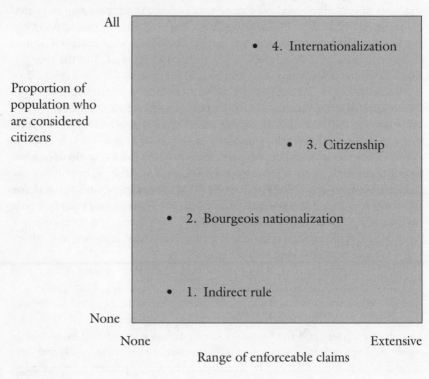

major businesses of government. Many European states became welfare states, states committed to providing services and guaranteeing income to large categories of their citizenry.

What of the next phase? If the effect of Europeanization is to displace resources and power toward larger compacts, including the European Union, that displacement should equalize rights among the citizens of different states, vest many rights in supranational entities, diminish differences between national citizens and European foreigners within any particular state, and therefore narrow the scope of national citizenship. We might schematize the phases as in figure 3–1. The diagram portrays a movement chiefly of inclusion for persons in the early phases, a movement chiefly of the range of entitlements in the later phases. If there is something to my argument, we should discover some version of this question mark–shaped curve in Europe as a whole over the last three or four centuries, but also in smaller areas of Europe at different times depending on the timing of military expansion and bourgeois strength.

Need I recall how empirical, cynical, and speculative my account of citizenship rights is? Rather than a general theory stating the principles by which rights should form, I have offered a quick gloss on European historical experience. Rather than draw out the noblest principles in which the process might be wrapped, I have insisted on the struggle, self-interest, and inadvertence involved. Rather than base my analysis on close, well-documented comparison, I have ridden high and fast across three or four centuries of history. The chronology itself requires enormous qualifications: formally designated serfs, for example, still existed in the Russia of 1860 but had disappeared from England and the Netherlands four or five centuries earlier; even today, rights of free speech vary enormously from Albania and Turkey to Norway and Finland. Most European states have found it expedient at some times in the twentieth century to define some putative citizens—communists, fascists, Gypsies, Jews, homosexuals, collaborators—as undeserving of their rights. A full theory of citizenship rights would account for these variations as well as broad trends over the whole continent. Please treat my account exactly as it deserves: as a provocative, historically grounded, theoretical sketch that invites confirmation, refutation, modification, and extension.

Extensions and Applications

This product of empiricism, cynicism, and speculation applies most surely to the creation of citizenship rights at a national scale during the emergence of consolidated states in Europe. Considering how shakily it walks its own terrain, perhaps we should simply leave the model there, and see if it gets anywhere. Nevertheless, it should be at least instructive to generalize from the specific historical terrain. The model says in general that rights—enforceable claims—arise from the repeated making of similar claims under certain conditions: (1) the claimant and the object of claims each can reward or punish the other in some significant way; (2) the two are in fact bargaining over those rewards and punishments; (3) one or both also bargains with third parties who have an interest in the claims being made, and will act to enforce future granting of the claims in question; and (4) the three or more parties to the claims thus constituted have durable identities and relations with each other.

This is not, I submit, a bad model—and there are many bad models—of how states become legitimate: not because citizens believe in rulers' virtue, divinity, or traditional authority but because third parties—especially powerful ones such as the rulers of other states—step in to support citizen-ruler bargains, particular when the disputed matter concerns states' demands on citizens rather than the other way round. A legitimate state is one whose domestic demands are supported by the rulers of most other states. Again, the model applies nicely to the way workers' rights vis-à-vis employers come into being, with the relevant third parties often being labor unions and the state. Even more generally, the model can provide a plausible account of how what James Coleman calls "disjoint constitutions" come into being, arrangements in which individuals transfer the rights to control certain of their actions to some collectivity, and accept the establishment of procedures to implement those rights—together with sanctions to enforce the norms and rules when the people ceding such rights differ, to some degree, from those whom the cession benefits.[13] The model tells us that disjoint constitutions result from coercive, unequal bargaining with third-party ratification.

The model also suggests how rights disappear. If any of the four founding conditions—claimant and object controlling relevant rewards and punishments, actual bargaining, interested third parties, durable identities and social relations—weakens significantly, so will rights. In the case of European citizenship, third parties to rights of religious diversity weakened significantly with the peace settlements of 1648, which ratified the establishment of Protestant or Catholic state religions, and denied rulers the rights to change them. With that arrangement, the chances that princely members of a sect would intervene in another state on behalf of their religious brethren diminished significantly, and the path to persecution of religious minorities widened. The rights of religious minorities declined through much of Europe, as rulers sought the organizational advantages of cultural homogeneity and exemplary intolerance. Although during the eighteenth century a number of states came to tolerate and to accept payoffs from formally proscribed minorities, no major changes in religious *rights* occurred until the French Revolution.

When the bargaining model is used to inform historical and comparative analysis, it helps make sense both of where rights come from and when they can disappear. This model of rights as the product of interest-driven bargaining looks at least as plausible as the common notions that rights derive from mentalities, Zeitgeisten, general theories, or the sheer logic of social life.

[13] James S. Coleman, *Foundations of Social Theory* (Cambridge: Harvard University Press, Belknap Press, 1990).

CHAPTER 4

Did the Civil War Further American Democracy? A Reflection on the Expansion of Benefits for Union Veterans

THEDA SKOCPOL

Scholars intrepid and knowledgeable enough to study the political development of the United States in comparative-historical perspective are few and far between. In this endeavor, Barrington Moore, Jr., has joined with a few other giants of contemporary historical social analysis such as Louis Hartz, Samuel Huntington, and Seymour Martin Lipset.[1] Even in this special company, however, Moore stands out for the originality of his focus on the Civil War in his monumental book *Social Origins of Dictatorship and Democracy*.[2] Other comparativists have placed more emphasis on the American Revolution and the formulation of the Constitution as defining moments in American political development.

"Passing over [the American Revolution] with but a few brief comments," Moore characterized it as "a fight between commercial interests in England and America" that "did not result in any fundamental changes in the structure of society." "What radical currents there were in the American Revolution were for the most part unable to break through to the surface."[3] In contrast,

---

[1] See Louis Hartz, *The Liberal Tradition in America* (New York: Harcourt Brace, 1955); idem, *The Founding of New Societies* (New York: Harcourt, Brace and World, 1964; Samuel P. Huntington, "Political Modernization: America vs. Europe," in *Political Order in Changing Societies* (New Haven, Conn.: Yale University Press, 1968); and Seymour Martin Lipset, *The First New Nation: The United States in Historical and Comparative Perspective*, expanded ed. (New York: Norton Library, 1979).

[2] Barrington Moore, Jr., *Social Origins of Dictatorship and Democracy: Lord and Peasant in the Making of the Modern World* (Boston, Mass.: Beacon Press, 1966), chap. 3, "The American Civil War: The Last Capitalist Revolution."

[3] Ibid., pp.112–13.

he saw the Civil War as "the last capitalist revolution," the most critical water-shed in the political development of the United States. "Striking down slav-ery," Moore maintained, "was a decisive step, an act at least as important as the striking down of absolute monarchy in the English Civil War and the French Revolution, an essential preliminary for further advances" in "competitive democratic capitalism."[4]

In this essay, I honor Barrington Moore's bold focus on the consequences of the Civil War for U.S. political development, reflecting critically and building upon it. First, I present Moore's arguments from *Social Origins* and briefly summarize some of the criticisms that other scholars have directed against his theses. Then I draw on my own recent research about the expansion of social benefits for Union veterans of the Civil War from the 1870s to the turn of the twentieth century.[5] Moore himself didn't know about this intriguing evidence concerning U.S. patronage politics and social welfare in the late nineteenth century. Yet the case of Civil War pensions reveals that Moore was basically correct when he argued that the Union victory in the Civil War furthered possibilities for socially inclusive democracy in the "re-United" States. Moore was insightful in ways that went beyond the terms of his own analysis.

Moore on the Consequences of the Civil War

Moore made his case about the U.S. Civil War in a nuanced way. The Civil War, he argued, was *not* essential to the purely economic development of U.S. industrial capitalism. "Plantation slavery in the South . . . was not an economic fetter upon industrial capitalism. If anything, the reverse may have been true; it helped to promote American industrial growth in the early stages." "But slavery was an obstacle to political and social democracy." For Moore, the historically conceivable alternative to a Union victory in the Civil War was a situation in which no violent conflict occurred at all, in which northern capital-ists continued to accommodate a southern planter class that was politically very powerful within the U.S. federal system. If "the conflict between North and South had been compromised," he argued, "the compromise would have been at the expense of the subsequent democratic development of the United States." He then went on to explain his view more fully: "One need only

---

[4] Ibid., pp.152, 153.

[5] This chapter incorporates some reworked excerpts from "Public Aid for the Worthy Many: The Expansion of Benefits for Veterans of the Civil War," chap. 2 of Theda Skocpol, *Protecting Soldiers and Mothers: The Political Origins of Social Policy in the United States* (Cambridge, Mass.: Harvard University Press, Belknap Press, 1992). To see the full development of the arguments presented here, as well as additional arguments about benefits for Civil War veterans and their consequences for later phases of U.S. social policy making, the reader should consult the book.

consider what would have happened had the Southern plantation system been able to establish itself in the West by the middle of the nineteenth century and surrounded the Northeast. Then the United States would have been in the position of some modernizing countries today, with a latifundia economy, a dominant antidemocratic aristocracy, and a weak and dependent commercial and industrial class, unable and unwilling to push forward toward political democracy.[6]

In Moore's view, the Union war effort against the South embodied an alliance between the industrialists and wage laborers of the Northeast, on the one hand, and the commercial farmers of the West, on the other. Both of these socioeconomic formations shared certain "competitive democratic" ideals in contrast to a "Southern society . . . firmly based on hereditary status as the basis of human worth." "With the West, the North, though in the process of change, was still committed to notions of equal opportunity. . . . Within the same political unit it was . . . inherently impossible to establish political and social institutions that would satisfy both" North and South. "Slavery was a threat and an obstacle to a society that was indeed the heir of the Puritan, American, and French Revolutions."[7]

That the Civil War was an incomplete and ambiguous victory for ideals of freedom and equality Moore readily acknowledges. He describes the defeat of the Radical Republicans, whose "demand for sweeping land reform [during Reconstruction] reflected realistic awareness that nothing else would break the power of the planters. . . . In the absence of confiscation and redistribution of land, the plantation system recovered by means of a new system of labor" as Negro tenants were forced into terribly exploitative sharecropping arrangements. Political "Thermidor" also came to "liquidate" the "Second American Revolution."[8] This was signaled by the electoral compromise of 1877, which allowed the Democrats to regain full control of the politically unreformed South, while the increasingly deradicalized Republicans gave up on protecting the newly enfranchised former slaves. If anything, Moore adopts an overly pessimistic view of where the United States ends up politically by the late nineteenth century:

> When the Southern "Junkers" were no longer slaveholders and had aquired a larger tincture of urban business and when Northern capitalists faced radical rumblings, the classic conservative coalition [i.e., between capitalist industrialists and labor-repressive landlords] was possible. . . . Much of the old repression returned to the South in new and more purely economic guises, while new forms

---

[6] Moore, *Social Origins,* pp. 112, 115, 153.
[7] Ibid., pp.152–53.
[8] Ibid., pp.145, 147.

appeared there and in the rest of the United States as industrial capitalism grew and spread. If the federal government no longer concerned itself with enforcing the fugitive slave laws, it either aquiesced [in] or served as an instrument for new forms of oppression. . . . [T]he federal government became a series of ramparts around property, mainly big property, and an agency to execute the biblical pronouncement, "To him that hath shall be given."[9]

Despite his acknowledgement of many antidemocratic tendencies in U.S. politics following the Civil War and its settlement, Moore did not back off from his basic thesis: "The Northern victory, even with all its ambiguous consequences, was a political victory for freedom."[10] The Civil War, on balance, furthered the prospects for political and social democracy in the United States.

Criticisms of Moore's Arguments

For the most part, Moore's arguments about the United States have simply been ignored by critics or by scholars more interested in extending or reworking his ideas about political transformations in Old World "agrarian bureaucratic" monarchies.[11] Yet there have also been very sharp dissents from Moore's conclusions about the consequences of the Civil War for U.S. politics. These have come especially from scholars interested in issues of political economy and class analysis, who stress exactly the same developments after Reconstruction that Moore himself regarded as ambiguities for his thesis. Thus, for the social historian Jonathan Wiener, the reimposition of labor-repressive agricultural forms and the disenfranchisement of former slaves in the South reveals that the Civil War failed to keep the United States off an antidemocratic path of capitalist industrialization.[12]

Along similar lines, the political-economist Richard Franklin Bensel has

[9] Ibid., pp.149, 150, 154.

[10] Ibid., pp.152–53.

[11] For examples, see Theda Skocpol, "A Critical Review of Barrington Moore's Social Origins of Dictatorship and Democracy," *Politics and Society* 4, no. 1 (Fall 1973): 1–34; idem, *States and Social Revolutions: A Comparative Analysis of France, Russia, and China* (New York: Cambridge University Press, 1979); Timothy Tilton, "The Social Origins of Liberal Democracy: The Swedish Case," *American Political Science Review* 68, no. 2 (1974): 561–71; Gregory M. Luebbert, *Liberalism, Fascism, or Social Democracy: Social Classes and the Political Origins of Regimes in Interwar Europe* (New York: Oxford University Press, 1991); and Brian M. Downing, *The Military Revolution and Political Change: Origins of Democracy and Autocracy in Early Modern Europe* (Princeton: Princeton University Press, 1992).

[12] Jonathan M. Wiener, "Review of Reviews: The Social Origins of Dictatorship and Democracy," *History and Theory* 15, no. 2 (1976): XX-XX, idem, *The Origins of the New South: Alabama, 1860–1885* (Baton Rouge: Louisiana State University Press, 1978).

recently emphasized the incoherence of class alignments in post–Civil War U.S. politics, with northern wage-earners split between the Republican and Democratic parties, and southern farmers and sharecroppers split racially between white Democratic loyalists and blacks who were coercively disenfranchised by the 1890s. Bensel concludes in *Yankee Leviathan* that

> Barrington Moore . . . erred in arguing that Union victory promoted the development of social democracy in the United States. . . . If the North had lost the Civil War, both the northern Union and the new Confederacy would have had internally coherent class coalitions as the basis of their respective major parties. Without the southern insistence on devolution of authority (states' rights), the post–Civil War Democratic party [in the North] could have embraced a state-centered program of social-welfare expansion and marketplace regulation that might have competed very successfully with Republican developmental policies. At the very least, the resulting major party debate over such proposals would have borne a much closer resemblance to that in contemporary European movements. Even more, such a class-coherent alignment might have radically changed the trajectory of American state development (in the North) in a more centralizing, interventionist direction.[13]

Alas, as things actually turned out according to Bensel:

> What little social-democratic potential the Civil War possessed was embodied in emancipation and largely abandoned during and after Reconstruction. . . . [S]ubsequent American development was debilitated by the legacy of southern separatism that imposed incoherent class coalitions upon the national political system. Thus the weak, decentralized social-welfare commitment of the American state was very much the product of the Civil War and Reconstruction political economy. . . . Union victory meant that the continuing dilemma of southern separatism, not social dislocation associated with industrialization, would be the major problem facing late-nineteenth-century state-builders.[14]

Not only political economy analysts, but also an adherent of Samuel Huntington's approach to U.S. political development has criticized Moore's argument about the consequences of the Civil War. In an interesting 1974 article called "'Revolutions May Go Backwards': The American Civil War and the Problem of Political Development," William G. Shade argues that "political stabilization following the Civil War was achieved at the cost of political

[13] Richard Franklin Bensel, *Yankee Leviathan: The Origins of Central State Authority in America, 1859–1877* (New York: Cambridge University Press, 1990), pp. 433–34.
[14] Ibid., p. 436.

modernization."[15] For Shade, the issue is not whether post–Civil War U.S. political parties represented class-coherent alignments. Rather, using conceptualizations borrowed from Huntington's classic 1968 essay on "Political Modernization: America vs. Europe," Shade argues that during the Civil War the Republican party briefly established a more centralized U.S. state that mobilized popular political support on a national basis and "fused" functions previously separated institutionally under the "Tudor" American Constitution.[16] There was indeed a burst of Huntingtonian "political modernization," but it was accompanied by instability and violence. For postwar U.S. political leaders, it was inherently difficult either to continue such political modernization or to reestablish a stable, peaceful polity after the end of Reconstruction, when the South re-entered the national electoral system. The upshot, according to Shade, was that the deradicalized postwar Republicans reverted toward the patronage politics and decentralized accommodations that were standard for nineteenth-century U.S. politics. "Republican leaders settled upon the tariff issue as the basis for party unity. It enabled them to focus nationalist sentiments, emphasize progress in terms of economic growth, and appeal to a wide spectrum of economic groups."[17]

Meanwhile, in the national polity as a whole, the "country rejected the Radicals and political modernization for a 'New Departure' version of the familiar Tudor polity." As Shade elaborates, "faith in the fundamental law [of the Constitution] persisted, unitary federal sovereignty was rejected, the sharing of functions among the branches revived, the political participation of blacks [was] curtailed." Moreover, within the "third party system" that prevailed between the mid-1870s and the mid-1890s, both the Democrats and the Republicans remained "'exterior' parties . . . [that] depended upon state machines; local issues played a much greater role than they had in the decade of political decay which immediately preceded the war. The . . . political structure once again reinforced the federal system; the parties participated in a silent conspiracy to prevent the expansion [of federal power] from departing too far from the eighteenth-century constitutional structure."[18] From this perspective, Huntington's failure to analyze the Civil War in his 1968 essay was understandable. The Civil War and Reconstruction were but an exceptional interlude in the long-term trajectory of U.S. political development.

Of course the Huntingtonian institutionalist William Shade and the political economist Richard Bensel disagree fundamentally about *why* U.S. national

---

[15] William G. Shade, "'Revolutions Can Go Backwards': The American Civil War and the Problem of Political Development," *Social Science Quarterly* 55, no. 3 (December 1974): 753–67. The phrase in the title is quoted from the abolitionist Thomas Wentworth Higginson.
[16] Huntington, "America vs. Europe.".
[17] Shade, "'Revolutions Can Go Backwards,'" p. 764.
[18] Ibid., p. 763, 765.

political development after Reconstruction took the directions it did. While Shade places the explanatory emphasis on the enduring racist, constitutional-ist, and localist values of the American people as a whole, Bensel stresses the logic of capitalist industrialization in a situation of politically "incoherent" class and regional alignments.[19] Despite these seemingly fundamental dis-agreements, however, these theorists—along with virtually all others who have criticized Moore's argument about the Civil War—agree that the one hope for progressive U.S. politics in the later nineteenth century lay with the Radical Republicans and with permanent victories for land reform and black voting rights in the South.

No one can gainsay that the defeat of radical efforts during Reconstruction was crucial—especially for explaining why American governmental and elec-toral developments did not converge toward European bureaucratic and social-democratic patterns by 1900. All the same, we can wonder whether this was the whole story about U.S. democracy and welfare-oriented national gov-ernmental action in the late nineteenth century. Did the political failures of Radical Republicanism and Reconstruction really bring an end to the modern-izing and democractic potentials of the gargantuan Union effort? Were the post-Reconstruction Republicans really just the agents of federal decentraliza-tion, "Tudor" constitutionalism, and established propertied interests that Shade, Bensel, and others make them out to be?

I maintain that consideration of one oft-neglected aftermath of the Civil War—namely, the expansion of generous federal pensions for Union veterans and their dependents—can help us to more fully appreciate what Shade has called the "ironic dimensions" of U.S. political development after the huge internal bloodletting of the 1860s. In my view, Barrington Moore's original thesis that the Civil War furthered American democracy, and even social democracy to some extent, can be supported in a way that Moore himself never imagined. We need to take more careful account than did Moore of the precise governmental, party, and electoral structures of the U.S. national polity in the nineteenth century. If we do this, we can come to understand why one of the crucial effects of the Civil War upon that national polity was to further the possibilities for the world's first generous regime of social spending. Although American national government and electoral politics did indeed revert after the abortive end of Reconstruction to well-established routines of patronage politics, the result was not just a revisiting of decentralized "Tudor" constitu-tionalism. Nor was it a commitment to government for the privileged and propertied alone. The well-being of many disabled and dependent ordinary Americans also became a central concern of the federal government during the era after the end of Reconstruction.

[19] Ibid., p. 767; and Bensel, *Yankee Leviathan,* chap. 7.

The Dimensions of Civil War Pensions

Between 1880 and 1910, the U.S. federal government devoted over a quarter of its expenditures to pensions distributed among the populace; aside from interest payments on the national debt in the early 1880s, such expenditures exceeded or nearly equaled other major categories of federal spending.[20] By 1910, about 28 percent of all American men aged 65 or more, more than half a million of them, received federal benefits averaging $189 a year.[21] Over three hundred thousand widows, orphans, and other dependents were also receiving payments from the federal treasury.[22] During the same period, thousands of elderly men and a few hundred women were also residents of special homes maintained by the federal government or their respective states.[23] Officially all of these benefits were granted under federal and state laws dealing with veterans of the Civil War.

Here we shall be concerned only with federal Civil War pensions, by far the most costly and expensive of the public programs for veterans and their survivors. The pattern and timing of the expansion of Civil War pensions reveal that this was not merely a military program, and not simply a mopping-up operation in the direct aftermath of the 1860s conflict. The human after-effects of the Civil War interacted with intense political party competition between the 1870s and the 1890s to fuel public generosity toward a fortunate generation of aging men and their family dependents—including less privileged as well as middle-class Americans, and including African-American as well as white Union veterans. As a result of the expansion of Civil War pensions, the United States during the late nineteenth century became for many of its citizens a kind of precocious social spending state: precocious in terms of the usual presumption of an absence of federal involvement in social welfare before the New Deal, and precocious in terms of how the United States around 1900 compared to other Western nations.

[20] Richard Franklin Bensel, *Sectionalism and American Political Development, 1880–1980* (Madison: University of Wisconsin Press, 1984), p. 67. Bensel computed his percentages from the 1936 *Annual Report of the Secretary of the Treasury on the State of the Finances* (Washington, D.C.: Government Printing Office, 1937), table 5, pp.362–63.

[21] In 1910 there were 562,615 invalid Civil War pensioners on the rolls, receiving $106,433,465, and the national population of males 65 years and over was 1,985,976. The sources for these figures are *Report of the Commissioner of Pensions,* included in *Reports of the Department of the Interior for the Fiscal Year Ended June 30, 1910,* vol. 1 (Washington, D.C.: Government Printing Office, 1911), pp.146, 149; and U.S. Bureau of the Census, *Historical Statistics of the United States,* bicentennial ed., pt.1, series A 119–134 (Washington, D.C.: Government Printing Office, 1975), p.15.

[22] *Report of the Commissioner of Pensions,* p. 272.

[23] Judith Gladys Cetina, "A History of Veterans' Homes in the United States, 1811–1930" (Ph.D. diss., Department of History, Case Western Reserve University, 1977), chaps. 3–7. Veterans' homes, as well as state and local benefits for Union and Confederate veterans and survivors, are discussed in Skocpol, "Public Aid for the Worthy Many."

The Civil War—Necessary but Not Sufficient

The basic precondition for the later widespread disbursement of military pensions to military veterans and the survivors of deceased soldiers was the duration, intensity, and mass-mobilizing quality of the Civil War itself. "With the national economies on both sides fully integrated into their respective war efforts, the American Civil War was truly . . . the first 'total' war in the modern sense."[24] The conflict not only joined industrial with human mobilization, but also the pattern of warfare, especially once Union forces drove deeply into the South, was relatively unlimited in that it was directed against civilians and economic targets as well as military formations. What is more, the American Civil War, like the earlier French revolutionary wars and the later world wars of the twentieth century, was "democratic," because the entire adult male citizenry was subject to calls to military service. At first, the calls in the North were voluntary; but in March 1863 conscription was instituted for men 20 to 45 years old who could not pay commutation or arrange for substitutes.[25]

The Civil War was also, by far, the most devastating war the United States has ever experienced. Some statistical facts about the North's experience of the Civil War can help to convey how traumatic it was. (White southerners suffered an even greater human impact, as we shall learn below.) About 2,213,000 men served in the Union army and navy.[26] This included about 37 percent of the northern men between the ages of 15 and 44 in 1860[27]—fully comparable to the massive one-third of British men who served in World War I, a quintessential total, modern war.[28] Overall, the Union side in the Civil War suffered 364,511 mortal casualties (including 140,414 battle deaths and 224,097 other deaths, mostly from disease).[29] These numbers translate into a ratio of about 18 northerners killed per thousand in the population, whereas only 1.31 Americans per thousand were to die in World War I, and 3.14 per thousand

[24] R. Ernest Dupuy and Trevor N. Dupuy, *The Encyclopedia of Military History from 3500 B.C. to the Present,* 2nd rev. ed. (New York: Harper and Row, 1986), p. 820.

[25] Eugene C. Murdock, *One Million Men: The Civil War Draft in the North* (Madison: State Historical Society of Wisconsin, 1971), chap. 1; and James W. Geary, *We Need Men: The Union Draft in the Civil War* (DeKalb: Northern Illinois University Press, 1991).

[26] *Bureau of the Census, Department of Commerce, Historical Statistics of the United States, Colonial Times to 1970,* bicentennial ed. pt. 2, series Y 856–903 (Washington, D.C.: U.S. Government Printing Office, 1975), p. 1140.

[27] The 37 percent figure was estimated as follows, from ibid., pt. 1, series 172–194, pp.22–23: I added the 1860 population in "15–24" and "25–44" for the Northeast, North Central, and West regions; then I multiplied by the proportion of males (51.36%) in the total populations of these regions in 1860. Then I divided the 2,213,000 who served on the Union side of the Civil War by the estimated 5,903,832 men, 15–44, who lived in the nonsouthern regions in 1860.

[28] Arthur Marwick, *War and Society in the Twentieth Century* (London: Macmillan, 1974), p.61.

[29] *Bureau of Census, Historical Statistics,* pt. 2, series Y 856–903, p. 1140.

would become mortal casualities in World War II.[30] As for the Union military's wounded who survived, they numbered some 281,881, or about 14 per thousand in the northern population.[31]

Throughout this discussion, therefore, we need to remember that the sheer dimensions of the Civil War as a martial event made possible the subsequent expansion of a generous pension system. This war created a large number of survivors of dead soldiers, along with many wounded and other veterans who might later claim rewards for latent disabilities or for their service alone. Nevertheless, no examination of the demographics of the war outside of the context of the nineteenth-century U.S. polity can account for the development of the pension system, as a contrast with the other major nation that experienced democratic military mobilization in early modern times can help to dramatize.

From 1792 through 1815, Revolutionary and Napoleonic France experienced mass-mobilizing wars. "Over two and a half million recruits passed through France's armies," most of whom died in combat or (especially) from disease, but some 150,000 of whom survived to be pensioned (along with an unknown number, in the thousands, who survived without pensions).[32] Benefits for French soldiers commenced in generous terms at the democratic height of the Revolution, much as still-more-generous U.S. veterans' benefits were later to commence in the democratic North in the midst of the Civil War. Laws passed in France in 1793 reflected a historically unprecedented concern to pension not just officers but also disabled and needy common soldiers and the widows of soldiers who died in service.[33] The subsequent historical trajectory of French veterans' benefits was, however, conditioned by fiscal constraints and, even more, by the revival of bureaucratic controls and elite patronage under Napoleon.

In France after 1803, a large backlog of pension applications was efficiently processed by the bureaucracy, but the rates of pensions were sharply lowered, and the eligibility of common soldiers and their widows to receive help was restricted, even as French officers received proportionately more under the 1803 laws and through special grants to favorites from Napoleon himself.[34] Despite the benefit cutbacks, as backlogs of previously wounded veterans moved through the system, overall French pension costs attributable to the

---

[30] I divided the northern mortal casualties by a total population figure of 20,310,000 outside the South obtained from ibid., pt. 1, series A 172–194, p. 22. Battle deaths in proportion to population for World Wars I and II come from J. David Singer and Melvin Small, *The Wages of War, 1816–1965: A Statistical Handbook* (New York: John Wiley and Sons, 1972), p. 260.

[31] *Bureau of Census Historical Statistics,* pt. 2, series Y, p. 1140.

[32] Isser Woloch, *The French Veteran from the Revolution to the Restoration* (Chapel Hill: University of North Carolina Press, 1979), pp. 206, 209–10, 308, and chap. 7.

[33] Ibid.; and also Isser Woloch, "War-Widows Pensions: Social Policy in Revolutionary and Napoleonic France," *Societas* 6, no. 4 (Autumn 1976): 235–54.

[34] Woloch, *French Veteran*, pp. 101–9; and Woloch, "War-Widows Pensions," pp. 244–51.

Revolutionary and Napoleonic Wars continued to rise modestly through the 1810s.[35] France continued during subsequent decades to do more for veteran common soldiers than did other European nations.[36] But its veterans' benefits did not for many years become as generous (in levels or coverage) as they had been at the height of the Revolution. And they would never become anywhere near as legally liberalized, socially far-reaching, or costly as those of the late-nineteenth-century United States. The contrast, I maintain, was between a mass mobilizing French Revolution that gave way to centralized bureaucracy and only episodically redemocratized postrevolutionary regimes, and a U.S. Civil War that entailed democratic mass mobilization without centralized bureaucratic controls and that subsequently gave way to a restoration of full-fledged federal patronage democracy.

Raising Massive Armies in a Nonbureaucratic Democracy

Generous responses by the Union side to the needs of the soldiers and sailors fighting for its cause commenced within the first year of the Civil War, well before anyone imagined that the conflict would drag on so long and become so costly. The United States was a full democracy for white males, and the Republican party had risen to power in the name of "free land, free labor, and free men."[37] Generous treatment for soldiers was in accord with the outpouring of nationalist sentiment in the democratic North. It was also a practical necessity for a nonbureaucratic state, especially once the first rush of patriotic volunteering was over and prior to the institution of conscription in 1863.

During 1861, preexisting regular army benefits were granted to the first volunteers for the Civil War, yet this was understood to be only a stopgap approach. In February 1862, a new law specifically addressing the needs of Union soldiers and their dependents was enthusiastically enacted by the Republican-dominated Congress.[38] Secretary of the Interior J. P. Ushur proudly declared it "the wisest and most munificent enactment of the kind ever adopted by any nation."[39] Subsequently, the 1862 law was rendered

[35] Woloch, *French Veteran*, pp. 206–7.

[36] See the report prepared for the U.S. Sanitary Commission during the Civil War: Stephen H. Perkins, *Report on the Pension Systems and Invalid Hospitals of France, Prussia, Austria, Russia and Italy, with Some Suggestions upon the Best Means of Disposing of Our Disabled Soldiers*, Sanitary Commission Report No. 67 (New York: William C. Bryant and Co., 1863).

[37] Eric Foner, *Free Soil, Free Labor, Free Men: The Ideology of the Republican Party before the Civil War* (New York: Oxford University Press, 1970).

[38] William H. Glasson, *Federal Military Pensions in the United States* (New York: Oxford University Press, 1918), pp. 124–25.

[39] As quoted in John William Oliver, "History of Civil War Military Pensions, 1861–1885," *Bulletin of the University of Wisconsin*, no. 844, History Series, no.1 (1917): 9–10, from House Executive Documents, 38th Cong., 2d sess., 1864–65, vol. 5, p. 11.

more generous and systematic by a steady stream of legislative tinkering; but it was destined to remain the baseline of the Civil War pension system until 1890.

Under the 1862 law, the award of pension benefits was directly linked to disabilities "incurred as a direct consequence of . . . military duty" or, after the close of combat, "from causes which can be directly traced to injuries received or disease contracted while in military service."[40] At the same time, widows, orphans, and other dependents of those who died for causes traceable to their Union military service also received pensions at the rates their relatives would have gotten for total disabilities.[41] The rates for dependents were very generous by preexisting historical standards in the United States and elsewhere; and the range of potential beneficiaries also became remarkably broad.

Patterns of Pension Growth after the Civil War

Given the generosity of the basic Civil War pension law, as well as the magnitude of the needs immediately generated by the war, it is hardly suprising that each year thousands of former soldiers and survivors of soldiers who had died applied for these military-disability pensions. Before pensioners from the Civil War started to be added to the rolls in 1862, the United States was paying benefits to 10,700 veterans and widows at a total cost of about $1 million per year; and beneficiaries and expenditures were declining each year.[42] By 1866, however, the Civil War enrollments had suddenly swelled the pension list to 126,722, with total disbursements mounting to about $15.5 million.[43] From 1866 through 1874, the numbers of pensioners and the cost grew steadily, as the human costs to the northern side of America's massive internal bloodletting registered in the public fisc.

The pension costs of the Civil War seemed to peak in the years after 1870— just as one might expect for a benefit system tied directly to disabilities incurred in wartime service. "We have reached the apex of the mountain," declared Commissioner of Pensions James H. Baker in 1872.[44] The numbers of new applications declined after 1870; the total number of pensioners stopped growing in 1873; and the total expenditures reached an apparent upper limit in 1874.[45] Although there were complaints about fraudulent pen-

[40] As quoted in Glasson, *Federal Military Pensions,* p. 125.
[41] Ibid., pp. 126–28, 138–42; and Oliver, "History of Civil War Military Pensions," pp. 10, 21–22.
[42] Glasson, *Federal Military Pensions,* p. 124.
[43] Ibid., p. 273.
[44] As quoted in Oliver, "History of Civil War Military Pensions," p. 39.
[45] Glasson, *Federal Military Pensions,* pp. 148–49.

sion claims even in this early period, the political impact of this concern was undercut when the system seemed to stop expanding.

Part of the reason for the mid-1870s pause in the expansion of the Civil War pension system must have been that the subjectively most pressing needs of the (then-youthful) veterans and survivors had already been addressed. True, the Pension Bureau refused to accept about 28 percent of the applications it received between 1862 and 1875.[46] Yet it is important to realize that large numbers of potential pensioners did not apply at all. Although the requirement to demonstrate service-connected disabilities obviously limited applications from veterans, many potentially eligible veterans and survivors failed to apply for pensions during the decade after the war's end. A desire to forget the war and get on with life, an absence of financial need, unfamiliarity with the possibilities or the application procedures, and a reluctance on the part of some to take handouts from the government—all of these factors may have been involved in the initially low "take-up rate" for Civil War disability pensions. And that rate truly was rather low. Among the survivors of the Union soldiers who were killed during the war, plus the survivors of the veterans who died by 1870, only about 25 percent were receiving dependents' pensions in 1875.[47] Also, we know that about 15 percent of the surviving former soldiers in 1865 had been wounded during the war.[48] Presumably most of them, if motivated, would have been in a very good position to claim some sort of disability benefits (and this does not include many others who could make the case for later disabilities that had remained latent during the war). Yet table 4–1 reveals that only 6.5 percent of all veterans, or about 43 percent of the formerly

---

[46] I calculated an acceptance rate of 72 percent (and a rejection rate of 28 percent) from figures presented for the years 1861 and after in the *Annual Report of the Commissioner of Pensions for 1888* (Washington, D.C.: Government Printing Office, 1888), p. 35, table 6. The number of applications filed is calculated for the years 1861 through 1875, and the number accepted is calculated for 1861 through 1876, in the conviction that many applications filed in 1875 may have been processed during 1876. Interestingly, the 28 percent rejection rate for 1861 to 1875 was considerably lower than the rejection rate of about 38 percent for the entire period from 1861 to 1888. Presumably, applications in the period during and right after the Civil War were more likely to be corroborated by hard evidence of death or disability.

[47] For the war's "mortal casualties" of 364,511, see note 33; for the 106,669 recipients of pensions for "widows and dependents" in 1875, see Glasson, *Federal Military Pensions*, p. 144. I divided the latter number by the former, to get a take-up rate of 29.3 percent. But actually, this percentage must be low, because about 100,000 more men died between 1864 and 1870, most presumably due to causes traceable to the war, and their relatives would have had time to apply for pensions before 1875. If these are included, the take-up rate for dependents' pensions in 1875 becomes 23 percent.

[48] I arrived at a percentage of 15.4 by dividing the number of wounded survivors of the Civil War (for which see note 37) by the number of "union veterans in civil life" in 1865 given in table 1. Of course, this is only a rough estimate, because some of the wounded surely died during 1864–65, and others of the originally wounded who later recovered may have remained in the regular military after the end of the war.

Table 4-1. Take-up rates for Civil War Pensions

	Union veterans in civil life	Disabled military pensioners	Percent of veterans enrolled as pensioners
1865	1,830,000	35,880[a]	1.96
1870	1,744,000	87,521	5.02
1875	1,654,000	107,114	6.48
1880	1,557,000	135,272	8.69
1885	1,449,000	244,201	16.85
1890	1,322,000		
1891		520,158	39.34
1895	1,170,000	735,338	62.85
1900	1,000,000	741,259	74.13
1905	821,000	684,608	83.39
1910	624,000	562,615	90.16
1915	424,000	396,370	93.48

Sources: Bureau of the Census, *Historical Statistics of the United States, Colonial Times to 1970,* bicentennial ed., pt. 2, series 957-970 (Washington, D.C.: U.S. Government Printing Office, 1975), p. 1145; and William H. Glasson, *Federal Military Pensions in the United States* (New York: Oxford University Press, 1918), pp. 144, 271, 272.
[a]Includes a few prior invalids.

wounded men who might have been especially eligible, had signed up for (disability) pensions by 1875.

Despite the initial reluctance of many veterans and surviving relatives to claim pension benefits, the "apex of the mountain" for Civil War pensions came not in the mid-1870s as Commissioner Baker declared, but two decades later. Table 4-1 and figure 4-1 show what happened to the Civil War pension system as it evolved from a generous, partially utilized program for compensation of combat injuries and deaths into an even more generous system of disability and old age benefits, which were ultimately "taken up" by over 90 percent of the Union veterans surviving in 1910. In contrast to what happened in France after the Revolution, the terms of eligibility for U.S. veterans' pensions became steadily more liberal in the decades after the Civil War. Accordingly, after the mid-1870s, the numbers of pensioners and the costs resumed upward trajectories and continued to grow until the facts of generational mortality overtook the ingenuity of politicians at channeling ever higher benefits to ever more people.

There were several notable legal watersheds along the way. The 1879 Arrears Act allowed soldiers who newly discovered Civil War–related disabilities to sign up and receive in one lump sum all of the pension payments they would have been eligible to receive since the 1860s. A decade later, the 1890 Dependent Pension Act severed the link between pensions and service-related inju-

Figure 4-1. The expansion of Civil War pensions, 1866–1917

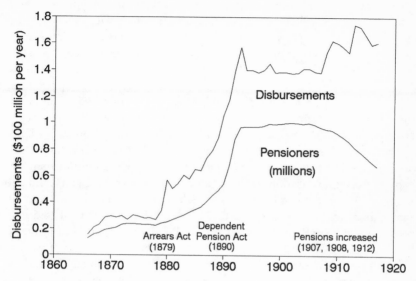

Source: William H. Glasson, *Federal Military Pensions in the United States* (New York: Oxford University Press, 1918), p. 273.

whether or not he had seen combat or been in any way hurt during the war, could apply for a pension if at some point in time he became disabled for manual labor. In practice, old age alone soon became a sufficient disability, and in 1906 the law was amended to state this explicitly.[49] After the turn of the century, moreover, Congress several times significantly raised the general benefit levels for both veterans and surviving dependents.

What happened after the mid-1870s to the Civil War pensions system? Clearly, pensions became caught up in politics, but how, exactly? Certain political mechanisms that might have fueled expansion have been suggested by several scholars who have examined the matter. Let me comment briefly on the ideas of some of these other scholars before I develop my own arguments.

One argument about the liberalization of Civil War pensions is a pressure group thesis.[50] After the Civil War, hundreds of thousands of former Union soldiers organized themselves into veterans' associations, which in turn repeatedly lobbied Congress to improve benefits. Indeed, this "social demand"

[49] U.S. Bureau of Pensions, *Laws of the United States Governing the Granting of Army and Navy Pensions* (Washington, D.C.: U.S. Government Printing Office, 1925), p. 43.

[50] James Q. Wilson, "The Rise of the Bureaucratic State," *The Public Interest*, no. 41 (Fall 1975): 88–89.

argument gains plausibility from the highly visible role that the most important northern veterans' organization, the Grand Army of the Republic, played
in lobbying for legal liberalization in the years prior to the Dependent Pension
Act of 1890, and the glee with which the organization greeted this law when it
passed.[51] Other facts militate against simple reliance on the GAR pressure
group thesis, however. During the 1870s, when the Arrears Act was urged
through Congress, the Grand Army of the Republic was at best limping along,
with many of its state-level "departments" in severe disarray and others avoid-
ing political entanglements by concentrating on local fellowship and charity.[52]
The national Grand Army of the Republic did not officially endorse or lobby
for the Arrears Act, which actually seems to have affected the GAR more than
vice-versa.[53] The new law stimulated thousands of applications for membership in veterans' associations (of which the GAR was the strongest), and also
intensified the interest of Grand Army leaders in pension legislation and administration. In 1881–82, the GAR set up a Washington, D.C.–based Pensions Committee to lobby Congress and the Pensions Bureau. The most rapid
expansion of the GAR came during the 1880s—"immediately after the society
. . . began its aggressive campaign for government aid to veterans"—and the
organization reached the peak of its membership in 1890, when it enrolled 39
percent of all surviving Union veterans.[54] After 1890, as during the decade
before, the GAR continued to pressure Congress on behalf of ever-more
liberalized pension laws. Yet the GAR never did get all that it asked Congress
to give; and even the Dependent Pension Act of 1890 fell a little short of the

---

[51] Mary Dearing, *Veterans in Politics: The Story of the G.A.R.* (Baton Rouge: Louisiana State
University Press, 1952), pp. 397–401.
[52] On the situation of the Grand Army in the 1870s, see Robert B. Beath, *History of the
Grand Army of the Republic* (New York: Bryan, Taylor, and Co., 1888); Dearing, *Veterans in
Politics,* chapter 6; Frank H. Heck *The Civil War Veteran in Minnesota Life and Politics*
(Oxford, Ohio: Mississippi Valley Press, 1941), pp. 11–12, and chap. 2; Edward Noyes,"The
Ohio G.A.R. and Politics from 1866 to 1900," *The Ohio State Archaeological and Historical
Quarterly* 55 (1946): 80–81; and George J. Lankevich, "The Grand Army of the Republic in
New York State, 1865–1898" (Ph.D. diss., Columbia University, 1967), chaps. 4–6.
[53] Stuart Charles McConnell, "A Social History of the Grand Army of the Republic, 1867–
1900" (Ph.D. diss., Johns Hopkins University, 1987), pp. 368–79; Elmer Edward Noyes, "A
History of the Grand Army of the Republic in Ohio from 1866 to 1900" (Ph.D. diss., Ohio State
University, 1945), pp. 79–89; and Lankevich, "Grand Army in New York State," pp. 142–56.
[54] Wallace Evan Davies, *Patriotism on Parade: The Story of Veterans' and Hereditary Organizations in America, 1783–1900* (Cambridge, Mass.: Harvard University Press, 1955), pp. 36,
160; and Stuart McConnell, "Who Joined the Grand Army? Three Case Studies in the Construction of Union Veteranhood, 1866–1900," in *Toward a Social History of the American Civil
War: Exploratory Essays,* ed. Maris A. Vinovskis (New York: Cambridge University Press, 1990),
p. 141. McConnell reports a slightly higher GAR membership figure for 1890 (427,981) than
does Heck, *Civil War Veteran in Minnesota,* p. 257 (409,489). I adjusted the percentage from
McConnell because Heck's figure cross-checks with the number officially given in *Journal of the
Twenty-fifth National Encampment, Grand Army of the Republic* (Rutland, Vt.: The Tuttle
Company, 1891), p. 66.

straight "service pension" (that is, for all veterans aged 62 and above, with no disability clause) that many within the GAR were demanding.[55]

Another argument stresses the link between protective tariffs and the expansion of pension expenditures. Generous Civil War pensions become in this view a way to siphon off the embarrassing fiscal "surpluses" that high tariffs incidentally produced. Those supposedly pulling the political strings were protection-minded businesses in the northeastern "core" region of the country. The Republican Party is pictured as controlled by such protectionist business interests, while the Democratic Party opposed both high tariffs and generous pensions because both worked to the fiscal disadvantage of the South and other places (including New York City) with a stake in free commerce.[56] Midwestern agricultural areas that might otherwise have had an interest in free trade are considered to have been "bought off" by the disproportionate flow of pensions, funded by tariff revenues, to veterans and survivors in those areas. In current scholarship, this argument is most clearly put forward by the political scientist Richard Bensel.[57]

What was the relationship between pensions and tariff revenues? Figure 4–2 shows that customs receipts constituted between 30 percent and 58 percent of federal revenues during the entire period between the Civil War and World War I. Figure 4–3 shows that there was, indeed, a federal budget "surplus"— that is, an excess of total receipts over current expenditures—from 1866 to 1893. The Dependent Pension Act of 1890, designed to make many more veterans eligible for pensions than under previous laws, passed after a decade of spectacular federal surpluses. Curiously, however, the Arrears Act of 1879 passed at a time when there was practically no surplus, that is, when the customs receipts of the day were actually being spent on other items (especially on retiring the debt). Supported by both Republicans and northern Democrats, this critical piece of pension legislation passed without a close connection to the spending of surplus revenues, and indeed there were many worries about how to cover its anticipated cost.[58]

Arguments pointing to organized veterans or tariff advocacy by protection-

[55] Although advocates of straight service pensions managed to get the National Encampments of the GAR to endorse that option in 1888 and 1890, key national GAR leaders preferred the more "moderate" disability-service pension that was actually enacted in 1890. Thus, during 1889, the GAR's national Pension Committee supported the introduction of both types of bills in the respective houses of Congress. See McConnell, "Social History of the Grand Army of the Republic," p. 377, and Lankevich, "Grand Army in New York State," pp. 235–37.

[56] See William H. Glasson, "The South and Service Pension Laws," *South Atlantic Quarterly* 1 (October 1902): 351–60.

[57] Richard Franklin Bensel, *Sectionalism and American Political Development, 1880–1980* (Madison: University of Wisconsin Press, 1984): chap. 3.

[58] Glasson, *Federal Military Pensions,* pp. 163, 166–73. In fact, because of the worries over costs, when the appropriations for the act were made, some new provisions were added to limit somewhat the amounts of arrears paid to successful applicants (see pp. 172–73).

Figure 4–2. Customs receipts as percentage of total federal receipts, 1866–1916

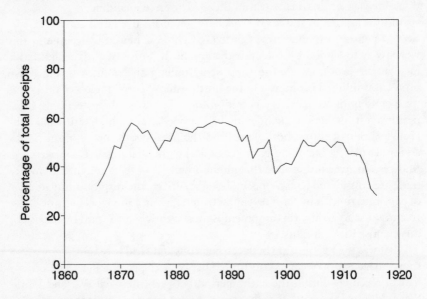

Source: Historical Statistics of the United States: Colonial Times to 1970, Bicentennial ed., pt. 2 (Washington: Bureau of the Census, 1975), p. 1106, series Y 352, Y 353.

ist northeastern industrialists are not so much wrong as incomplete and under-specified. Such groups were part of the Republican-orchestrated coalition behind the 1890 Dependent Pension Act. But there were other instruments in the band; and the party leaders who set the tune had their own organizational interests above and beyond those of the GAR and business groups.[59] The expansion of Civil War pensions must be understood in relation to the structure of the nineteenth-century U.S. state and situated in terms of the dynamics of political party competition after the Civil War. The expansion of Civil War pensions reflected the proclivity of the nineteenth-century U.S. political parties to enact distributive policies—policies that allowed the spread of some-times carefully timed and targeted benefits to key supporters in their geographically widespread cross-class constituencies.[60] The important legal watersheds also reflected the changing competitive strategies of the major

[59] For a political dispute in which the preferences of party politicians differed from those of business groups advocating tariff reform, see S. Walter Poulshock, "Pennsylvania and the Politics of the Tariff, 1880–1888," *Pennsylvania History* 29 (July 1962).

[60] See Richard L. McCormick, *The Party Period and Public Policy: American Politics from the Age of Jackson to the Progressive Era* (New York: Oxford University Press, 1986), esp. chap. 5. For a discussion of how nineteenth-century U.S. political arrangements furthered distributive social policies, see Skocpol, *Protecting Soldiers and Mothers,* chap. 1.

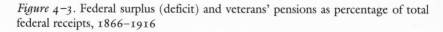

Figure 4–3. Federal surplus (deficit) and veterans' pensions as percentage of total federal receipts, 1866–1916

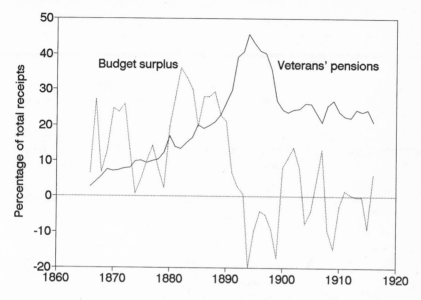

Source: Historical Statistics of the United States: Colonial Times to 1970, Bicentennial ed., p. 2 (Washington: Bureau of the Census, 1975), p. 1106, series Y 352; p. 1104, series Y 337; and William H. Glasson, *Federal Military Pensions in the United States* (New York: Oxford University Press, 1918), p. 273.

political parties; and the forms of new legislation maximized possibilities for using pensions to recruit voters.

After the end of Reconstruction, the Republicans became locked in tight national-level competition with a revived Democratic Party for control of the presidency and the Congress. This was a competition which lasted until after the realignment of 1896, when the Republicans again became nationally dominant. The initial major liberalization of Civil War pensions through the Arrears Act was spurred by the revival of tight party competition. Yet the ensuing expansion of pensioners and pension costs soon worked differentially to the advantage of the Republican party, which learned the uses of the Pension Bureau in managing the application backlog spurred by the Arrears Act. After the mid-1880s, the national Democrats emphasized tariff reductions and backed off from pension liberalization, while the Republicans became the champions of a politically as well as fiscally complementary set of generous distributive policies, including pensions along with tariffs. The Dependent Pension Act of 1890 was very much a Republican-sponsored measure, an intraparty compromise; and later slight changes in this law also came under Republican auspices.

From the Arrears Act to Congressional and Party Patronage

Supported by both Republicans and northern Democrats at a moment soon after the end of Reconstruction when national electoral politics had again become intensively competitive, the Arrears of Pension Act was signed into law by President Rutherford B. Hayes on January 25, 1879. According to this law (as later amended in the appropriations process), whenever it was found that applicants for pensions had been awarded benefits starting some years after the war, their cases should be reopened and payments made back to the date of their discharge from the military or the death of the family breadwinner. What is more, anyone who applied for a new pension (up until July 1880) would, assuming it was eventually granted, automatically receive as part of the first payment all of the "arrears," or previous pension payments, to which he or she would have been entitled from the time of discharge or death. "The average first payment in 1881 to army invalids was $953.62; [and] to army widows, minor children, and dependent relatives, $1,021.51."[61] At a time in U.S. history when the average annual money earnings of nonfarm employees totaled about $400, these were considerable windfalls that could be put to excellent use.[62] As Hayes would later write in defense of this legislation: "Look at the good done. In every county of the North are small but comfortable homes built by the soldier out of his arrearage pay."[63] With the passage of the Arrears legislation, veterans and survivors had new motives to apply for both monthly pensions and the hefty initial lump-sum payments. "Before 1879, new claims had been filed at the rate of 1,600 a month; after the new act took effect, new claims rose to over 10,000 a month."[64] And the avalanche of new applications was to be processed by a U.S. Pension Bureau that had few means at its disposal to detect fraudulent claims by pension applicants.

The consequences of the Arrears Act in 1879 transformed Civil War pensions from relatively straightforward compensation for wartime disabilities into fuel for patronage politics. Pension patronage flourished both through Congress and through party controls over the leadership and nonroutine practices of the Pension Bureau. An ideal "distributive" policy is one in which benefits are given to many particular recipients and politicians have some discretionary

---

61 Glasson, *Federal Military Pensions*, p. 175.

62 Bureau of the Census, *Historical Statistics*, pt. 1, series D 735–738, p. 165.

63 From Hayes's December 14, 1881 letter to William Henry Smith, as quoted in Glasson, *Federal Military Pensions*, p. 164.

64 Robert McElroy, *Grover Cleveland: The Man and the Statesman* (New York: Harper and Brothers, 1923), p. 190.

control over the timing and targeting of those benefits. Civil War pensions may not seem to fit this profile very well, if one assumes that conditions of eligibility were set by statutory law and potential recipients exercised all the discretion: that once they applied, they would automatically get the benefits if their qualifications fell within the statute. In fact, however, the statutes quickly became so bewilderingly complex that there was much room for interpretation of cases. Interior Department officials and Commissioners of Pensions might apply more or less stringent interpretations of existing statutes; they might even invite whole classes of old cases to be reopened to allow more generous pension awards.[65] In addition, individual cases (or groups of cases) might be speeded up or slowed down in their passage through the Bureau of Pensions. As a result of the many reapplications and new applications stimulated by the Arrears Acts, a backlog of several hundred thousand claims piled up for processing, and such massive backlogs continued to hang over the system into the nineties. This situation allowed considerable space for the manipulation of the timing of case processing.[66]

If a given applicant did not feel that his or her case had been correctly processed by the Pension Bureau, or if he or she thought that things were moving too slowly or that existing statutes did not quite cover the special merits of the case, a petition to a congressional representative might result. In 1882, Representative Roswell G. Horr of Michigan observed: "I think it is safe to say that each member of this House receives fifty letters each week; many receive more. . . . One-quarter of them, perhaps, will be from soldiers asking aid in their pension cases, and each soldier is clear in his own mind that the member can help his case out if he will only make it a special case and give it special attention."[67] Robert F. La Follette estimated in his autobiography that he spent from a quarter to a third of his time in Congress from 1885 to 1891 "examining testimony and untangling . . . records" for the "many old soldiers" in his district. Such help to a veteran from a Congressman could be just as important to the recipient's welfare as help to an unemployed worker from an urban political boss. As La Follette explained, "I recall one interesting case.

[65] On reinterpretations across administrations, see George Baber, ed., *Decisions of the Department of the Interior in Cases Relating to Pension Claims and to the Laws of the United States Granting and Governing Pensions,* vol. 4, (Washington, D.C.: Government Printing Office, 1891). The editorial preface to this volume states that it was intended to highlight disagreements about legal interpretation with the previous administration of Democratic President Grover Cleveland, differences flowing "from a spirit of larger liberality exercised by the present administration [of Republican President Benjamin Harrison] in applying the pension system to those entitled to its benefits" (p. iii).

[66] Heywood T. Sanders, "Paying for the 'Bloody Shirt': The Politics of Civil War Pensions," in *Political Benefits,* ed. Barry S. Rundquist (Lexington, Mass.: Lexington Books, D.C. Heath, 1980), p. 146.

[67] Leonard D. White, *The Republican Era, 1869–1901: A Study in Administrative History* (New York: Macmillan, 1958), p. 72.

An old man, by the name of Joseph Wood, living in Madison, very poor, had a claim pending for an injury received at Pittsburgh Landing. His case had been repeatedly rejected because the records of the War Department showed that his regiment had not arrived at Pittsburgh Landing until forty-eight hours after the claimant swore he had been injured." La Follette found that his captain and twenty-five other soldiers agreed with the claimant, and so did the memoirs of General Sherman. But the War Department would not question its records. "I seemed up against it, when it flashed across my mind that the [War Department] document looked too new to be the original record. Upon inquiry, I found this was true. The old worn records had been stored away some years before. Some one was detailed to examine them, and sure enough, there had been a mistake in copying. General Sherman and my old soldier friend were right. Thirty-six hundred dollars back pension brought comfort to that old man and his wife."[68] With a proliferation of cases such as these, the "volume of correspondence between the Pension Bureau and members of Congress was immense. In 1880 it was reported as amounting to nearly 40,000 written and personal inquiries; in 1888 it had more than doubled (94,000 items); and in 1891 it reached a peak of 154,817 congressional calls for information on the condition of cases, an average of over 500 for each working day."[69]

Pension patronage went beyond congressional interventions in individual cases. During the 1880s, when competitive patronage democracy was at its height, party-appointed leaders of the Pension Bureau exercised a certain amount of partisan discretion in the handling of categories of cases. Appointed in 1881 by Republican President James A. Garfield, Commissioner of Pensions Colonel W. W. Dudley proved to be a key innovator in the political use of the Pension Bureau. Not only did Dudley champion the rapid expansion of the Pension Bureau to facilitate the processing of claims; he also worked with the Grand Army of the Republic to draw up lists of potentially eligible veterans in each state, and he made lists of veterans' addresses available to new applicants so that they could locate witnesses. Commissioner Dudley determined that, as of 1882, over a million living Union veterans and almost 87,000 pensionable relatives had not yet applied for benefits; and he realized that two-fifths of existing pensioners, along with over half of the 300,000 claims then pending at the Bureau, came from the electorally crucial states of Illinois, Indiana, New York, Ohio, and Pennsylvania.[70] Moving from investigation of the political

68 Robert M. LaFollette, *La Follette's Autobiography: A Personal Narrative of Political Experiences*, (Madison: University of Wisconsin Press, 1968; orig. 1911), pp. 37–38. For other instances of particular congressional representatives who took pride in helping pension applicants, see Heck, *Civil War Veteran in Minnesota*, pp. 185–90.

69 White, *Republican Era*, p. 75.

70 My account of Dudley's activities draws on Oliver, "History of Civil War Military Pensions," pp. 105–17, and Sanders, "Politics of Pensions," pp. 146–50.

potential of the pension system to practical applications, Commissioner Dudley directed Pension Bureau officials not to refuse claims until after the 1884 presidential election, and told them to speed up the processing of applications from Ohio and Indiana, where the election was sure to be very close. In September 1884, moreover, Dudley went on a paid "leave of absence" from Washington, taking large numbers of pension examiners first into Ohio and then into Indiana. Prospective pensioners were sought out, urged to apply, and told to vote for the Republican ticket to ensure the rapid processing of their claims. Several Democrats later told congressional investigators that they voted Republican in the election out of fear for their pension applications![71]

Commissioner Dudley's efforts may have helped the Republicans to carry Ohio by 15,000 votes, but they failed by about 6,500 votes in Indiana.[72] The Democratic presidential candidate Grover Cleveland was elected, and Dudley had to resign his post. Nevertheless, Colonel Dudley's "performance was not lost on the Republican Party. [Thereafter] the party used its incumbency of the White House as a vehicle for boosting the outputs and generosity of the Pension Bureau. . . . If the Republicans were able to create an enduring alliance with the ex-soldiers and build a national political machine, it was largely because they were willing and able to employ the pension bureaucracy in a partisan fashion."[73] There were also reports of Democrats using the Pension Bureau to help former soldiers when they were in office and facing elections.[74] Nevertheless, Heywood Sanders presents rough evidence that the expansion of Pension Bureau budgets and personnel, and higher rates of approval for new pension claims, corresponded to years of Republican control of the executive branch between 1878 and 1899. "For the individual veteran," he concludes, "the choice was obvious. . . . Electoral support for Republican candidates promised a better pension, delivered more quickly."[75]

Republican Sponsorship of the Dependent Pension Act

Indeed, the Democrats and the Republicans increasingly parted company on the issue of pension generosity after the early 1880s. Although many northern Democrats in Congress continued to vote in favor of pension legislation, from the time of Grover Cleveland's presidency onward, the national Democratic Party and Democratic presidents stressed controls on pension

---

[71] Oliver, "History of Civil War Military Pensions," pp. 111–12, citing *House Report,* 48th Congr., 2d sess., vol. 3, No. 2683, pp. 6–9.

[72] Oliver, "History of Civil War Military Pensions," pp. 112, 117.

[73] Sanders, "Politics of Pensions," p. 150.

[74] According to Glasson, *Federal Military Pensions,* p. 224, President Cleveland's Commissioner of Pensions, John C. Black, attempted to use the bureau to aid the Democrats in 1888, especially in Indiana.

[75] Sanders, "Politics of Pensions," pp. 147–50, quotation on p. 150.

expenditures and the need to attack fraud in the system. Meanwhile, the Republicans waxed ever more eloquent in their advocacy of generosity to the Union veterans. As the 1888 Republican platform put it, "The legislation of Congress should conform to the pledges made by a loyal people and be so enlarged and extended as to provide against the possibility that any man who honorably wore the Federal uniform shall be the inmate of an almshouse, or dependent upon private charity. In the presence of an overflowing treasury, it would be a public scandal to do less for those whose valorous service preserved the government."[76]

"In the presence of an overflowing treasury." This phrase signals an important reason for major party differentiation on the question of further pension liberalization. After the 1870s, the rapid growth of the industrializing U.S. economy brought plentiful revenues into the federal treasury. As we saw in figures 4–2 and 4–3, tariff revenues accounted for between 30 percent and 58 percent of all federal revenues between the Civil War and World War I, and the decade of the 1880s was a time of huge surpluses in the federal budget. Even with efforts made to "retire the outstanding national debt as quickly as possible," nevertheless, in the words of Morton Keller, "the most pressing fiscal problem of the 1880s was the large revenue surplus generated by rising tariff receipts."[77] This rising surplus easily covered the unanticipated costs of the Arrears Act and left high-tariff advocates, mostly Republicans, looking for new ways to spend money, while Democratic advocates of lower taxes and tariffs could argue that the revenues were no longer needed.

The Republicans understood themselves to be the party of those who had saved the nation and could best represent its postwar interest in a strong, growing economy.[78] The party benefited by the 1880s from an ideally complementary set of distributive policies, using some measures such as protective tariffs and the expansion of federal services to generate the money and jobs that could be distributed through other policies, including the pension system. By finding popular new uses for the surpluses piling up in the 1880s, the Republicans hoped to maintain the tariffs that helped them build coalitions across industries and localities. If a way could be found to spread Civil War pensions to still more people, that would be ideal. After the Arrears Act, many veterans and survivors had applied for pensions but could not prove that disabilities or

---

[76] Donald Bruce Johnson, *National Party Platforms*, vol. 1, *1840–1956*, rev. ed. (Urbana: University of Illinois Press, 1978), p. 82.

[77] Keller, *Affairs of State*, p. 381.

[78] See Lewis Gould, "The Republican Search for a National Majority," in *The Gilded Age*, revised and enlarged ediition, ed. H. Wayne Morgan (Syracuse, N.Y.: Syracuse University Press, 1970), pp. 171–87; and a contemporary party statement, John D. Long, ed., *The Republican Party: Its History, Principles, and Policies*, (n. p., 1888).

deaths were directly connected to Civil War military service.[79] Additional pensions would flow overwhelmingly to the northeastern and midwestern states where the Republicans were strong (and wanted to stay strong), including states where they found themselves in close competition with the Democrats.[80] Furthermore, pensions apparently would go disproportionately to townspeople and farmers, the sectors of the Republican coalition that did not benefit as directly from tariffs as many workers and businessmen did (or believed they did).[81]

For the 1888 election, the Republicans mobilized the Grand Army of the Republic, whose membership stood at 372,960 in 1888.[82] They made strong promises about liberalized pensions and protective tariffs.[83] And they nominated a "soldier president," General Benjamin Harrison, who ran a campaign that linked tariffs to appeals to the veterans, as illustrated by a political song of the day:[84]

> Let Grover talk against the tariff, tariff, tariff
> And pensions too
> We'll give the workingman his due
> And pension the boys who wore the blue.

This combination worked for the Republican party in 1888. In an across-the-board victory widely attributed to the "old soldiers'" vote, the Republicans took both houses of Congress; and they won the presidency by detaching Indiana and New York from the states that had gone for Cleveland in 1884. Without controlled statistical studies, we cannot really tell whether pension politics made the difference in such key states in 1888. But we do have the necessary kind of evidence for Republican fortunes across 88 Ohio counties in elections from 1892 to 1895. Heywood Sanders found that, even when the veteran population was controlled for, the prior distribution of pensions up to 1890 significantly affected both turnouts and election results in favor of the Republicans.[85]

---

[79] Glasson, *Federal Military Pensions,* pp. 204–5.

[80] See Bensel, *Sectionalism and American Political Development,* p. 68, map 3.1, and pp. 62–73.

[81] We do not have good data on the precise social characteristics of pensioners, but suggestive findings along these lines appear in Sanders, "Politics," pp. 151–52.

[82] The GAR membership figure comes from Heck, *Civil War Veteran in Minnesota,* App. A, p. 356.

[83] See the 1888 Republican platform in Johnson, *National Party Platforms,* vol. 1, pp. 79–83.

[84] Quoted from Dearing, *Veterans in Politics,* pp. 382–83. For more on the 1888 election and its aftermath, see Donald McMurry, "The Political Significance of the Pension Question, 1885–1897," *Mississippi Valley Historical Review* 9, no. 1 (June 1922): 19–36.

[85] Sanders, "Politics of Pensions," pp. 150–54.

After the 1888 election, Republican President Harrison put a Union veteran and member of the GAR Pension Committee in charge of the Pension Bureau,[86] and he resubmitted liberalized pension legislation to the Congress. As the Pension Bureau forged ahead with granting pensions under loose interpretations of existing laws, the Republicans' "Billion Dollar Congress" enacted monetary reforms that helped knit together western and eastern Republicans, along with the the Dependent Pension Act, and the McKinley Tariff of 1890, which embodied the highest rates up to that point in U.S. history. The Dependent Pension Act was a "service-disability" measure, which relaxed the previous requirement that veterans must show disabilities originating in injuries actually incurred during the Civil War. Henceforth, monthly pensions could, in the words of the Act, be obtained by "all persons who served ninety days or more in the military or naval service of the United States during the late war of the Rebellion and who have been honorably discharged therefrom, and who are now or who may hereafter be suffering from a mental or physical disability of a permanent character, not the result of their own vicious habits, which incapacitates them from the performance of manual labor."[87] With this watershed legislation, the door was opened for many new successful applicants—exactly what the Republican party wanted.

Both the numbers of pensioners and overall expenditures on Civil War pensions leapt upward again after 1890 (see figure 4-1 above). By 1893, there were 966,012 pensioners, and the federal government was spending an astounding 41.5 percent of its income on benefits for them. This was the peak of expenditures, and of course, natural attrition was pruning the ranks of actual and potential beneficiaries. But new veteran pensioners also continued to apply throughout the 1890s. As table 4-1 documents, the percentage of Civil War veterans receiving benefits grew from 39 percent in 1891 to 74 percent in 1900. By 1915, 93 percent of Civil War veterans who were still living were signed up for federal benefits.

Over time, Civil War pensions became more and more obviously old-age and survivors' benefits for all those Americans fortunate enough to be able to claim service in the Union armies (or a connection to a man who had so served). Administrative rulings making age alone a "disability for manual labor" commenced soon after the Dependent Pension Act and were later confirmed by a 1906 law that declared simply "the age of sixty-two years and over shall be considered a permanent specific disability within the meaning of the pension laws."[88] Of course, even at its height the Civil War pension system was not the equivalent of the social insurance and old-age pension systems that

---

[86] Donald L. McMurry, "The Bureau of Pensions during the Administration of President Harrison," *Mississippi Valley Historical Review* 13, no. 3 (December 1926): 343–64.

[87] Bureau of Pensions, *Laws of the United States Governing Pensions,* p. 38.

[88] Ibid., p. 43.

were emerging in the fledgling European and Australasian "welfare states" of the late nineteenth and early twentieth centuries. While Americans fortunate enough to receive Civil War pensions actually got more generous payments on better terms than the first beneficiaries of foreign welfare-state policies, nevertheless the U.S. pensions did not reach all—or even most—less-privileged or working-class Americans.[89] Former Confederate white southerners were left out of the system, even though they were much poorer than northern whites during this period.[90] And less skilled wage-earners who had immigrated into the North after the Civil War were also ineligible for benefits. If they became impoverished due to disability or old-age, these immigrant wage-earners had no alternatives except to seek private charity or enter poor houses.

Yet Civil War pensions did help many former wage-earners and their dependents, along with many farmers and middle-class people. Perhaps most telling, Civil War pensions were available on surprisingly universalistic terms to African-Americans, 186,000 of whom had served in the Union military effort.[91] Barrington Moore and others have assumed that all possibilities for racial equality in the late-nineteenth-century United States disappeared when radical Reconstruction failed. But actually a flicker of interracial brotherhood did live on in and through the implementation of Civil War pensions. The U.S. Pension Bureau tried to apply its laws fairly to all veterans, including free northern blacks and the southern ex-slaves who fought for the Union. And the Bureau itself employed quite a number of African-American veterans on its large staff in Washington, D.C.

Looking back over the entire expansion of the Civil War pension system, it seems apparent that the dynamics of party-run patronage democracy spurred that expansion. Close competition between the Republicans and the Democrats in the late 1870s helped to bring about the passage of the Arrears Act, whose effects, in turn, fueled the emergence of the Republican "old soldiers'" machine. The major parties continued to be very closely competitive through the mid-1890s, and in this context it was especially advantageous for the Republicans to combine tariff protection with the increased distribution of social-welfare benefits under the Dependent Pension Act.

To be sure, in any polity—and certainly in any democracy—there would have been pressures to to provide for elderly and impoverished veterans to-

[89] For an analysis of the social incidence of Civil War benefits, and a comparison to benefits offered by early European welfare states, see Skocpol, *Protecting Soldiers and Mothers*, pp. 130–39.

[90] During the late 1880s and 1890s, the formerly Confederate southern states established minimal, needs-based pensions for their disabled military veterans. But there was never any southern analogue to the the the federal Dependent Pension Act of 1890. See the discussion in Skocpol, *Protecting Soldiers and Mothers*, pp. 139–40.

[91] See ibid., p. 138, and chap. 2, nn. 128, 129, 130, and 131.

ward the end of their lives. Such pressures in the 1830s and 1840s, for example, led to modest and very belated benefits (more than fifty years after the war!) for nonofficer Revolutionary War veterans and their survivors.[92] For Union Civil War veterans, however, this expectable movement toward universal-service coverage was speeded up and made much more generous. A military-disability system originally tailored to mobilize unprecedented masses of soldiers eventually became enmeshed in the intense competition of the distributively inclined parties that dominated both legislation and administration in the United States from the mid-1870s to the mid-1890s. Thus Civil War pensions became one of a handful of major distributive policies that helped to fuel and sustain late-nineteenth-century U.S. patronage democracy—and, especially, to further Republican fortunes within it.

Histories of U.S. social provision have mostly failed to notice that the national government was a major welfare provider at the turn of the century—no doubt because the relevant expenditures were officially categorized as military costs. Yet as Isaac Max Rubinow declared in 1913, five years after the British launched national old-age pensions, "when our [Amercan] pension roll numbers several thousand more names than that of Great Britain. . . . [and] when the cost of our pensions is . . . more than three times as great as that of the British pension system, . . . it is childish to consider the system of war pensions as a sentimental problem only, and to speak of the millions spent for war pensions as the cost of the 'Civil War.' We are clearly dealing here with an economic measure which aims to solve the problem of dependent old age and widowhood."[93]

Rubinow was right. Civil War pensions became one of the politically most successful social policies ever devised and sustained in the United States. These social benefits were expanded early in the country's modern national history, during the post-Reconstruction period when the radical tendencies of the "democratic capitalist" coalition that had achieved Union victory in the Civil War had petered out, but when other progressive possibilities still lived on through competitive electoral politics and the Republican Party. The expansion of Civil War pensions signaled the potential for honorable, cross-class, and cross-racial social provision to flourish in U.S. democracy.[94] These pensions at

92 John P. Resch, "Federal Welfare for Revolutionary War Veterans," *Social Service Review* 56, no. 2 (June 1982): 171–95.
93 I. M. Rubinow, *Social Insurance, With Special Reference to American Conditions* (New York: Arno Press, 1969; originally 1913), p. 404.
94 For a discussion of how Civil War pensions fit into patterns of more and less politically successful social policies in U.S. history, see Theda Skocpol, "Targeting Within Universalism: Politically Viable Policies to Combat Poverty in the United States," edited by Christopher Jencks and Paul E. Peterson, ed., *The Urban Underclass*, (Washington, D.C.: Brookings Institution, 1991), pp. 411–36.

their height were America's first system of federal social security for the disabled and the elderly.

Of course, federal social benefits of this scope and generosity were not to be sustained beyond the lifetime of the generation that fought to save the Union. All the same, the expansion of these public benefits during the late nineteenth century did exemplify—very much as Barrington Moore might have said, had he considered the matter—a little bit of "social democracy" in an era otherwise marked by "Thermidorean" government by and for the privileged. This little bit of social democracy practiced by the U.S. federal government was very much a legacy of the Union struggle in the Civil War, played out in the context of America's distinctive brand of patronage-oriented democratic politics. Until the late 1890s, U.S. politics remained extraordinarily electorally competitive and rooted in democratic popular support among a generation of northerners who had experienced directly the clash of freedom and national unity against slavery and separatism. For this generation—and for the Republican Party that even after Reconstruction continued to embody many of its ideals and interests—Barrington Moore's vision of the Civil War as the last democratic capitalist revolution surely made sense.

CHAPTER 5

Development, Revolution, Democracy, and Dictatorship: China Versus India?

EDWARD FRIEDMAN

In *Social Origins,* Barrington Moore, Jr., doubted that the peaceful British transfer of power to a democratic India would produce successful modernization because violence was needed to explode obstacles blocking development.[1] While British colonialism had disrupted a potential fascist route to modernization, Moore concluded that the "democratic capitalist" route was "an historical formation . . . past its zenith."[2] Only a Soviet Russian style Leninist dictatorship, following a nationalistic peasant revolution, as in China, could, for Moore, smash trammels and speed development. The "backward countries . . . want to go through Russia to reach America."[3] A Leninist command economy could win the material blessings of modernity.

Moore's pessimism about the prospects for Indian democracy was the conventional wisdom. Social scientists tended to agree that Mao's revolutionary China was a successful modernizer and Nehru's capitalistic democratic India a failure. In fact, India was politically democratic, but it was also economically

[1] One reviewer of *Social Origins,* Edith Link, pointed out, "An overriding theme of the book is . . . the peculiar position of India, where, without such revolutionary force as brought about capitalist democracy in England, France and America, democracy has been established on an admittedly shallow base. Moore shares the general doubts as to whither India" (*Journal of Economic History* [1967]: 262). Another reviewer, Jonathan Wiener, stated "India's move toward authoritarianism in 1975 confirms Moore's thesis that democracy cannot survive without social revolution" ("Review of Reviews," *History and Theory* 19 [1976]: 169).

[2] Barrington Moore, Jr., *Social Origins of Dictatorship and Democracy: Lord and Peasant in the Making of the Modern World* (Boston: Beacon Press, 1966), p. 483.

[3] Barrington Moore, Jr., "On the Notion of Progress, Revolution, and Freedom," *Ethics* 72 (1962): 114.

Leninist. Only in the 1990s did India begin to reform its Leninist economy. Dictatorial China, however, began reforming its Leninist economy already in 1978. The standard contrast of China as revolutionary, socialistic, and developmental and India as evolutionary, democratic, and stagnant obscures what is clarified by understanding India as a political democracy with a largely Leninist economy. Seeing it in this perspective clarifies the relations of democracy, dictatorship and development.

Democracy or Dictatorship

No reviewer challenged Moore's assertion about the superiority of socialist dictatorial China.[4] No one noted that India's economy was Leninist. Even though Leninist economics eventually failed everywhere, in the 1960s, it was not unusual to treat a Leninist economy as a success. Theory sees with glasses whose focal power is fixed by the grinding force of that moment's assumptions and preoccupations. In retrospect, the sources of astigmatism which saw Leninism as a success seem overdetermined. In the 1960s, U.S. President Kennedy's Alliance for Progress was smashed by military coups, while Castro's Leninism found strong appeal in Latin America; the Soviet Union reached nuclear parity with the United States, and China defeated India in a war; Moscow and Beijing backed victorious Leninists in Vietnam; America aligned with right-wing forces in South Korea and Taiwan, which seemed at the time like economic wastelands.

Actually, the export-oriented industrializations of Taiwan and South Korea turned out to be successes, while Leninist-like dictators, Ghana's Nkrumah, Indonesia's Sukarno and Algeria's Ben Bella, all of whom practiced self-defeating import substitution during their industrialization, fell in the mid 1960s. No one understood Leninism as an economic dead end when they fell or when Khrushchev's economic reforms were thwarted in 1964 by conservative Leninists, or when Mao denounced China's reformers as capitalist-roaders in 1966 and imposed an economic autarky that locked poor Chinese into stagnant misery. Indira Gandhi's Congress Party also extended Leninist economics. The political kingdom seemed everything. Modernization was to be advanced via an extensive mobilization of labor and resources by the state. These ideas were followed by most anti-imperialist governments seeking rapid development. Democratic India and despotic China had learned similar economic lessons; they were not economic opposites.

[4] Even Samuel Huntington in *Political Order in Changing Societies* (New Haven: Yale University Press, 1968), who disagreed with Moore on everything from methodology to politics, agreed that Leninism was a successful modernizing strategy. Huntington treated Leninists as such capable modernizers that a non-Leninist South Korea could not compete with a Leninist North Korea.

At the outset of the 1990s, in response to India's command economy maladies, the head of a Farmers Movement, Sharad Joshi, described Indian development policies as "Praebrozenskian squeezing of the peasantry," that is, pure Stalinism, and Joshi called for "chipping away at the socialist monolith." Already in the 1930s, the Nehru group embraced "the importance of centrally coordinated planning for rapid industrialization."[5] Nehru, in power, chaired the State Planning Commission that worked out five-year plans. Heavy industry was privileged, agriculture and consumption goods slighted. Moore knew that India's economy resembled that of Lenin's last years in power[6] and that in 1959 the ruling Congress Party took a form of collective agriculture as a goal.[7] India's economy combined a logic of centralization with extensive state regulation, which included the control of inputs, financial resources, and key prices, thereby becoming "the largest employer in the country."[8] "Import substitution industrialization, comprehensive control and regulation of the private sector, suspicion of foreign investment and socialist rhetoric," all helped to legitimate the state.[9] The "socialist economic policies adopted in the Nehru-Gandhi era . . . virtually bankrupted India by 1991."[10] In economics, Nehru's Leninist India, as Mao's China, emulated much in Stalin's Russia. Illusions about an economically potent Leninism persisted into the end of the 1980s, when Gorbachev still looked toward East Germany as a model to copy.[11]

Already in 1954, Moore presciently saw the forces undermining Soviet Russia's command economy. "Stagnation . . . appears built into the structure of the Soviet economy and lies continually just beneath the surface."[12] He concluded that the future would either be controlled by rationalist (more technocratic) forces or traditionalist ones, either of which would "do their work of erosion upon the Soviet totalitarian edifice."[13] Soviet Russia's socialism was a dead end. Yet in the mid-1960s, in *Social Origins,* Moore treated the Leninist socialist path as a successful route to modernization. He overlooked the importance of freedom.

[5] Jyotirindra Das Gupta, "India" in Larry Diamond et al., *Democracy in Developing Countries* (Boulder, Colo.: Lynne Rienner, 1989), p. 78.

[6] Moore, *Social Origins,* p. 405.

[7] Ibid, p. 399.

[8] Das Gupta, "India," p. 84.

[9] Stanley Kochanek. "The Transformation of Interest Politics in India," *Pacific Affairs* 68, no. 4 (Winter 1995–96), p. 544.

[10] John Burns, "India's Prime Minister Wages Uphill Campaign," *New York Times,* April 5, 1996.

[11] Marshall Goldman, *Gorbachev's Challenge* (New York: Norton, 1987), chap. 6.

[12] Karl Deutsch, "Cracks in the Monolith," in Carl Friedrich, ed., *Totalitarianism* (Cambridge: Harvard University Press, 1954), p. 71, likewise insisted that Leninism would inevitably implode.

[13] Barrington Moore, Jr., *Terror and Progress USSR* (Cambridge: Harvard University Press, 1954), p. 231.

In contrast to his views in *Social Origins,* Moore insisted at the end of the 1960s that democracy was so central to a decent life that its lack was nightmarish.

The most important issues on which I disagree [with radicals] concern the radical rejection of liberal democracy, and more particularly the liberal ideals of tolerance and protection against the arbitrary abuse of authority.

. . . [A]ny future society that does not preserve and extend the achievements of liberalism . . . will not be a society worth living in. . . . [T]he possibility of *effective* criticism and complaint may be the best criterion with which to judge human societies. . . . [T]he Bolshevik Revolution turned into a vicious form of oppression . . . . [Without] the achievements of liberalism . . . revolutionary activism . . . will be tragic.[14]

Moore found Leninism a stagnant, inhuman tragedy and welcomed evolutionary democratization as a reason "for hope" about humanity's future, as progress in "justice and human freedom."[15]

Hence it was only in *Social Origins* that Moore looked favorably on the Soviet way as something more than a dead end. In the 1960s, Moore forgot his earlier insights on a stagnating Leninism and put aside his continuing appreciation of freedom. Only in *Social Origins* did he equate violence under Leninism with liberal modernization and ignore the basic difference between dictatorship and liberty. That logic was in tune with the preoccupations of the time; and no one commented on it.

While writing *Social Origins,* Moore found that the most important problem "was whether violence can be justified on behalf of freedom." He justified "the terrible price" of the French Revolution's Reign of Terror for leading on to modernization and democratization, in contrast to the "tragic price" of "the mere continuation of the existing social order" as supposedly occurred in India. Presuming that Stalinist revolutionary socialism, treated as a politico-economic unity, would do better for the rural poor in China than evolutionary democracy would do for the poor in India, Moore asked rhetorically of democratic gradualism, "How many children die in India each year as part of the price of a 'reasonable' rate of economic advance?"[16] He did not notice that India, as China, had a Soviet style economic system, that "the structure of the capital goods industry in India is comparable to . . . China."[17]

[14] Barrington Moore, Jr., *Reflections on the Causes of Human Misery and Some upon Certain Proposals to Eliminate Them* (Boston: Beacon Press, 1970), pp. 114, 192.
[15] Barrington Moore, Jr., *Authority and Inequality under Capitalism and Socialism* (Oxford: Clarendon Press, 1987), p. 92.
[16] Moore, "On the Notion of Progress," pp. 106–19.
[17] Das Gupta, "India," p. 86.

Moore asked whether the French Terror of 1793–94 could be justified because it eventually facilitated democracy. But Stalin's terror did not facilitate democratization. In *Social Origins,* India was not judged by the French standard of destroying obstacles to democratic freedoms. India was a political democracy. It was, however, economically Leninist.

If Stalinism sped growth, including a lowering of the death rate at birth and a raising of life expectancy, would that make its tyranny life-enhancing? Life under Stalin was an endless terror. It was precisely in terms of babies saved that Trotsky justified the Bolshevik violence that subverted a fledgling democracy, which had been built out of Russia's democratic February 1917 revolution. How much of life is lost in daily fear and trembling under tyranny?[18] While economic inequities can kill, so can political inequity. The economic and political should be analytically separated.

Leninist systems, after an initial equalization tend to polarize resources such that the elite monopolizes benefits, while life for the majority of the excluded actually tends to worsen. By the 1970s, life expectancy in the Soviet Union was decreasing. Under Mao's despotism, China's poor benefitted from a onetime gift but lacked any political means subsequently to express or impose their interests. They had no say on revenue-raising or budget expenditures. A gift is not empowerment. Eskimos say "Gifts enslave." Democracy—that is, experientially fair rules by which citizens choose officials to run government in a publicly accountable way such that people with incommensurable ultimate ends can live in peace—enhances life.[19]

Social Origins's equation of violence in democratizing France and in Leninist dictatorships is problematic. Violence in Mao's China created an entrenched dictatorship that monopolized resources and locked the poor into misery. The conventional wisdom of the 1960s, however, held that the economic results of Leninism were positive. Yet on the creation of wealth, compare South Korea with North Korea, West Germany with East Germany, Thailand with Vietnam, Austria with Czechoslovakia, and the island of Taiwan with mainland China.

While writing *Social Origins* in 1962, Moore found that in Leninist Russia, "violence was a means to catapult an agrarian country into the modern world, eliminating disease, famine, and illiteracy." Such socialism he dubbed a "success," "a new social order."[20] Yet collectivized countrysides were disasters. Chinese villagers were re-enserfed on socialist latifundia. The tillers did not

---

[18] Saving babies is also how the mass murderers of Sendero Luminoso justify their slaughtering. But military dictatorships in antisocialist Korea, Taiwan, and Chile have actually produced similar or higher levels of enhanced life as measured by infant mortality and life expectancy. This did not impress the apologists for Leninist tyranny.

[19] Edward Friedman, ed., *The Politics of Democratization* (Boulder, Colo.: Westview Press, 1994), p. 14.

[20] Moore, "On the Notion of Progress," pp. 106–19.

own the land and could not leave it. In China, famine killed. More villagers died of starvation and slaughter in socialist Russia or China than in post-independence India. Democracy saves lives. A government in India would fall if the political opposition, the free media, and the organized interests of a robust civil society revealed that malnutrition had become deadly famine. While democracy in India prevented a large famine, China's dictatorship hid and buried its many millions of famine victims.

By the Gorbachev era, Moore had long since dropped his idea in *Social Origins* of successful modernization via Leninist socialism and again found it a failed and decaying system. He took democracies in India and elsewhere as "objective reasons for hope about the future of human institutions."[21] Why then did comparative social history not reveal to Moore the cruel tragedy in Leninist dictatorships and the preciousness of political freedom while he was writing *Social Origins?* What misled Moore in that one, short time seems to lie in the massive U.S. armed intervention in Vietnam.

Moore, in the 1960s, believed that American democracy had been neutered, leaving it incapable of significant progress (this at the height of the American civil rights movement). He found that capitalist material success was premised on a war economy that required an enemy and therefore missed opportunities for detente with Nikita Khrushchev (actually Europe and Japan were growing faster than the United States and investing less in the military, so analysts would soon wonder if America's war spending hurt the American economy). For Moore, America threatened "another major war," in which "all life, may be destroyed." Morally outraged, Moore blamed Washington for a war-prone nuclear arms race, civil defense mobilization, the sending-up of Gary Powers' U-2 spy plane prior to a summit with Khrushchev, the Bay of Pigs invasion, and the beginning of escalation in Indo-China. Moore ridiculed America as a society of "brainwashing and super-patriotism" which believed it could survive "in air-conditioned bomb shelters." Since Leninist socialism was also morally defective and both sides were "absolute political dinosaurs," Moore wished "a plague on both your houses."[22]

Premised on this amoral equivalence, *Social Origins* equated the cost of all paths to modernization. Moore celebrated deadly violence and understated Leninist cruelty. He slighted democratic achievement. Looking astigmatically out from within, Moore wrote from the inevitably prejudiced palace of the present.

In search of a basis for morally informed political choice, Moore imagined an observer as in a helicopter caught in a crowd, hearing words, catching the color, but finding no pattern. He argued that a scholar, like the helicopter,

---

[21] Moore, *Authority and Inequality,* p. 123.
[22] Moore, "On the Notion of Progress," pp. 109–16.

should rise above the details. However, if one goes too high, one loses touch with living dynamics and sees only dead abstractions. The goal is to hover at a point where one can both see the general pattern and also hear the human cries of pain.

But what if the mid point is both too low to discern a pattern and too high to hear the discourse? What if there is no perfect distance for seeing the past as a way to gain insight on the present and future? What if the comparative historical project is based only on metaphorical rhetoric, an epistemology without foundation?

Comparative social history is not a panacea. It also is not a nostrum. A search for large historical patterns within changeable societal totalities helps to situate our judgments on what is more or less possible. It is misleading to list all factors and then seek correlations. As Moore said, a shopping list is not a recipe. It matters when an ingredient is added and how it interacts with other ingredients. Moore's approach to understanding what he took to be the modern era may be just as applicable to the subsequent era.

Democratic Europe versus Barbaric Asia

What distinguished Moore was that he did not privilege or demonize Europe or Asia. He was skeptical of theories that ascribed moral superiority to "Western 'advanced' culture."[23] His knowledge of ancient achievements and modern failures made him both less worshipful of modernity and more pessimistic about the permanence of democracy. Democratic Athens had been subverted from within more than once.

As had John Stuart Mill in *On Liberty,* Moore found freedom-promoting wisdom in non-Christian ancients. Considering Pericles' defense of Athenian freedom, Moore commented that "not even the victory of Christianity . . . destroyed this proud standard," and he found of the old Testament, "that Yahweh is an arbitrary brute." Moore did not find the seeds of rational freedom in a Judeo-Christian tradition.[24] For him, democracy—as fascism or communism—was an option for all humanity. That insight made Moore's work superior to conventional American or European social theory which insisted on Protestant conscience as the only cultural base of liberal democracy. Those theorists could not hear the voices of Indian democrats who understood Hindu civilization as a nondogmatic culture of inclusion. These Indians saw the early Muslim conquest and Moghul empire as un-Indian in its sectarianism but claimed that it was Indianized subsequently under Akbar's inclusive toleration. They then saw India wounded again by British colonialism, which

[23] Moore, *Reflections on Causes of Misery,* p. 145.
[24] Moore, "On the Notion of Progress," p. 115.

manipulated sectarian communities for the purpose of dividing and ruling the nation. In establishing a secular democracy in 1947, Indian democrats could see themselves as returning to tolerant Hindi cultural wisdom.[25]

For Moore, all humans are capable of the broadest range of good and evil. *Social Origins* was based on the awareness of a common potential. Moore understood Calvin's Christian Geneva as totalitarian, just as analysts in the 1990s might similarly regard other revivalist communalisms. Although a victory of the "liberal bourgeoisie" and political freedom had been possible in Geneva, instead what happened was that a skewed "balance of power among clergy, feudal elements, and the bourgeoisie" led to a popular totalitarianism, a "theocratic dictatorship" backed by "the power of the executioner," in which "it was regarded as a conspiracy to speak in opposition to the list of candidates presented by the clergy." "Like the Bolsheviks, the true Calvinists had a deadly fear of error and its social consequences." In both Bolshevism and Calvinism "sham democracy and mutual repression" were "reinforced by a central apparatus of terror."[26] Looking even further ahead, Moore found that a Leninist party permitted yet more thorough tyranny.

The dangers in a purist communalist takeover of politics are alive in the dictatorial project of India's Hindu chauvinists and of post-Mao Chinese nativists who promote purist Confucian authoritarianism at the end of the twentieth century. As the history of Irish Catholics and English Protestants or of European Americans and African Americans reveals, reconciling communalism and democracy is not easy anywhere.

All democratizers must grapple with historically defined divisions within communities. The American Constitution, for example, could not peacefully contain the division between North and South, an issue that Moore explored in *Social Origins*. The problem of communalism bedevils crafters of democracy from Quebec, the Lombard and Northern Ireland to Sri Lanka, Kashmir, and the Punjab. Sadly, Moore is silent on the politics of regions and communities in India.

Development: China versus India

In November 1989, as peaceful democratization began to transform Eastern Europe, Moore saw how large scale violence could undermine liberating

[25] Amartya Sen, "The Threats to Secular India," *New York Review,* April 8, 1993, pp. 26–32; idem, "The Debate Over Hindu Nationalism," *Contention* 4, nos. 2 and 3 (Winter and Spring 1995).

[26] Barrington Moore, Jr., *Political Power and Social Theory* (Cambridge: Harvard University Press, 1958), chap. 2; On Calvin's ecclesiastical dictatorship of intense "bigotry and inhumanity," see Leonard Levy, *Blasphemy* (New York: Knopf, 1993).

change.[27] In contrast to *Social Origins*'s privileging of violent change, India's evolutionary democracy now seemed hopeful. The peaceful democratic transitions of the 1970s in South Europe and Latin America and of 1989–90 in Mongolia, Albania, and the nations once dominated from Moscow further belie *Social Origins*'s claim of a necessary link between violent destruction and democratic construction.

Revolutionary violence can polarize a society into irreconcilable forces and delay the reconciliation required for a democratic consensus. The violence of the French Revolution, the 17th century English wars, and the American Civil War did not only explode obstacles to democratization. Moore ignored the insight of his analysis of Calvin's Geneva. Balance, reconciliation, and compromise advance the cause of liberty.[28]

Federalist accommodation with the communities of an overly centralized India has "compartmentalized friction," given more Indians a stake in a legitimate democratic polity and proven "remarkably successful in accommodating cultural diversity."[29] But democracy is never guaranteed. "Success in balancing requires an imaginative leadership which no system ensures."[30] Some analysts fear that overcentralization (insufficient federalist accommodation) and weakened national party organization are furthering demagogic appeals to antidemocratic tendencies in Indian communalism.[31] Communalist inclusion strengthens democracy and advances equity. India must grapple with how to "balance between majority preference and minority protection," how to balance center and region, group and individual,[32] dilemmas for all nations. Because Indian democracy left rural social relations in place, *Social Origins* expected a Chinese type revolution that annihilated landlords to bring faster and more thorough modernization. He did not see how compensatory discrimination and social welfare could win the allegiance of India's rural poor to democracy. Peasant democrats seemed an oxymoron; peasant revolutionaries seemed the future. "The peasants provided the dynamite that finally exploded the old order . . . [furnishing] the main driving force behind the victory of a party dedicated to achieving through relentless terror a supposedly

---

[27] Barrington Moore, Jr., *Liberal Prospects under Soviet Socialism: A Comparative Historical Perspective* (New York: Columbia University Harriman Institute for the Advanced Study of the Soviet Union, 1989).

[28] On the centrality of reconciliation to democratization, see Lawrence Weschler, *A Miracle, A Universe* (New York: Penguin, 1990).

[29] Robert Hardgrave, "India: The Dilemma of Diversity," *Journal of Democracy*, 4, no. 4 (October 1993), pp. 54–68.

[30] Das Gupta, "India," p. 96.

[31] Atul Kohli, "Centralization and Powerlessness: India's Democracy in a Comparative Perspective," in Joel Midgal et al., eds., *State Power and Social Forces* (New York: Cambridge University Press, 1994), pp. 89–107.

[32] Hardgrave, "India," p. 65.

inevitable phase of history in which the peasantry would cease to exist."[33] In fact, collectivization froze China's peasantry in place more than a lack of land reform locked Indian villagers at the bottom of society.

Socialist collectives, a kind of plantationlike reenserfment lock a peasantry into misery. Chinese starved to death in three political famines of the Mao era, the national famine of 1959 to 1961, and regional famines in Anhui in 1963, and in Sichuan from 1974 to 1976. At the end of the Mao era, China was no more industrialized than India. China lacked India's high-level corps of scientists and technicians that permitted India to become the leader in Third World computer software exports. In China's capital, at Mao's death, only 2 percent of government offices had telephones. Leninist states, after exhausting the productivity of dragooned corvée labor, left in place wasteful, militarized, heavy-steel economies incapable of efficiency, innovation or moving up the value-added ladder. Reforming such economies is painful. This is true both for India and China. A key problem for India's future could not even be imagined if India were seen as a capitalist democracy: can India reform its Leninist economy without devastating its democratic polity?

In addition to misconceiving the Leninist command economy as a success and violence as a prerequisite of democratization, Moore also erred in treating peasants as a "political plague."[34] Polls show peasants in India most committed to the democracy. Treating peasants as an economic moment of a dying past or a disease to be extirpated rather than as a rooted society, an integral culture, or an ethnonational community can energize murderous wars on the supposedly petit bourgeois peasantry. If culture is epiphenomenal and economics alone is real, then the extirpation of various peasantries in the Ukraine or Kazakhstan or in Cambodia can be presented as progressive historical inevitability. Democratic critics of such genocidal policies dub Leninist polities fascist socialism.[35]

Of course, Moore never had illusions about the inhumanity of Leninist-Stalinism. His two studies of the Soviet system are masterpieces. Moore's deepest intention was to be sensitive to comparative miseries, to calculate societal suffering as carefully as possible. His was a scholarship of humane responsibility—except in treating the annihilation of peasants as an amoral inevitability.

When Moore wrote *Social Origins*, almost 85 percent of Chinese were

[33] Moore (1966), *Social Origins*, p. 227.
[34] Ibid., p. 426. Ronald Dore puts the point gently: "Moore just doesn't *like* peasants." Ronald Dore, review of *Social Origins, Archieves Europeenes de Sociologie* (1969).
[35] Edward Friedman, "The Societal Obstacle to China's Socialist Transition," in David Mozingo and Victor Nee, eds., *State and Society in Contemporary China* (Ithaca, N.Y.: Cornell University Press), 1983.

locked up in the countryside by a household registration and internal passport system that was as confining as South African apartheid. Because they lived as reenserfed peasants on socialist latifundia called collective farms, such people are usefully analyzed as the victims of feudal socialism or feudal fascism.

Cambridge University economist Suzie Paine argued that India's peasants were better off than China's because they could confront their plight, flee, organize, seek other work or join a political struggle, whereas China's peasants on collectives, much as in a serf society or an apartheid system, were left immobile and dependent on arbitrary, all-powerful party lords. Groveling and sycophancy were the only legal paths to family survival.[36]

Under China's dictatorship, to speak against regime policies required martyrlike courage. The dictatorship's responses could run a gamut from torture, slave labor, and death to persecution of family members. Leninism fostered a debilitating dependency that made for passivity, fawning, self-blame, and self-doubt. Yet, Moore's commitment in the 1960s to a plague on both Washington and Moscow led him to equate English enclosures with the Stalinist collectivization famine. He slighted the value of liberty, of physical mobility, and of a commercialized peasantry. Peasants have been central to democratization.[37] In East Asia peasantries have been engines of both growth and democratization.

A blind spot on peasantries—most of humanity in most of recorded history—does not obscure the breadth of Moore's commitment to dignity for all humanity. *Social Origins* explored a similar array of human possibilities. Japanese and German fascism reflected similar social forces, east and west. Likewise, in a study of privacy, Moore found "a desire for privacy as a panhuman trait." Human dignity required space for personal development. "The great civilizing achievement in the concept of privacy has been its questioning of social concerns. That was mainly an achievement of western civilization."[38] But the achievement was no more peculiarly western than was penicillin, first discovered in Britain. All humanity could value the contribution wherever it happened first. Coercive communitarianism everywhere led to its opposite, an intensified "demand 'for more freedom, for the cultivation of individuality, for closer contact among family members.'"[39] This surely is true of post-Mao China.

Democracy is not the fruit of cultural seeds that grow only in western soil. More poor rural people enjoy democracy in India than do rich urban ones in

[36] Edward Friedman, Paul Pickowicz and Mark Selden, *Chinese Village, Socialist State* (New Haven: Yale University Press, 1991).

[37] Dankwort Rustow, "Transitions to Democracy," *Comparative Politics* 2 (1970): 337–63.

[38] Moore, *Privacy: Studies in Social and Cultural History* (Armonk, N.Y.: M.E. Sharpe, 1984), pp. 275–76.

[39] Moore, *Authority and Inequality,* p. 305.

Europe and America combined. Moore found that in Japan, as "in the United States and earlier in England," any people can craft a pact of compromise and legitimate opposition.[40] For democracy, politics and policy are decisive.

Continued citing of four words from *Social Origins*, "No bourgeoisie: no democratization," misleads. Already in 1970 Moore found that liberal democratic "ideals have much less to do with capitalism and the rise of the bourgeoisie than has often been supposed."[41] Moore looked to political crafting.

For Moore, in contrast to standard western theory,[42] Hindu culture was not the major obstacle to India's democratization. Dictatorship might win if rural landowners could prevent land reform and agricultural commercialization, thus keeping the rural poor locked into misery, thereby creating a social base for a Leninist project or for fascism.[43]

Land reform was central to the postwar rise of East Asia in Japan, Taiwan, and Korea. Latifundia (including the socialist kind) tend to impose a politics that overvalues the currency in order to make luxury imports inexpensive for the rural elite, a situation which in turn inadvertently prices domestic manufactures out of foreign markets, thereby restricting economic development. As Moore stressed in *Social Origins*, a prospering democracy is premised on a market-oriented agriculture.

India's command economy of administrative suffocation ("the license raj"), parastatals and agricultural marketing boards resembles the economies of much of the Third World.[44] It is less destructive—India did not collectivize agriculture—than a full-scale Leninist economy with dead money, a war on culture, trade minimalization, little physical mobility, state enterprises, and nationalized food markets. Still, India's ever more corrupt bureaucracy, centralized state-sponsored industrialization, and massive protectionism likewise tended to stifle the most productive farmers. Treating world market involvement as evil imperialism, Nehru and Mao locked India and China out of major forces of progress and wealth expansion. Parastatal enterprises lost money and were subsidized and privileged by marginalizing other sectors. Both India and China built an administrative structure whose work ethic was ever more subverted by unaccountable and personalistic power.

Rigid, hierarchical centralization, the suffocation of money and the market, the physical distribution of material goods in quantitative terms, and the construction of a late-nineteenth-century, German-style, military-oriented steel economy to defend against imperialism—that is, the Leninist-Stalinist

[40] Moore, *Liberal Prospects*, pp. 15–16.
[41] Moore, *Reflections on Causes of Misery*, p. 113.
[42] Standard western theory can be taken to refer to the work of Samuel Huntington. His work on the democratic potential of developing countries is the most frequently cited.
[43] Actually, fascist forces in India do best in urban areas.
[44] A good overview of economics in Africa is Richard Sandbrook, *The Politics of Africa's Economic Stagnation* (Cambridge: Cambridge University Press, 1988).

economic system that poor nations copied—precluded modernization. Without modernization, nations did not have the flexibility needed to innovate in the permanent revolution of science and technology or to reward consumers with the material blessings of modern life. Yet the Soviet Union's launch of Sputnik in 1957 made the Leninist command economy seem ahead in science and technology. In the early 1960s, the Soviet Union's lead in heavy-steel rocket technology—a missile gap—made Leninism seem to be a successful path toward modernization in the era of *Social Origins.*

Hidden from view were the items sought after by KGB spies; the computer and other electronic and information technologies that were beyond the reach of the evermore outmoded late-nineteenth-century heavy steel system that rendered Leninist economies evermore backward in a postindustrial or post-steel era. In the 1980s, while democratic India remained locked in an outmoded economic Leninism, China's post-Mao dictators attacked command economy inefficiencies. A policy choice for economic reform is possible with dictatorship or democracy.

Yet the conventional wisdom at the end of the twentieth century holds, as did the conventional wisdom in the 1960s, that dictatorship furthers China's growth, and democracy hurts India. In fact, "neither East Asian authoritarianism nor Indian democracy explains . . . the differences in their level of economic performance."[45] Democracy does not block progress; dictatorship does not quick-start development. Institutional and policy adaptations to the economic imperatives of a new age are at issue. Can India reform without losing its democracy? Can Moore's approach to comparative social history offer clues to the future?

Imperatives of the Era after Modernity

Since no one foresaw the implosion of the Leninist system, Moore grew pessimistic about the worth of comparative social history. How could it not foresee such a major event? Yet Moore understood that "predictions are [not] very feasible in the social sciences."[46] He wanted, nevertheless, to comprehend the major human possibilities.

Moore's approach and the global imperative of reform economics suggest that a basic question for the so-called postmodern age is, what institutions and policies will prove most successful? This is the same question Moore asked when he approached routes to modernity. His approach remains relevant. Anti-imperialists who became cognizant of the stagnant despotism of the

[45] Jagdish Bhagwati, "Democracy and Development," *Journal of Democracy* 3, no. 3 (July 1992), p. 43.
[46] Moore, *Reflections on the Causes of Misery,* p. 5.

Brezhnev era erred in looking to Mao's more autarkic and cellular economy as an advance over Moscow's hypercentralization. The new age demanded economic reform. After Mao died, China's rulers looked to East Asia where so many nations responded well to the end of the Bretton Woods–dollar era, to oil price spikes, to a world recession, and to a debt crisis, while rigidly centralized, statist economies, from Cuba to North Korea stagnated or declined.

Post-Mao Chinese rulers initiated decollectivization, agricultural commercialization and international economic openness. Living standards rose even for most of the poorest. China became the world's fastest growing economy.[47] A lack of economic reform meanwhile kept areas of rural India mired in stagnant poverty, while a lack of export competitiveness made India the world's number two debtor nation. Revivalist communalism spread.

By the 1990s, democratic Russia committed itself to institutional and policy reform. Moore worried that in "a world dominated by anti-rationalism, fundamentalism and chauvinist religious beliefs," Gorbachev might "turn out to be the last flare-up from the ashes of the Enlightenment."[48] If reform is blocked in India and vengeful communalist forces rise, then, democracy could be snuffed out in India too. Indeed, in India, as in Russia or Serbia, reform transition dilemmas can prod socialists to try to hold power by appealing to communalism, a red-brown alliance. India's vicissitudes since the economic crisis of the 1960s foreshadow similar dilemmas throughout the reforming, once-Leninist world.

Through oil, debt, and other crises, India's democracy has proved resilient. Amazingly, after half a century of democracy in India, the conventional wisdom still finds that preconditions to democracy include high income and at least middling levels of economic development, conditions not met by democratic India. It is still dismissed as a "most dramatic exception."[49] The conventional wisdom of social theorists keeps expecting the "establishment of an authoritarian regime in India."[50] Yet specialists in Indian politics find that democracy has given the poor an experiential stake in a free India, and even facilitated a strengthened federalism, while China's dictators struggle to maintain rigid central control.

A crucial issue is social equity, both as a basis for democracy and as an integral element in East Asian development (that at the end of the twentieth

---

[47] Kristof Nicholas, and Sheryl Wu Dunn, *China Wakes* (New York: Random House, 1994).

[48] Moore, Liberal Prospects, p. 28.

[49] Samuel Huntington, *The Third Wave: Democratization in the Late Twentieth Century* (Norman: University of Oklahoma Press, 1991).

[50] Previously Huntington found that Indian democracy was preserved because liberal cosmopolitans were defeated by a leader responsive to communal demands who "had never been outside his country." In contrast, most analyses of Indian politics found the communalist focus and the loss of a truly national party appeal most threatening to Indian democracy. See Kohli, "Centralization and Powerlessness."

century both India and China would copy).[51] The equity question is hidden because Western elites tend to blame their problems in competitiveness on their humane "welfare capitalism" in contrast to economically successful Asia's supposedly "harsher" capitalism.[52]

As the conventional wisdom on Leninism's developmental superiority had missed decisive data, so the late-twentieth-century consensus overlooks what should be obvious. By the 1990s democratization was succeeding in Muslim Albania, Buddhist Mongolia and Confucian South Korea. It had already established its viability in Shinto Japan, Africa's Botswana and animistic groups in the South Pacific islands. The binary opposition of civilized Europe to barbaric Asia ignores xenophobic, racist, and other intolerant forces in Europe that, as Moore notes, actually threaten democracy. Taking Europe as the model of civilization obscures its savage antidemocratic elements. French can hate Arabs, English can discriminate against South Asians, Germans can attack Turkish people. Imagining the East as cruel and barbaric obscures East Asia's humane superiority in terms of economic equity.

"Singapore, Taiwan and South Korea (and Japan as well) managed to raise living standards for all . . . achieving a remarkable degree of economic equality." China is erroneously taken as an East Asian success story when, by contrast, it has seen a "rapidly widening gap between haves and have-nots, accompanied by debilitating corruption and abuse of power."[53] Perhaps China's rigidly centralized Leninist dictatorship will prove an obstacle to a needed flexible development in the new epoch.[54]

In the new era, global tendencies of production for niche, luxury, and high-tech markets are strongly polarizing. Products are no longer made that the median wage manufacturing worker can purchase. Profits are maximized at the high-priced end. Innovation comes from ever more costly research with long periods of expensive development. Microelectronic advances that free capital from national controls provide tremendous advantages vis-à-vis labor that permit capital to bid down wages. Stable development may require balancing policies against the forces of economic polarization to assure equity. Democracy is an art of balance.

Yet a current neoliberal consensus promotes a free market, presuming that wealth turns into democracy, a great error in the new era. A perspective ignoring the technologic of polarization is oblivious to the need for policies that maintain the social equity that is basic to democratic strengthening and to

[51] Edward Friedman, "What Asia Will and Will Not Stand For," *Osaka Journal of Foreign Studies* (Summer 1996).

[52] Editorial, *Financial Times* (London), December 24, 1993.

[53] Arnold Isaacs, "China, Inc." *New York Times Book Review,* November 28, 1993.

[54] Edward Friedman, *National Identity and Democratic Prospects in Socialist China* (Armonk, N.Y.: M.E. Sharpe, 1995), chap. 10.

East Asian–style economic progress, the most equitable the world has seen. A continuing commitment to social equity in India, aided by democratically participating communalists, could help democracy continue to prosper in India and ease the trauma of economic reform.

Moore's illuminating notion of different eras with distinct dynamics can raise the question of whether success in the new post-modern era might go to states capable of maintaining social equity to contain polarizing forces. Moore's "story of the transition from the preindustrial to the modern world"[55] meant a transition through textile manufactures to steel technologies. Authoritarian, hierarchical statism could work for steel in Meiji Japan, Bismarckian Germany, and Stalinist Russia, but it could not work anywhere in the post-steel era. The Japanese tend to define the new age in terms of information technologies which privilege software over hardware and brain power over manual labor. A top-down centralized state suited the economy of the modern era. Might China be politically stuck in that era while democratic India can do more in a postmodern era to accommodate federalist forces?[56]

To the extent that East Asian state institutions were crafted for steel era problems, they too may be outmoded. Moore noted "that any society . . . is destined to become antiquated." He found technology the major source of progress and argued that "changes in technology [were] accompanied by changes in social structure."[57] Since Moore noted that "modern times do differ qualitatively from pre-industrial times,"[58] his approach implies a subsequent qualitatively different, postmodern, postindustrial era.

Moore concluded "that it is impossible to repeat the capitalist and democratic solution to the problems of modernization."[59] All have to adapt to postmodern imperatives. In the new era, equity may facilitate economic success. Thinking of India as democratic capitalism misleads. A notion of capitalism covering half a millennia of changing technologies, social relations, markets, and their combined, exponentially unique consequences cannot depict the diverse dynamics of different eras. *Social Origins* tried to comprehend a transition from the premodern to the modern, "the decline of one kind of civilization and the rise of a new one."[60]

In this new era, democratic equity may be crucial. For decades, however, Japan was wrongly deemed undemocratic.[61] "Japan . . . is governed by a permanent alliance between the Liberal Democratic Party and the state bu-

---

[55] Moore, *Social Origins,* p. 3.
[56] Ayesha Jalal, *Democracy and Authoritarianism in South Asia* (New Delhi, India: Cambridge University Press, 1995).
[57] Moore, "On the Nation of Progress," pp. 106, 107.
[58] Moore, *Reflections on Causes of Misery,* p. 151.
[59] Moore, *Social Origins,* p. 4.
[60] Ibid., p. 5.
[61] Friedman, *Politics of Democratization,* chap. 1.

reaucracy that effectively blocks any meaningful voter influence on public policy. Marx would probably join the many current observers . . . who have asked whether it makes sense to call this arrangement democracy.[62] Others acknowledge that governments in Seoul and Taipei combine democracy and development, but then dismiss the achievement as anomalous. "Yet while such accomplishments are not impossible, they have been exceedingly rare."[63] This dismissal of central facts as anomalies reveals the error in the conventional wisdom that will not comprehend Asia as democratic.

In fact, Japan was democratized by political reforms following defeat in World War II in a way facilitating great economic equity. Taiwan's development was even more equitable. Democracy with social equity may permit the flexibility needed to adapt to rapid technological and world market change in the post-steel era because citizens are then less threatened. Consequently, if democratic India eventually succeeds in enhancing federalism and reforming out of its command economy while China remains locked into the political rigidities of the inordinately inegalitarian Leninist dictatorship, then India could surpass China. China's Leninist polity, as Tito's Yugoslavia and Kadar's Hungary, could find the real gains of economic reform incapable of getting past the brick wall of Leninist dictatorial rigidities.[64]

Rather than being caused by dictatorship, as the conventional wisdom has it, China's post-Mao successes can be ascribed to other factors: (1) China promoted rural decollectivization and marketization of a peasant dominated agricultural sector, a process in which farmers succeeded in spite of the regime.[65] (2) It avoided a massive overhang of wasteful production from state-owned enterprises as existed in the Soviet Union. (3) It fostered tendencies that led toward success in the global market. By 1961, the Sino-Soviet split combined with an American embargo of China and compelled China to compete for export earnings on merit. Thus, Chinese exports have long been market oriented. (4) In contrast to the Soviet Union where, for decades, people were paid for work with worthless money, since there was nothing to buy—a condition leading eventually to skyrocketing inflation when Russia opened up to the world market—Mao destroyed money, such that latent inflation did not explode when China opened to the world market. (5) China benefits from its location in the world's most dynamic economic region at a propitious moment and from diaspora spread effects. Other East Asian societies moving up the value-added and technology ladders seek to hold global

62 Kyung-won Kim, "Marx, Schumpeter and the East Asian Experience." *Journal of Democracy* 3, no. 3 (July 1992): 22.

63 Adam Przeworski, "The Neoliberal Fallacy," *Journal of Democracy* 3, no. 3 (July 1992): 56.

64 Yu-shan Wu, *Comparative Economic Transformations* (Stanford: Stanford University Press, 1994).

65 Kate Xiao Zhou, *How the Farmers Changed China* (Boulder: Westview, 1996).

market shares by investment in neighboring, low-wage Chinese labor.[66] Russia lacks these advantages.

India, however, may have both a diaspora potential and a geographic advantage since East Asian dynamism has now spread toward India through Southeast Asia. South Asians migrate to Taiwan and Japan as laborers. India could yet prove a great success if it combines democracy, social equity, and horizontal coordination with a market-oriented rewarding of winners instead of a market-disregarding subsidization of losers. Its information technology achievement could prove a harbinger of yet more success.

While China still has great growth potential, Leninist obstacles remain. The administration is not run by a professional technocracy but by the politically loyal. No efficient banking or tax system has been built. Money-losing state enterprises increase as does their burden on all. The turn to market-oriented farming is incomplete and insecure. The countryside is full of hate-filled explosions against cruel, thieving party bosses. Leninist conservatives insist that reversing reform is the price of stability. The regions demand a devolution of power. Leninist centralizers reject it. Consequently, China's political future remains in question.

The imperatives of a postmodern stage sped the undermining of Leninist regimes, intensifying long-existing debilitating factors in the command economy. The postmodern era belies grand narratives of a once and forever transition to modernity, a rather chiliastic notion that, as with Marx's communism or Hitler's Reich, misleadingly assumed a final solution to the pains of permanent change. What has been conceived as the modern was a moment in a persistent social crisis of ever faster change out pacing consciousness. This analysis and projection emulates Moore's comparative social history, investigating the limited possibilities of a particular era. There is so much to learn from Barrington Moore.

Moore's abiding contributions in *Social Origins* include his insistence on transcultural explanations that cover the human species, his finding that different patterns of state-society relations were more or less successful responses to technological and other challenges in different eras, and his insistence on democracy as a political form that decreases the likelihood of human misery. These contributions are a legitimation of scholarship driven by morally informed concerns over big questions infused with extensive learning combined with profound skepticism. They do not embrace presentist romanticism, dogmatism, cynicism, or utopianism.

Moore opposed those who could not see how political democracy enhanced human dignity. "Democracy has been a weapon of the poor and the many

[66] Friedman, *National Identity.*

against the few and the well-to-do ever since it surfaced in ancient Athens."[67] Moore did not see that this would be true for India, too. Still, he never found anything humane in the Soviet system. In contrast, numerous theorists who investigated revolution following the publication of Moore's *Social Origins* treated market-oriented democracies as inhuman and exploitative and were silent on the inhuman, counterproductive, and cruel character of nationalized agricultural markets and collectivized farm production.[68] Moore's moral equation in the early 1960s of all paths toward modernity misled.

Yet Moore was wise in his comprehension of the vicissitudes of democracy. He reminds us of how fragile and incomplete any existing democracy is. His study of the American Civil War showed that the gains of the initial 1789 breakthrough to democracy could be lost. In fact, democratic political institutions are no guarantor of the solution of any particular problem. Democracy is but an opportunity. From Moore's realist perspective, it is smug and ignorant to believe that a particular political system guarantees the solution to basic human problems.

Aware of how close France came to going fascist despite the 1789 revolution, Moore dismissed the post–1989/90 euphoria about global democratization as a guarantor of prosperity and world peace. Protofascist and antidemocratic forces are active in any nationalistic society. It is true in Europe. It is true in India and China. Yet, rather than promoting massive violence as a solution, as did *Social Origins*, Moore found in 1989 that there is almost no prospect for political freedom in Russia if "violence on any large scale is necessary to uproot the Soviet elite."[69]

Bracketing Moore's errors of the 1960s shows that, as with his study of Calvin's Geneva, his work comprehends democracy as a political outcome of a balance of forces. Democracy is a consequence of struggle, compromise, and conscious crafting.[70] Moore called attention to "England from the late eighteenth to the early twentieth century" when industrialization was accompanied by "older elites" sharing their power first with "the middle classes" and then with "the industrial working classes." This transition was but one of a number of possibilities. During "the period roughly 1793–1830," civil liberties were "suspended" and England "became a land ruled by a repressive oli-

---

[67] Moore, *Liberal Prospects,* p. 25.

[68] In 1990, Moore was still being attacked for finding that Leninist-led "socialist revolutions . . . led only to dictatorship," when, supposedly, this "great socialist transformation" emanates in "the expansion of human freedom" (Jeffery Paige, "The Social Origins of Dictatorship, Democracy and Socialist Revolution in Central America," *Journal of Developing Societies* 6 [1990]: 42).

[69] Moore, *Liberal Prospects,* p. 10.

[70] Giuseppe DiPalma, *To Craft Democracies* (Berkeley and Los Angeles: University of

garchy." The democratic opening, despite violent revolution, could have been closed. But a section of the elite then found politically innovative ways to satisfy the disenfranchised.[71] So it may be with India.

Political democracy requires continuous political crafting. In Europe, at first, it required "a balance to avoid too strong a crown or too independent a feudal aristocracy."[72] Democracy is not the result of structural continuities, but of human interventions requiring "reconciliation" between elites and challengers.[73] Too much violence can produce long-term alienation. Moore concluded already in 1962 that democracy may require "a rate of 'progress' slow enough not to frighten unduly the defenders of the status quo and rapid enough to satisfy at least moderately those who suffer under the prevailing system." Democratization is thus a political craft which involves "sweeping aside the remnants of an outmoded social order [in a way that] would not be so bloody and difficult a process as to make subsequent reconciliation and the operation of a free society impossible."[74]

As with any fledgling democracy (imagine 1789 America), India's original democratic breakthrough was far from complete. Rural elites were reassured by Congress Party limits on rural reform. The peripheralized and dependent peasants in the countryside, however, also won gains from the democracy. A process of democratization began. It is never easy. It is never consolidated. If progress is too slow for challengers or too fast for elites, democracy can be lost (imagine Civil War America).

In *Social Origins*, Moore saw early democracies on the North Atlantic as part of an era of commercial expansion and industrialization (pre-steel) that weakened the hold on power of anticommercial authoritarian elites and of centralized autocracies. The commercial and coastal could balance the administrative center. Such democratic balance occurred in different cultures at diverse levels of economic development, proof of a panhuman capacity to craft democracies.

Indian democracy must reform its Leninist economy. Norberto Bobbio is "convinced that it is even more difficult to achieve democracy in a socialist [i.e., Leninist] system."[75] Should democratic India succeed in economic reforms, it may have developmental advantages in the post-steel era that dictatorial China does not have because a Leninist polity is so polarizing.

Moore's approach to theory captured probable patterns and limited possibilities. To limit the polarizing tendencies inherent in the new post-steel

---

[71] Moore, *Reflections on Causes of Misery*, pp. 155–61.
[72] Moore, *Social Origins*, p. 430.
[73] Moore, "On the Nation of Progress," p. 112.
[74] Ibid.
[75] Norberto Bobbio, *Which Socialism?* (Minneapolis: University of Minnesota Press, 1987).

forces requires action on behalf of equity. Without equity and the reconciliation of groups, that is, without meeting the imperatives of democratization of the new era, it may be difficult to combine democracy and development.

China's dictatorship is incapable of persuading the Chinese that equity rules. Polls show 80 percent of the people declaring that government policies do not improve their lives. Favoritism and incompetence are inherent in Leninist administrative structures staffed by a nomenklatura chosen and promoted on the basis of personal and political loyalty. Consequently, state actions, understood as purely personal maneuvers, seem unjust and corrupt. Cynicism prevails. Dictatorial China, therefore, for all its extraordinary growth, may be undone by its political system which tends toward corruption and chaos, which keeps in place political interests that block equity and honesty. India, of course, faces similar problems of delegitimation, patronage and corruption. The future is frighteningly open as both countries try to reform out of their Leninist economies.

Barrington Moore knew that history is not a problem with a solution. He wondered how people could avoid worst case outcomes. He asked us to keep in mind the costs, the negative potentials, the limited options, and the preciousness of the achievements that limit terror, misery, and dictatorship and provide ever greater access to the material blessings of applied science and the creation and expansion of wealth. Moore has courageously sought to comprehend how to avoid the worst and make the better a bit more likely. He challenges social theorists to be neither the flag-carrier of ideological apologias, nor the banner-waver of dogmatic critiques. His skeptical realism permits moral agents to define less bad possibilities.

Moore understood an era's patterned dynamics as a new whole remaking the content and meaning of particular parts. The human species has been shaped since sometime around the 15th to 17th centuries by a modern world economy in which a continuing process of scientific and technological revolutions keeps redefining political prospects. The Leninist system, built in the Soviet Union, locked countries which emulated it, such as India, into a late-nineteenth-century German-like economy, an economy good for heavy steel and related military products but unsuited to the post-steel era.

Starting in the 1960s, the great Andrei Sakharov found that only openness and democracy permitted material success in the new scientific and technological era of rapidly changing, horizontally enmeshed, global information economies.[76] Sakharov's hope is threatened by a dynamic of income polarization, not yet visible in the 1960s. A society shaped only by the postmodern market associated with polarizing dynamics can become increasingly inequitable and prod people to seek solace in alternatives to liberal democracy by

---

[76] Andrei Sakharov, *Sakharov Speaks* (New York: Vintage, 1974).

promoting the scapegoating of, secession from, or war upon other communities. What is needed to preserve democracy and cushion rapid change are, as democratic theorists Robert Dahl and Adam Przeworski argue, interventions on behalf of social equity.

Combining growth, equity, and democracy will require creative political action. Neoliberal orthodoxies may make it almost impossible for policy action and funding to provide the equity which alone can strengthen the democratic breakthroughs Sakharov foresaw. Moore confronted such painful realities that make it difficult to advance toward a democracy worth cherishing.

Moore sought morally informed scholarship without illusions. He told his students that mere criticism was worthless and that prophecy was also useless, since history would make a fool of the future-oriented projections of even the greatest social theorist. The challenge for people committed to advancing knowledge was to be clear on what one has learned, what values one cherishes, and what traditions of thought facilitate a continuing quest for truth, progress, and freedom. A review of Barrington Moore's passionately committed work reveals how vitally important it is to pursue the painful quest for enough knowledge to permit informed, moral action, action which will further the limited prospects for freedom with less misery.

P A R T I I

GROUPS AND SOCIAL IDENTITIES IN POLITICS

CHAPTER 6

Intellectuals, Social Classes, and Revolutions

MICHAEL WALZER

Most Marxist writing about revolution, by academics as well as militants, has focused on the great question: how to get started? What are the causes of revolution? There has been less interest, surprisingly little, in outcomes. A certain agnosticism about outcomes seems to be a feature of leftist thinking, dating at least from the era of 1789. Thus, St. Just's dictum, adopted by, and one would think more suitable to, Napoleon: *On s'engage et puis, on voit.* Marx gave this agnosticism a historicist rationale, though only with reference to the last or proletarian revolution. The world whose laws science could discover and explain lay this side of that cataclysmic event, and what lay on the other side was largely unknowable. Or, rather, it could be understood only by negation—the withering away of the state, the abolition of private property, the achievement of classlessness—and not in any positive or substantive way. "The dictatorship of the proletariat" remained a phrase without content, and the political, administrative, and economic character of communist society was never seriously discussed.

Lenin and Trotsky laid the foundations for a theory of outcomes but did not develop it in any detail; nor did they acknowledge its political implications. To have done so would have undercut their own activity. And yet, they must have had some idea, before they committed themselves, of the sort of regime they would be creating. In any case, such an idea is implicit in their writings, and I shall try to expound it. I do not claim that what follows is an account of "what Lenin and Trotsky really meant." It is only one possible working out of an argument they began. I merely follow certain familiar clues, turning sometimes to historical examples that the Bolshevik leaders would never have chosen. The clues have to do, first, with the internal structure of revolution—with the sequence of events and the relations of forces within the process—and second, with two very different kinds of revolutionary endings.

The term *revolution* obviously does not cover every attack upon an established order or every seizure of power. Military coups are not revolutions; nor are most anticolonial struggles. In a world in which political turnovers are common, the term covers only a small number of cases: conscious attempts to establish a new moral and material world and to impose, or evoke, radically new patterns of day-to-day conduct. A holy commonwealth, a republic of virtue, a communist society—these are the goals revolutionaries seek. So I shall focus on the great revolutions—the English, French, Russian, and Chinese—in which modern radicalism reached its fullest substantive expression and the new world came most clearly into view. The argument about structures and endings is essentially similar in these four, whatever other differences exist among them. Now that we have seen Lenin's revolution, and Mao's, agnosticism is no longer a practical or a justifiable option. Nor, unhappily, have the most recent revolutions carried us into a world of freedom, beyond the grasp of social analysis.

The Relationship between Class and Vanguard

Revolution, then, is a project, and it is important to say whose project it is. This is the question Lenin addressed in *What Is To Be Done?* When we study the forces that make or try to make a revolution, he suggests, we immediately discern two groups with different sorts of political capacities and ambitions: a revolutionary class whose discontent provides the energy and whose members supply the manpower, and an intellectual vanguard that provides ideology and leadership.[1] The vanguard is formed only in part, perhaps in small part, by men and women drawn from the revolutionary class. The extent of recruitment depends largely on the social composition of the class, the availability of education to its members, and so on. Thus, a significant number of Puritan clerics came from the lesser gentry; an insignificant number of Chinese Communist intellectuals come from the poorer peasants. By and large, while classes differ fundamentally from one revolution to another, vanguards are sociologically similar. They are recruited from middling and professional groups. The parents of the recruits are gentlemen farmers, merchants, clerics, lawyers, petty officials. Recruitment begins at school, not in the streets, or in shops and factories, or in peasant villages.

[1] V. I. Lenin, *What Is To Be Done?* (Peking: Foreign Languages Press, 1975), esp. pt. 1. Lenin draws freely here upon arguments first developed by Kautsky.

Lenin argues, though explicitly only for the proletariat and the Marxist intelligentsia, that each of these groups has its own consciousness. Class consciousness develops as the spontaneous assertion of the shared interests of the members, as these interests are perceived by men and women still living in the old order and still thinking only about its possibilities. They have little choice; they are ambitious but hemmed in, or hard pressed simply to survive. They have to make out, or they have to earn a living today and then tomorrow. Their shared awareness of their predicament moves them to associate for protection and short-term advance. Hence the parliamentarianism of the English gentry and the trade-unionism of the modern working class. Though the life patterns of the revolutionary class may point toward a new social order, its conscious activity is shaped within the old order and aims at accommodations thought to be possible. Class consciousness rarely inspires an innovative politics. The idea of radical transformation is carried into the revolutionary class by the men and women of the vanguard.[2]

Vanguard consciousness is the work of intellectuals somehow cut loose from the constraints of the old order—or of intellectuals who cut themselves loose. These are people, usually young people, who respond to the decadence of their world by withdrawing from it. They give up conventional modes of existence, conventional families and jobs; they choose marginality; they endure persecution; they go into exile. They are receptive to radical and, as their opponents rightly say, foreign ideas: Calvinism in sixteenth- and seventeenth-century England, English liberalism and Genevan republicanism in eighteenth-century France, Marxism in Russia and China. Revolutionary thought nowhere develops indigenously. Nor does the will to revolution—at least, it does not arise in the center but at the furthermost edges of the prerevolutionary world. If the new class grows in the womb of the old society, its delivery ("Force is the midwife . . . ") comes from outside.

Class and vanguard consciousness are very different, and they are different in characteristic ways. An analogy with the Israelite Exodus from Egypt, used frequently by Puritan radicals and occasionally still by the Jacobins, illustrates the difference. A double consciousness guides the Exodus. The people (the oppressed and revolutionary class) are moved by the vision of "a land of milk and honey"; Moses and the Levites (the vanguards) are moved by the vision of "a nation of priests and a holy people." Both these groups and both these visions are necessary for success. Without the people there would have been no new nation; without Moses and the Levites the land would never have been conquered. As the biblical account makes clear, the people alone would probably not have left or would quickly have returned to the fleshpots of Egypt. It

---

[2] I have tried to illustrate this thesis with regard to the English case in Michael Walzer, *The Revolution of the Saints* (Cambridge, Mass., Harvard University Press, 1965), chap. 4.

would be wrong to think about this as a simple conflict between popular interests and intellectual idealism. For it is possible to be very idealistic about milk and honey, and groups like the Levites quickly acquire a vested interest in holiness. Each side has interests and ideals which overlap in complex ways and make cooperation between priests and people, vanguard and class, possible. The two forms of consciousness reflect two different experiences—that of the slaves in Egypt, that of Moses in exile in the desert—which are nevertheless the experiences of people tied to one another and capable, at some level, of understanding one another.

The two different experiences produce two different sorts of political association. Class politics is catholic and inclusive. Gentlemen, merchants, workers, and peasants in the old order share a common life—share experiences, willy-nilly, without reference to the opinions or feelings of individuals. It is a matter of collective location, not of private volition. Hence, class organizations are open, and their internal life usually takes shape, at first, as a democracy of the members, loosely governed.

Vanguard groups, by contrast, are closed and exclusive. Joining the vanguard is a matter of choice, but it requires also the acceptance of new members by the old. And the old have, through choices of their own, established certain criteria. They need to make sure of the commitments of their would-be brethren or comrades in order to guarantee the special character of their group. Here, collective location or class origin hardly matters. What does matter is opinion, ideology, zeal, readiness to accept a common discipline. Crane Brinton has said that Jacobin ideology amounts to a call for a nation of smallholders and shopkeepers, "a greengrocers' paradise."[3] That is true, up to a point, and one would expect all greengrocers to be welcome. The Jacobin intellectuals, however, had in mind a republic of virtuous greengrocers—tested and certified at meetings of the Jacobin clubs. The two notions overlap but are not the same.

The inner history of the revolution is in large part the working-out of the tension between these different notions and between the two groups of men and women who carry them. "The shift in different stages of the revolution," Trotsky has written, "like the transition from revolution to counter-revolution, is directly determined by changing political relations between . . . the vanguard and the class."[4] These relations in turn are shaped, I shall argue, by the different social compositions and the relative political strengths of the two groups. The thrust toward revolutionary dictatorship, the pursuit of holiness, virtue, or communist discipline, the use of terror, the possibility of a Thermidorean reaction, success or failure in the establishment of responsible govern-

[3] Crane Brinton, *A Decade of Revolution: 1789–1799* (New York: Harper & Brothers, 1934), p. 136.
[4] Leon Trotsky, "Hue and Cry over Kronstadt," *New International* 4 (1938): 103.

ment—all these depend upon the interaction of vanguards and classes and then on the historical factors that determine the interaction.

The analysis cannot begin, then, with either vanguards or classes considered alone, for what is crucial is the relation between a particular vanguard and a particular class at a particular moment in time. The balance of forces, the relative strength and competence of the two groups, shapes the revolutionary process. Ideally, the balance should be described in careful detail, but I obviously cannot do that here. I can only offer a quick historical survey of class/vanguard relationships in the great revolutions.

A clerical vanguard, like that of the Puritan ministers, holds a strong position over and against any lay group. It stakes a claim to special knowledge, though no longer to magical powers, and it possesses a considerable capacity for collective discipline. This capacity was evident when young and radical clerics established the first underground organizations in modern European history. Protestant ministers, however, are vulnerable to the appearance of lay saints, who may either join and reshape the vanguard or organize to resist its initiatives. The appearance of born-again Christians among gentlemen and merchants quickly undercuts the more extreme forms of clerical pretension. Lay vanguards, led most often by lawyers and journalists, hold a weaker position relative to gentry-merchant groups, for their knowledge is not so special and is shared almost from the beginning by the men and women with whom they interact. It is among these middling social groups that intellectuals are most likely to fulfill the task that Lenin first assigned to them—which he and the Bolsheviks were never able to fulfill: "The task of the intelligentsia is to make special leaders from among the intelligentsia unnecessary."[5] Hence, the weakness of radical intellectuals as a distinct and disciplined group during the French Revolution and the virtual nonexistence of vanguard politics in 1830 and 1848.

Organization requires more than competence, however; it also requires practice. The hundred years of Protestant experimentation with conferences and congregations—roughly the period of gentry self-assertion in Parliament—goes a long way toward explaining the precise form of the interactions of the 1640s and the 1650s. In the years immediately following 1789, by contrast, the radicals were compelled to innovate on the spot. Eighteenth-century French society had only the most rudimentary sorts of lay political or intellectual organization (the salons, literary and scientific societies, Masonic lodges). The Jacobin clubs, split and purged several times, represented a first approximation to the party cells that facilitated later vanguard activity. But they lacked trained and disciplined cadres and members sufficiently differenti-

5 V. I. Lenin, *What the "Friends of the People" Are* (Moscow: Progress Publishers, 1951), p. 286.

ated by experience or conviction from their immediate social surroundings. The short life of the Jacobin republic, and its failure to leave any significant institutional residues, has to be connected with the short history of Jacobinism before the republic was founded.

In more recent revolutionary upsurges the independence of the vanguard has been enhanced by its contact with poorly educated and unorganized social classes. Vanguards have a much stronger position relative to new industrial workers and traditional peasants than to gentlemen and merchants, and a stronger position relative to peasants than to workers. Selig Perlman has argued, also using a Leninist sociology, that the power of a radical intelligentsia within or over the working class declines in close connection with the rise of unionism.[6] The more organized the class, the less powerful the vanguard. If that is so, then it follows that the proletariat of a developed industrial society will resist vanguard initiative more strongly than other social groups, and for what may properly be called Marxist reasons: everyday life tends to produce among workers very high levels of solidarity and political sophistication and relatively tight defensive organizations. Perhaps that is why there has never yet been a revolution in which a mature working class provided the mass base.

The conditions under which social classes yield to vanguard direction resemble those that make for other sorts of elite dominance. First, class balance: that moment in history when an older ruling class can no longer maintain its political position, while the coming class cannot yet assert its own authority. Engels refers to this balance of forces in explaining early modern absolutism.[7] He might have added that it helps explain the role of radical intellectuals in the struggle against absolutism. Once that struggle has begun, however, the balance is likely to shift rapidly toward the rising class, and if that class is sufficiently cohesive and well organized, the vanguard upsurge will be brief. It can be prolonged only if no social class can assert its own right to rule. Second, then, class underdevelopment: the essential prerequisite of sustained vanguard dictatorship. A wide variety of factors come into play here. Class size, resources, education, organizational structures, and traditions of struggle determine the specific revolutionary capacity of burghers and proletarians. Mass illiteracy, geographic dispersion, and a purely local solidarity determine the general incapacity of a traditional peasantry.

Modern radicalism has tended to reach out for a peasant base—to bring into political life a social class far less capable of organization and independent activity, more in need of and more at the mercy of vanguard leadership than any other. Not that the vanguard is ever entirely free of class control: I only

---

[6] Selig Perlman, *A Theory of the Labor Movement* (New York: Macmillan, 1928).
[7] F. Engels, *The Origin of the Family, Private Property and the State* (Moscow: Foreign Languages Publishing House, 1952), p. 281.

want to suggest a comparative judgment. A Puritan minister was locked into a tight connection with, in part a dependence on, the English gentleman. Every move he made had to be negotiated. He had very limited powers of experimentation. Even when he succeeded in getting Puritan morality enacted into law, he could not get it enforced. The seventeenth-century gentry provide a classic example of a group resistant to vanguard initiative. Already in control of the Commons, politically sophisticated, well educated, and economically powerful, it and its merchant allies were the agents of the first and perhaps the most successful Thermidorean reaction. Even this class, however, needed the clerical vanguard, at least for a time. For the ministers provided the decisive innovations in revolutionary politics and the zeal without which the monarchy could never have been overthrown.

It is easy to imagine how much more such men are "needed" when they interact with a disconnected class radically deprived of resources, education, and leadership. Peasants can mount Thermidorean pressures, such as those that forced the introduction of the New Economic Policy in Russia. But it is critically important that NEP was a Bolshevik policy aimed at appeasing the peasants, not a peasant policy aimed at overthrowing Bolshevism: "The concessions to the Thermidorean mood and tendency of the petty bourgeoisie," Trotsky wrote in 1921, " . . . were made by the Communist party without effecting a break in the system and without quitting the helm."[8] There was no Russian (as there is no Chinese) equivalent of the gentry or of the French bourgeoisie, no indigenous class capable of generalizing its own way of life, asserting its ideological and organizational supremacy, and replacing the vanguard regime.

Thermidor decisively tests the class/vanguard relationship, and I should say a word about its general character. It is not to be identified too literally with the political intrigue of the summer of 1794. What made that intrigue possible was the defection of revolutionary forces from the Jacobin dictatorship and the widespread sense of alternatives short of a restoration of the *ancien régime*. Thermidor is not a counterrevolution, though it may open up possibilities for counterrevolutionary politics; it is rather the self-assertion of the revolutionary class against the politics of the vanguard.[9] If, in the Russian case, the proletariat is the revolutionary class, then Kronstadt and the Workers' Opposition represent failed Thermidorean tendencies. If we prefer the peasants, then NEP is as close as Thermidor ever came. The politics of the vanguard shapes the period of revolutionary history called—the name is a triumph of antivanguard feeling—the Terror. This term too should not be identified in any simple sense

[8] Quoted in Isaac Deutscher, *The Prophet Outcast* (London: Oxford University Press, 1963), p. 317.

[9] See Georges Lefebvre's summary statement in *The Thermidoreans* (New York: Vintage Books, 1966), chap. 11.

with the proscriptions and judicial murders of the Jacobin regime.[10] The Terror is the dictatorial imposition of vanguard ideology. So Thermidor marks the end of dictatorship, and its success or failure is determined by the "changing political relations" of the vanguard and the class. If Thermidor fails, the Terror becomes permanent.

The Character of Vanguard Ideology

Vanguard ideology, and therefore the political character of the Terror, has a similar form in each of the great revolutions. Its specific content reflects shifting intellectual traditions—Reformation theology, neoclassical republicanism, Leninist political theory. But the basic structure and the general themes of vanguard argument persist, even when radical intellectuals address different social classes. For the placement of the intellectuals with reference to the different classes, and to the old order as a whole, remains fundamentally the same. The presentation of the argument changes, of course, and it is probably worth noting a general decline in the intellectual quality, and a restriction in the referential range, of revolutionary literature from the seventeenth to the twentieth centuries. (I refer here only to the propaganda of the vanguard, not to its more reflective and theoretical work.) The rigorously argued and heavily annotated sermons of the Puritan ministers have no analogues in the popular writings of contemporary Chinese Communists. The debased aphoristic style—as it appears in English—of the *Little Red Book* is not imaginable in either the English or the French revolutions. Calvinism found popular expression at a fairly high level because the social classes for which it was popularized already possessed a substantial literary culture. Marxism has found popular expression at a low level because its vanguards have written for classes without a literary culture of their own.

But all such differences are less important than the deeper similarities in vanguard ideology. It is the similarities that make revolution the sort of event it has consistently been. The first is simple enough. Calvinism and Marxism, and republicanism too, though to a far lesser degree, impose upon their adherents a genuine intellectual regimen. Each of these creeds has behind it a tradition of learning; it requires study; and when studied it imposes order upon a wide range of historical, cultural, and political phenomena. Life in the vanguard is an educational experience. Its members come to possess a doctrine that they apply and manipulate with great skill, and this possession is crucial to their bid for power. Members of the revolutionary class remain doctrineless until they go to school with the vanguard. They share socially widespread interests and

---

[10] But Deutscher was surely right to argue, against Trotsky, that the Stalinist purges were a feature of the Russian Terror and not of the Russian Thermidor (*Prophet Outcast*, p. 316).

aspirations and hold common opinions; they do not need a doctrine. But the vanguard intellectuals, socially disinterested and often disdainful of common opinion, are likely to be, perhaps need to be, doctrinaire. Their zeal is first of all intellectual in character.

That zeal takes three different though related forms:

1. It is puritanical. Vanguard ideologies place an enormous emphasis on self-control, collective discipline, and mutual surveillance (what the Puritans called "holy watching"). They aim to produce high standards of methodical work and to curb or limit all forms of the dissipation of energy through play. The vanguard's ideas about the range of revolutionary activity are likely to be fixed by their ideas about the number of people capable of sustained discipline of this kind. The range widens, at least in theory, as workers and peasants enter the revolutionary coalition. Thus, Lenin's *State and Revolution* suggests that everyone can internalize self-control and make it habitual, and that everyone can watch everyone else, so that policemen, like vanguard intellectuals, will one day become superfluous. But Lenin is not willing to wait for that wonderful day: "No, we want the socialist revolution with human nature as it is now, with human nature that cannot do without subordination [and] control."[11] The vanguard will have to do the controlling—there is no one else. In preparing its members for this task, Lenin often sounds like the prophet of a Weberian Protestantism, preaching vehemently against "this slovenliness, this carelessness, untidiness, unpunctuality, nervous haste, the inclination to substitute discussion for action, talk for work, the inclination to undertake everything under the sun without finishing anything."[12] For Lenin, the true sign of a "proletarian" was not his class background or his specific relation to productive forces, but his self-control.

Exactly how well self-control works, we do not know. It has not made policemen superfluous, but clearly there have been periods in the history of every vanguard when holiness, virtue, or Communist discipline has been maintained at a high level. And clearly too, the class with which the vanguard interacts always resists this difficult morality. Not, by any means, unanimously: the vanguard does make converts, especially during moments of crisis and heroism; modified versions of virtue do fit the experienced needs of particular classes or sections of classes; and the enforcement of morality can be turned into an expression of existing class conflicts (especially when the old ruling class was leisured, aristocratic, and "decadent"). So vanguard intellectuals find gentry, merchant, worker, and peasant collaborators. Nevertheless, the history of every revolution is in part the history of popular resistance to virtue. Once again the Exodus story is illustrative. According to a folk legend, on the day

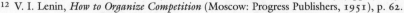

11 V. I. Lenin, *State and Revolution* (New York: International Publishers, 1932), pp. 42–43.
12 V. I. Lenin, *How to Organize Competition* (Moscow: Progress Publishers, 1951), p. 62.

that the Israelites left Mt. Sinai, they marched at double speed in order to get as far away as possible. They wanted no more laws.

2. Vanguard ideology expresses a zeal for political activism and participation, for self-government, often understood as a consequence of or a parallel to self-control. It is almost as if a dialogue were going on between the autocrats of the old order and the vanguard of the new. The autocrat, like a good Hobbist, says, "Absolute power is necessary to social order; therefore I will repress you." The vanguard intellectuals reply, "Holiness or virtue or Communist discipline is necessary to social order; therefore we will repress ourselves." Self-government, understood as collective self-repression, must be the work of men and women who have already learned the discipline of the self, or who are locked into groups that enforce such discipline. Hence, the role assigned in vanguard political practice to the congregation, the club, and the party. By contrast, members of the class generally seek a more immediate form of self-government in parliaments, assemblies, and soviets. Hannah Arendt is right when she claims that freedom is the very essence of revolution.[13] But two different kinds of freedom are at stake in the revolutionary process. For the class, freedom is a natural or a human right already possessed; all that is necessary is to create conditions under which it can be exercised—to open up arenas for democratic politics. For the vanguard, freedom has to be earned; men and women become free over a long period of internal (religious or psychological) and external struggle.

Vanguard intellectuals, therefore, willingly repeat the arguments of older elites: that the people are not ready for self-government, free elections, a free press. Ever-present Thermidorean pressures, called counterrevolutionary by the vanguard, prove the unreadiness. The classic response to these pressures is the purge, which clears the political arena of men and women who, it is alleged, would vote if they could to return to Egypt. But the purge is ostensibly a temporary measure—permanent only for those who are killed in its course. Ultimately, and in principle, the band of brethren, citizens, or comrades ought to include everyone.

3. The vanguard has deep egalitarian tendencies. Its activity calls into question all conventional social distinctions. Its members make war upon traditional hierarchies of birth and blood and denounce all claims to rule based on wealth rather than virtue. A hatred of personal dependency, a strong sense of the value of individual effort—these constitute the central features of every vanguard ideology. They are connected with the voluntarist character of the revolutionary struggle, and they are given symbolic expression in the new titles assigned to all participants, whatever their social background. Revolutionary classes, though they share for a time the excitement of the struggle, aspire to

---

[13] Hannah Arendt, *On Revolution* (New York: Viking, 1963), pp. 21ff.

something simpler and less demanding. Consider, for example, two titles from the era of bourgeois radicalism: mister and citizen. The first reflects class consciousness and is nothing more than a demand for equal respect. The second reflects vanguard consciousness and, far more heavily loaded, implies a shared concern and a shared activity. And it is not clear, in the second case, how much respect there can be if shared concern and activity do not in fact exist.

When the vanguard reaches out to radically oppressed social classes, its moral egalitarianism generates also a commitment to material equality. Puritans and Jacobins never seriously challenged the property system, though the political prerogatives of private ownership would surely have been eroded in a holy commonwealth or a republic of virtue. Communist vanguards obviously go much further, though they in turn stop short of acknowledging the prerogatives of collective ownership. They do not yield power to the workers and peasants whom they recognize as equal owners of the means of production. Indeed, worker and peasant attempts to give their new equality a political form are likely to be treated as counterrevolutionary, especially after Communist vanguards take over the task of economic development.

In the earlier revolutions, development was not a political issue, for the expansion of the economy resulted from the freely chosen activities of individual members of the revolutionary class. They required the support of the political authorities, but not their positive direction, the coercion of others, not of themselves. The case is very different in both Russia and China, where the liberation of class energy and the assertion of class interest could not readily have produced anything more than an equality of the impoverished (in vanguard ideology—Maoism may be an example—an equality of the virtuous poor).[14] Hence, the vanguard is driven to take on the role played, under radically different circumstances, by the Western bourgeoisie. It generates hierarchical structures of roughly the sort that exist in advanced bourgeois society, though with different ideological justifications and disguises. Liberty and equality disappear from its creed. What is left is a commitment to the forms of self-control and labor discipline necessary for industrialization.

Thus, Lenin wrote in 1918, "The task which the Soviet government must set the people in all its scope is—learn to work."[15] Here, government and people have replaced vanguard and class, but the relation of the first two is fixed by the relation of the second two. The government determines the tasks of the people, not the other way around. Once again, this pattern is possible only in the absence of an economically independent and politically advanced social class. The commitment to industrialization is also rooted in the van-

[14] See Benjamin I. Schwartz, "The Reign of Virtue: Thoughts on China's Cultural Revolution," *Dissent* 16 (1969): 239–251.
[15] V. I. Lenin, *The Immediate Tasks of the Soviet Government,* in *Selected Works,* vol. 7 (New York: International Publishers, 1935), p. 331.

guard's desire to maintain its new political position and to strengthen and develop the country it has come to rule. Vanguard intellectuals now seek to serve the long-term interests of their subjects. At the same time, they must ignore or repress the immediate demands of those same subjects. They are at war with "backwardness."

In the course of this war the members of the vanguard become more and more like the members of other ruling groups (modernizing elites?), increasingly accustomed to the prerogatives of government, increasingly isolated from their own people. Hence, the process that follows upon the seizure of power might be called—the term is obviously not Lenin's or Trotsky's—the routinization of vanguard consciousness. But routinization in this case can be a harrowing business, for the militants of the vanguard carry over into their new bureaucratic roles a deep conviction of their own superior understanding (their *correct* ideological position), a contempt for their enemies, and a disciplined readiness for combat. And they are, in the short run at least, steeled against the temptations of sentimentality and corruption.

The Outcome of Revolution

The argument thus far has assumed a single, readily identifiable vanguard and a single revolutionary class. Actual experience has been far more complex. The group of vanguard intellectuals shades off on the one side into the more responsible leadership, the directly controlled agents of the class (e.g., trade-union officials), and on the other into the exotic world of "new notionists," isolated sects and eccentric geniuses, without any social base at all.[16] The revolutionary class is itself a plurality of groups, perhaps a plurality of classes, including rising and falling, modern and traditionalist elements, not gentry, merchants, or workers only, but artisans and peasants too. These different elements form an unstable coalition and come into conflict with the vanguard on different schedules; they also come into conflict with one another.

The revolutionary world, then, is more pluralist than I have suggested. And yet, it also yields regularly to an act of personal unification—to a dictatorship different from that of the vanguard, the dictatorship of a leader who seizes upon the disruption and disorder of the moment. The leader imposes on the revolution something of his own character, but he also reflects the dominant tendencies of his society. Sometimes, he accommodates himself to the rising class and presides over the Thermidorean reaction, as Cromwell did in his last years. Sometimes, he intensifies and personalizes the Terror, as Stalin did before and after World War II. As with vanguards, so with dictators: their

[16] The phrase is quoted from Robert Purnell, *A Word to the World* (1649), in Christopher Hill, *Milton and the English Revolution* (New York: Viking, 1978), p. 108.

power is greatest where the mass base of the revolution is least organized and cohesive. The cult of personality grows where class political culture is underdeveloped. But why, in these circumstances, vanguard power cannot be sustained on a collective basis remains unclear. It is as if the radical intellectuals, for all their zeal and discipline, share in the political underdevelopment of their society—and if they do share that underdevelopment, they are likely, as in the Soviet Union, to suffer its consequences.

Still, personal rule is probably a temporary condition, and when we try to appraise the long-term outcomes of revolutionary activity, the class/vanguard scheme resumes its central importance. We can now distinguish two different sorts of outcomes. First, the vanguard wins and holds power, making its dictatorship permanent, dominating and controlling weak social classes. It attempts for a while to act out its radical ideology but undergoes a gradual routinization. Leaving aside the precise history and character of the routinization, it is fair to say that this was the foreseeable outcome of the Bolshevik revolution. The dictatorial rule of the vanguard was determined by the radical inability of any social class to sustain a Thermidorean politics. Thermidor, then, represents the second possibility: the revolutionary class resists and replaces the vanguard and slowly, through the routines of its everyday life, creates a new society in its own image. It reabsorbs the vanguard intellectuals into the social roles occupied by their parents, that is, into professional and official roles without any special political significance.[17]

The second of these outcomes seems to me the preferred one. Popular resistance to vanguard ideology, even when it is unsuccessful, has been sufficiently emphatic and so often reiterated as to demand serious attention. One of the central features of the revolutionary process, it determines what we can think of as a revolutionary law: *no vanguard victory is possible without radical coercion*. Given that law, it is best to insist, if one can, and as early as one can, upon the superfluity of the vanguard. The best revolutions are made by social groups capable of articulating their own collective consciousness and defending themselves against the initiatives of radical intellectuals. Thermidor is the work of such groups—an optimal outcome since it generates a limited and socially responsible government, more or less democratic depending upon the size and confidence of the newly dominant class. Thermidor represents the fulfillment of Marx's vision of revolutionary politics—the moment when power is "wrested from an authority usurping pre-eminence over society itself, and restored to the responsible agents of society."[18]

Short of Thermidor, only two other possibilities might raise similar hopes.

---

[17] See Crane Brinton, *The Jacobins* (New York: Russell and Russell, 1950), pp. 23ff., for an account of the later activities of Jacobin militants.

[18] Karl Marx, *The Civil War in France,* in Karl Marx and Friedrich Engels, *Selected Works,* vol. 1 (Moscow: Foreign Languages Publishing House, 1951), p. 472.

We might imagine an absconding vanguard, which withdraws from political power even in the absence of overwhelming class resistance. Like Machiavelli's ideal prince, it founds the republic, the new moral world, through its own heroic efforts, but then it "confides the republic to the charge of the many, for thus it will be sustained by the many."[19] Or, we might imagine a vanguardless revolution, carried out by a social class free from any lingering attachment to the old order, with a fully developed sense of its own future, capable of producing leaders of its own, loyal to itself—Marx's (but not Lenin's) industrial proletariat.

The Vanguardless Revolution

We have, as yet, no experience of either one of these possibilities. Let us, nevertheless, imagine a vanguardless class, for it is at least imaginable; its members would require only a strong and sophisticated sense of shared interests and a collective idealism. (The absconding vanguard, on the other hand, belongs to the realm of political mythology, for it would require an almost saintly self-effacement, extremely unlikely from men and women capable of seizing power in the first place.) What might a vanguardless revolution be like? I will describe it in the future tense, foregoing the conditional, though I don't mean by that to make predictions about the future. It has to be stressed, first, that vanguardless does not mean leaderless. It only means that the leaders of the revolution will not form a closed ideological group, responsible to one another and to no one else. They will be responsible to the men and women they lead; they will be agents and representatives; they will co-exist within the movement or party with oppositional elements; their authority will be temporary and revocable. Leaders of this sort might still be brilliant, outstanding, capable of bold initiatives, but they will share the consciousness of their followers—express it more coherently, perhaps, or bring it to a point in a more dramatic way, but share it still.

Of course, there will also be radical intellectuals with their own consciousness and their own visions of possible futures; I would not wish them away. And the intellectuals will still form groups of their own: clubs, sects, parties, and editorial boards. But these will be ginger groups, attached to the larger movement in one way or another—generating new ideas, stirring things up— but unable to control it. Barred from conspiracy (not so much by the police as by the strength and solidarity of the new class), they will be forced to argue, persuade, and exhort; they will be limited, that is, to those activities that even they might one day come to regard as morally and politically appropriate to the

[19] Niccolò Machiavelli, *The Discourses,* ed. Bernard Crick, trans. Leslie Walker (Hammondsworth: Penguin Books, 1970), ix.

intellectual vocation. Small numbers of them might break away for political adventures on the side, so to speak, acting out the old arrogance. But the more cohesive the class, the more brief these will be. As writers and teachers, the intellectuals will have some influence on class consciousness—and that will probably be all to the good—but they won't be able to replace that consciousness with their own—and that will certainly be all to the good.

But if class consciousness, as I have already argued, takes shape within the old order and aims in its politics at accommodations thought to be possible, how can it ever form a revolutionary creed? Assuming that particular sorts of success are in fact possible, I don't think it can be doubted that a vanguardless revolution will be a gradual movement, a "long march." It will take the form of a succession of accommodations in each of which the new class will find larger scope for its political activity and an increasing cultural influence. Without ever intending a total transformation, its members will slowly make their own way of life, their daily routines, into the common way of life. And one day, they will find themselves inhabiting, let's say, a workers' republic. They will have taken over or decisively reshaped the forms of everyday work and the means of production and then generalized that takeover in other areas of social and political activity. The process will develop in stages, but it is unlikely to be staged. It will include moments of tumult and upheaval, but it almost certainly won't culminate in anything like a one-stroke seizure of power.

All this suggests a pattern of revolutionary transformation appropriate to the highly industrialized countries; only there is the work force sufficiently skilled and sophisticated, organized and disciplined for the kind of politics that would be necessary. And even there, it remains an open question whether the workers—or anyone else—can in fact sustain the long march. Won't they get tired? Won't they get bored? Won't they be tempted, some of them, to join some vanguard adventure? Or to stay at home and let a new elite—recruited from their own ranks, perhaps, but no better for that—take over the movement? Certainly, Marxist writers have had intimations of such outcomes. One of Trotsky's close associates, Jean Vannier, wrote of the working class in the aftermath of World War II:

It has shown itself capable of outbursts of heroism, during which it sacrifices itself without a thought and develops a power so strong as to shake society to its very foundations. . . . But by and by, whatever the consequences of its action, whether victory or defeat, it is finally caught up in the sluggish quotidian flow of things. . . . Its courage and self-sacrifice are not enough to give it what, precisely, is needed in order to act out the role assigned to it by Marx: political capacity.[20]

[20] I owe this quotation to Irving Howe: see his *The Critical Point* (New York: Horizon Press, 1973), p. 18.

The quotidian flow of things, the demands of the everyday: here is the deepest source of on-going political subordination. Vannier's lines suggest the inevitability of vanguards and then of bureaucratic elites, and the permanent possibility of terrorism. But we should never be too quick to agree to such suggestions. For there are ways of institutionalizing Thermidorean politics, not only in the state, but also in the movement, forms of political life that impose restraint and responsibility: periodic elections, oppositional activity, freedom of speech and assembly. Most Marxist writers have radically under-estimated the importance of such things, treating them as if they were merely mechanical arrangements, useful or not at any given time. In fact, they are vital all the time; they are the beginning and the end. If the revolutionary move-ment is to create a democratic society, its advance must be an expansion from a center already democratic. Open membership, internal freedom—the forms of the future must be routinized in the present, so that as the routines spread, the forms take hold, reinforcing political with economic self-government.

The test of a "rising" class, then, is its ability to maintain democratic pro-cedures in its own organizations. It probably has to be said that the Western working class has not passed that test. Nor, however, has it failed and suc-cumbed (like the masses of Russians and Chinese) to vanguard leadership. By and large, it has been governed by its own bureaucrats, and that is a govern-ment less and less stable as educational levels rise within the working class and as more educated (white collar) workers are organized. So the future is still open, and the vanguardless revolution, as I have described it, is still an imagin-able process.

CHAPTER 7

Building, Bridging, and Breaching the Color Line: Rural Collective Action in Louisiana and Cuba, 1865–1912

REBECCA J. SCOTT

In his classic study, *Social Origins of Dictatorship and Democracy,* Barrington Moore, Jr. sought to understand the genesis and survival of specific political systems by examining the ramifications of the relationship of "lord and peasant" in eight widely varying societies. His goal, it seems, was both interpretive and normative: to understand complex historical processes, and to identify those conditions which might nourish democratic structures and culture. Following in that spirit, but taking a narrower focus, this essay examines the building of alliances and the mobilization of collective action in two postemancipation societies, focusing on the sugar plantation sector. The aim is to explore those conditions which nourished cross-racial collaboration and those which, by contrast, led to the construction and politicization of what was long referred to as "the color line."[1]

Any full understanding of these phenomena would require a detailed examination of class relations and a close study of the larger political context in which each sugar region was embedded. This preliminary essay can only sketch the lines of such a comparison. But it may begin to suggest the range and variability of paths out of slavery and provide evidence for the argument that both cross-racial alliances and bitter racial conflict are contingent phenomena,

---

[1] I thank Judith Allen, Sueann Caulfield, Ada Ferrer, Jeffrey Gould, Thomas Holt, Louis A. Pérez, Jr., Lawrence Powell, Peter Railton, Karen Robert, David Scobey, William Sewell, Jr., and John Shy for their comments on earlier drafts of this and related works, and for discussions of the interpretive issues that underlie this study. An earlier version of this essay appeared in Portuguese translation in *Estudos Afro-Asiáticos* (Rio de Janeiro) 27 (April 1995): 111–136. An expanded version appeared in Spanish in *Historia Social* (Valencia) 22 (1995): 127–149, as part of a special issue on race and racism in historical perspective.

powerfully shaped by evolving patterns of class relations and by the conscious choices of political leaders.

The selection of Louisiana and Cuba for the comparison is rooted in the centrality of plantation production of sugar in both of their economies, first under slavery and then with juridically free labor. They also share parallel histories of widespread rural mobilization in the postemancipation period, though it took quite distinct forms. At the same time, race, labor, and politics were intertwined in each case in very different ways.

Louisiana in the decades after slavery saw the emergence of an electoral majority of newly enfranchised freedmen, and a series of tumultuous strikes in the cane fields, in some cases carried out by coalitions of black and white workers. Like much of the rest of the South, Louisiana during Reconstruction underwent a halting experiment in interracial democracy, one which ended in retreat and repression. By the 1890s, white supremacy was entrenched, and the labor movement in the cane fields was crushed.

Cuba in the decade after emancipation saw the coalescence of a powerful anticolonial movement, aimed at ending Spanish rule on the island. Black, white, and mulatto rebels served side by side, and a central ideological tenet of the insurgent leadership was the repudiation of racism. By the early twentieth century an explicitly interethnic and interracial labor movement had begun to develop in Cuba's central sugar-growing regions. In 1912, however, the suppression of an armed protest in eastern Cuba degenerated into murderous racially specific violence by the Cuban army, and thousands of black and mulatto Cubans were murdered within a matter of months.

Postemancipation Louisiana and Cuba both evidently possessed the social and ideological elements necessary for building cross-racial alliances, yet at the same time possessed social divisions and ideological constructs that could nourish violent racism and white supremacy. A comparison of the two experiences illuminates the genesis and interplay of these various elements. Such a comparison need not treat "race" itself as having a fixed meaning or significance; indeed, it may reveal something about "race" as a signifier, since the boundaries and meanings of racial categories were being contested precisely during the volatile period of transition from one social and economic system to another.

A few initial words about method may be in order. Much has been written by social scientists about comparative perspectives, comparative approaches, and what is sometimes denominated "the comparative method." I will not attempt to situate this comparison—or the larger study of which it forms a part—in any of the taxonomic categories advanced in that debate. This essay simply takes as its starting point the observation by Barrington Moore, Jr., that comparison can provide "a rough check on accepted explanations" or, more broadly, the conviction that the history of one case can importantly inform the reading of another.[2] National and regional historiographies tend to have distinctive audiences and narrative structures. Thus the history of postbellum Louisiana generally culminates in the collapse of Reconstruction and the triumph of white supremacy. The history of late-nineteenth-century Cuba builds toward the development of a cross-class and cross-racial nationalist movement, with an epilogue on its suppression and manipulation under U.S. military occupation. One value of comparison may be to help expose the limitations of the hidden structures of such national narratives and to cast some doubt on their implicit teleology.

The model of comparison employed here is thus not the retrospective scientific experiment in which variables are identified, values determined, and outcomes explained. Important as such work may be, my goal here is somewhat different: to encourage a succession of rereadings of historical events in which old evidence is examined in the light of new questions, pointing the way to areas in which new evidence may be unearthed. Reading events through these new questions and evidence, in turn, draws attention to the paths not taken, thus challenging the sense of inevitability about the paths that were taken. What follows is an effort to "problematize," as the current clumsy phrase goes, the familiar narratives of "racial conflict" and "cross-racial alliance" through an exploration of the histories of the cane regions of southern Louisiana and of central and eastern Cuba.

Louisiana

Slave emancipation came to the sugar regions of Louisiana in the midst of civil war and complex ideological struggles. In the spring of 1862, Northern forces occupied the Confederate city of New Orleans and began to push their way up the Mississippi River. Soon virtually all of the major sugar-producing parishes of Louisiana were under Union control, and army and civilian officials attempted to improvise labor arrangements that would maintain production even as slavery was collapsing.[3] Shortly after the war ended, the establishment of the Freedmen's Bureau gave authority to a new set of federal officials, who then supervised and, to a lesser extent, enforced labor contracts.

In the early stages of the transition, some of the freed people found space in which to experiment with cooperative agriculture and independent leasing.

---

[2] Barrington Moore, Jr., *Social Origins of Dictatorship and Democracy: Lord and Peasant in the Making of the Modern World* (Boston: Beacon Press, 1966), p. xiii.

[3] For a careful analysis of this process, and a revealing set of documents, see Ira Berlin et al., eds., *Freedom: A Documentary History of Emancipation, 1861–1867,* series 1, vol. 3, *The Wartime Genesis of Free Labor: The Lower South* (Cambridge: Cambridge University Press, 1990), esp. chap. 2.

But both planters and bureau agents were firmly committed to annual wage labor contracts, and the predominant form of organization of production remained the work gang, now paid in wages. Planters generally refused to sell or rent land to freed people and often withheld wages to try to ensure compliance with the plantation work regime. The result was vulnerability for sugar workers, who had hoped for greater mobility and access to productive resources, and instability for employers, who aimed to reassert control over the pace of work and the deportment of workers.[4]

Each year freed men and women, hoping for better terms, delayed signing contracts, and planters sought to persuade them or to find substitute workers. At the same time, small strikes of workers on individual plantations provided some upward pressure on wages, and occasional informal work stoppages asserted the laborers' new autonomy. Paul DeClouet, a plantation manager in St. Martin Parish, wrote scornfully that the workers were "too pious" to work on Good Friday, and that they took time off on election day in 1868.[5]

With capital for expansion short, labor more demanding, and planters initially reluctant to replant, production was slow to recuperate. Many male former slaves, however, continued to work year-round on the plantations, and some women returned to paid work at the harvest. Planters hired some workers from out-of-state to substitute for those who left, but the work force remained predominantly African-American. Planters seem to have been thoroughly committed to a model of long-term, resident, low-wage labor, subjected to a strict plantation discipline. Though some sharecroppers and small-holders might join the plantation work force at harvest time, there was little to induce long-term migration. One can trace through DeClouet's daybook, for example, his experiment with hiring workers from Virginia—and their successive departures following day after day of cleaning ditches, spreading manure, and cutting wood, often in the cold and the rain.[6]

The initial catastrophic decline in sugar production was arrested, though output in 1870 was still less than two-thirds of the average annual output for 1855–59. In 1873 a national and worldwide economic crisis challenged this

[4] For a more detailed discussion, see Rebecca J. Scott, "Defining the Boundaries of Freedom in the World of Cane: Cuba, Brazil, and Louisiana after Emancipation," *American Historical Review* 99 (February 1994): 70–102. An important recent interpretation is found in John C. Rodrigue, "Raising Cane: From Slavery to Free Labor in Louisiana's Sugar Parishes, 1862–1880," (Ph.D. diss., Emory University, 1993).

[5] See Paul DeClouet's diary of 1867–68, vol. 2, in box 2, Alexandre E. DeClouet and Family Papers, Louisiana and Lower Mississippi Valley Collection, Special Collections, LSU Libraries, Louisiana State University (hereafter LLMVC).

[6] Many of the former slaves on the DeClouet plantations departed at the beginning of 1870, and DeClouet hired "Virginia men" to replace them. Several left within less than a month, and others left after a wage settlement in March. See entries for early 1870 in De Clouet's diary, 1869–70, vol. 5, in box 2, Alexandre E. DeClouet and Family Papers, LLMVC.

fragile recovery. Again, the question of how to respond was widely contested. Agricultural reformers, among them the vocal Dan Dennett of the *Daily Picayune,* argued throughout the 1870s that the sugar regions should turn away from reliance on wage labor and look to smallholdings. He envisioned a system in which plantations would freely subdivide their land into small leaseholds, and cane farmers would provide cane to a central mill for processing. But instead of subdividing the land, larger planters generally sought to compress costs. And the conspicuous element that seemed liable to compression was wages.[7]

Faced with generalized deflation and a decline in sugar prices, planters in individual parishes began to collaborate in the 1870s to try to cap or lower monthly rates of pay. One employer from St. James Parish candidly wrote to the *Daily Picayune* to announce that while wages the previous season had been $18 monthly plus rations, he and his neighbors were now paying $13 per month. "Please publish this, so that the change may be made in other districts, as, by being general, it may become permanent at least until better times."[8]

Workers responded with organized anger. In Terrebonne Parish several hundred laborers met in Zion church to form an association, refusing to work for less than $20 a month, and seeking to form sub-associations that could collaboratively rent lands to work on their own. Then they went on strike. Planters were alarmed, spread rumors of murder and mayhem, called on the governor to send in the militia, and had the leaders arrested. Eventually an agreement was reached, but workers did not get the right to rent lands collectively.[9]

In trying to arrange to lease land, workers in Terrebonne were reiterating a demand that had been made unsuccessfully several times before. During the Union occupation, groups of former slaves had often sought to occupy lands and produce subsistence and market crops.[10] In the 1860s, the editorialists of the New Orleans *Tribune,* representing certain sectors of the urban *gens de couleur,* had called for the subdivision of lands among the freedmen. Some delegates to the Louisiana Constitutional Convention of 1868 had proposed breaking up large estates by placing an upper limit on the size of tracts that

---

[7] Noel Deerr, *The History of Sugar,* vol. 1 (London: Chapman and Hall, 1949), p. 250, provides production figures for Louisiana. See also J. Carlyle Sitterson, *Sugar Country: The Cane Sugar Industry in the South, 1753–1950* (Lexington: University of Kentucky Press, 1953). On Dennett, see William Ivy Hair, *Bourbonism and Agrarian Protest: Louisiana Politics, 1877–1900* (Baton Rouge: Louisiana State University Press, 1969), pp. 37–38.

[8] Letter from H. O. Colomb, dated January 9, 1974, printed in the *Daily Picayune* (New Orleans), January 11, 1874.

[9] The strike is described in detail in the *Daily Picayune* (New Orleans), January 14, 15, 16, 18, and 20, 1874.

[10] See Berlin et al., *Wartime Genesis: The Lower South,* pp. 357–59.

could be bought at distress sales as a means of facilitating the purchase of land by freedmen, but their initiatives were defeated.[11]

Efforts to build land distribution into social policy had been unsuccessful, but the desire for land had not disappeared. The sugar workers of Terrebonne seem to have been adopting a strategy of seeking multiple sources of support: garden plots, leasehold land if possible, and reasonable terms of work when they did work on estates. In this respect they closely resembled their counterparts on the postemancipation sugar plantations of Jamaica, Cuba, and Brazil, who often sought some mix of wage labor and independent production.[12]

In 1874, however, workers had to adjust to the lowered wages, and the New Orleans *Price-Current* observed smugly that the fieldhands, "having been taught the necessity of thrift and economy, have really saved more from their two thirds, than they formerly did from full pay while the relations between them and their employers, have been more satisfactory than at any time since the war." Planters in St. Mary Parish attempted wage reductions the following year, and wages of $13 a month were common during 1875 and 1876.[13] Nevertheless, competition among employers, combined with resistance by workers, tended to undermine planter-imposed wage caps, and wages recovered slightly in 1877.[14]

Workers' challenges were thoroughly intertwined with Reconstruction politics and with the broader pattern of assertion by the freed people and their allies. One African-American state legislator was reported to have addressed "inflammatory" speeches to the Terrebonne strikers, urging them to resist wage cuts.[15] Two months later, in March, 1874, the formation of a black militia in Lafourche Parish caused equal alarm. Benjamin Lewis, described as "of mixed negro and Indian blood, the Indian in him clearly predominating," led the militia unit. The local paper of the town of Thibodaux later recalled the militia as a "sable band of terrorists" and evoked a picture of "the wives and sisters and mothers of those licensed banditti, going about our town armed

[11] See Roger Wallace Shugg, "Survival of the Plantation System in Louisiana," *Journal of Southern History* 3 (August 1937): 311–25, and Ted Tunnell, *Crucible of Reconstruction: War, Radicalism and Race in Louisiana, 1862–1877* (Baton Rouge: Louisiana State University Press, 1984).

[12] See Thomas C. Holt, *The Problem of Freedom: Race, Labor, and Politics in Jamaica and Britain, 1832–1938* (Baltimore: Johns Hopkins University Press, 1992); Rebecca J. Scott, *Slave Emancipation in Cuba: The Transition to Free Labor, 1860–1899* (Princeton: Princeton University Press, 1985); and Jaime Reis, "From *Bangué* to *Usina*: Social Aspects of Growth and Modernization in the Sugar Industry of Pernambuco, Brazil, 1850–1920," in Kenneth Duncan and Ian Rutledge, *Land and Labour in Latin America* (Cambridge: Cambridge University Press, 1977), pp. 369–96.

[13] Sitterson, *Sugar Country*, p. 246.

[14] For a general discussion of the fate of planter combinations, see Ralph Shlomowitz, "'Bound' or 'Free'? Black Labor in Cotton and Sugarcane Farming, 1865–1880," *Journal of Southern History* 50 (November 1984): 569–96.

[15] See *Daily Picayune* (New Orleans), January 16, 1874.

with cans of coal oil and cane knives."[16] The imagery of terror and murder was part of the standard white-supremacist demonology, but in this case it is unclear which was thought more dreadful—the fact of armed African-American men, or the brazenness of the African-American women.

For the white elite, relief from Reconstruction came with "Redemption" in 1877, as the state government reverted to the Democratic Party, the last remaining federal troops withdrew, and groups like Benjamin Lewis's militia were disbanded. But the years of African-American assertion were not erased, even by the paramilitary and vigilante violence that could now be exercised with impunity. Although the ideology of white supremacy seemed to be riding high, the next major efforts at collective action in the sugar cane fields would openly cross the color line.

In 1880 an estimated 500 black workers went on strike in St. Charles Parish, moving in a body from estate to estate to stop work. The group was apparently an imposing one, with some workers on horseback and many armed with sticks. Planters appealed successfully to the governor to call out the militia.[17] Then, in 1881, in St. Bernard Parish, black workers and white workers joined forces to press for wage increases. Similar strikes emerged in the years that followed.[18]

In 1886 the Knights of Labor began organizing black and white locals among railway workers in Louisiana, opening the way for a more formal cross-racial alliance. The Knights' "anti-monopolist" platform rapidly gained adherents, and candidates affiliated with the order won elections in the town of Morgan City, where the railroad monopoly made an obvious target. The Knights soon moved out into the sugar plantations, organizing around the themes of worker unity, cooperativism, and opposition to monopolies. The task of organizing among black and white sugar workers highlighted the strategic value of the Knights' commitment to interracial solidarity, while raising the question of just how far that commitment extended.[19]

Schreiver Local Assembly was organized in Terrebonne Parish in August of 1886 with a nucleus of black workers, later to transform itself into the region's first integrated local. The local of Little Caillou similarly had 32 charter members identified as black in July 1887, but 80 members, black and white, male and female, by October. Other assemblies, however, were segregated. The

[16] *Weekly Thibodaux Sentinel* (Thibodaux, La.), September 17, 1887.
[17] The early events of the strike are described in the *New Orleans Democrat*, March 19, 1880, reprinted in *St. Charles Herald*, February 15, 1973, p. 22. I am grateful to Robert Paquette for calling this item to my attention.
[18] See Jeffrey Gould, "'Heroic and Vigorous Action': An Analysis of the Sugar Cane Workers' Strike in Lafourche Parish, November, 1887," unpublished. I am very grateful to Prof. Gould for sharing this essay with me.
[19] See Gould, "'Heroic and Vigorous Action'" and Melton Alonza McLaurin, *The Knights of Labor in the South* (Westport, Conn.: Greenwood Press, 1978), esp. chap. 7.

leaders of the local assemblies in the sugar region included laborers, farmers, artisans, and at least one plantation school teacher; among them were individuals described as black, mulatto, and white. Most were literate, and their work experiences generally reached beyond the plantations, creating important linkages to small farmers, who could provide food during strikes, and to nearby towns, which could provide refuge in case of evictions.[20]

In the fall of 1887, in the face of new efforts by planters to reduce wages, District Assembly 194, in Morgan City, proposed negotiation. When planters refused, the assembly called together workers from the surrounding sugar parishes and formulated a series of demands. These included a daily wage of $1.25 without board or $1.00 with board, plus 60 cents for nighttime "watch," if required; an end to payments in scrip; and more regular payment of wages due. Leaders at this point seem to have been uncertain as to whether a strike would be necessary. They declared themselves willing to compromise, but set a deadline of October 29 for planters in Lafourche, Terrebonne, St. Mary, Iberia and St. Martin parishes to respond to their demands.[21]

The threat of a strike at the moment of harvest brought Democratic and Republican members of the elite together, and planters meeting in Lafourche Parish formulated a counterplan, committing themselves to ignore the demands, blacklist fired workers, and evict strikers from their plantations. They invoked the contractual obligations of the workers and the "depressed condition of the sugar industry" to justify their opposition, and referred to the Knights of Labor District Assembly representatives as "a committee of people claiming to represent a secret organization." They asked the sheriff to request that the governor send in the militia. A similar meeting of planters in St. Mary's parish declared that "after the planters have employed laborers during the whole cultivation of the crop, it is flagrantly unjust and illegal to demand extortionate wages to harvest the same."[22]

On November 1, 1887, militia forces under Brigadier-General William

[20] The description of local leaders is based on the evidence compiled by Jeffrey Gould and described in " 'Heroic and Vigorous Action.' " I have also drawn on Jonathan Garlock, *Guide to the Local Assemblies of the Knights of Labor* (Westport, Conn.: Greenwood Press, 1982). Information on membership of local assemblies is contradictory and needs further work. Among other things, the usual labels of "black" and "white" need to be examined more closely for regions like Little Caillou where additional socio-racial categories such as "mulatto" may have been used locally.

[21] The text of the demands can be found in the New Orleans *Daily Picayune,* Sunday, October 30, 1887. The description of the strike that follows is based on the newspapers, report, and manuscripts cited below, and on Hair, *Bourbonism and Agrarian Protest* , esp. pp. 175–84; Jeffrey Gould, "The Strike of 1887: Louisiana Sugar War," *Southern Exposure* 12 (November-December 1984): 45–55; Gould, " 'Heroic and Vigorous Action' "; and Covington Hall, "Labor Struggles in the Deep South," unpublished, in the Labadie Collection, Harlan Hatcher Library, University of Michigan.

[22] See *The Daily Picayune* (New Orleans), October 31, 1887, for the resolution of the meeting of "influential people" in Thibodaux on October 30.

Pierce took the train to the town of Thibodaux with the aim of "restoring peace in the sugar districts from Berwick's Bay to New Orleans, then seriously threatened by the belligerent attitude of strikers."[23] All was in fact relatively peaceful in the region, but work on most plantations had been halted by the strike. The press estimated the number of participants in the strike at around 10,000, and some accounts specified that around 9,000 of them were "colored."[24]

From early in the strike, class and racial divisions appeared within the Knights of Labor, whose members included some professionals and shopkeepers as well as wage workers. Local 6295 in St. Mary's and white Local 10499 voted to disregard the strike call.[25] Some white sugar workers did heed the call, however, and the strike was clearly a cross-racial one. Although the hostile *Daily Picayune* tended to portray the strikers as black, even it denounced "white mischief-makers" for their role in the events.[26]

In the first days of November planters attempted to oblige strikers to vacate their plantation cabins; at the same time, the strikers attempted to block the importation of strikebreakers. Birdshot was fired from ambush at strikebreakers who tried to operate mills, and groups of strikers were apparently prepared to challenge strikebreakers who arrived by train. General Pierce was distressed to find "a very large body of negroes lounging around the depot" at Schreiver. In the town of Thibodaux, a large crowd of strikers "black, white, and curious" watched as the militia disembarked.[27] Although the presence of the militia could be used to back up arrests and evictions, it did not prevent symbolic challenges: General Pierce reported that when troops arrived on one plantation "the negroes hooted and used violent language, the women waving their skirts on poles, and jeering."[28]

Planters were by now divided and uneasy. Some small-scale planters settled quickly; others brought in strikebreakers. The nephew of one planter in Terrebonne recalled of his uncle: "He gave in to the demands, not because he

---

[23] See *Report of Brig-Gen. William Pierce Commanding State Troops in the Field in District from Berwick's Bay to New Orleans to General G. T. Beauregard, Adjutant General of the State of Louisiana, November 28th, 1887.* (Baton Rouge, La.: Leon Jastremski, State Printer, 1887), p. 3.

[24] *The Daily Picayune* reported that "It is intimated that over 10,000 laborers in this district quit work this morning" (*The Daily Picayune* [New Orleans], November 2, 1887). The *Weekly Pelican*, a Republican newspaper from New Orleans, reported on November 5, 1887, that "Ten thousand laborers throughout the sugar district are on strike. Fully nine-tenths of these laborers are colored men and all are members of the Knights of Labor organizations." Although the claim that nine-tenths were "colored men" seems to imply that one-tenth were white men, I have found no direct evidence that permits a more precise estimate of the number of white strikers.

[25] See *The Daily Picayune* (New Orleans), October 31 and November 2, 1887.

[26] See *The Daily Picayune* (New Orleans), November 2, 1887.

[27] See Pierce, *Report*, p. 4, and the French-language section of the *Weekly Thibodaux Sentinel*, November 5, 1887. ("A peu près 500 grévistes noirs, blancs, et curieux assaistaient au débarquement de la force armée. . . .")

[28] Pierce, *Report*, p. 11.

wished to, but because he had no other option. He would have lost the crop and everything else, including the place, if he had not done so. Immediately all the neighboring planters denounced him as 'disloyal to his class,' declaring he should be willing to lose everything in defense of his class interests. But he could not see it."[29] Similarly, planters in lower Lafourche Parish, where most estates were relatively small, quickly settled with the strikers. The plantation workforce of lower Lafourche included workers identified as black, white, and mulatto, some of whom were resident on plantations, and others of whom occupied small farms in the areas. Many of the white fieldworkers who followed the Knights of Labor were apparently located in this zone.[30]

In upper Lafourche, which held the largest and most technologically advanced plantations, employers were not inclined to compromise. Some thought that the workers would respond to the mere presence of the militia and return to work; others counted on strikebreakers. The local press of Lafourche Parish denounced the leaders of the Knights of Labor as "wolves" who preyed on innocent workers.[31] At one level, events were simply stalemated. From the point of view of the white elite, however, such a stalemate was intensely distressing, both because it publicized their incapacity to impose their will, and because it delayed a harvest increasingly threatened by frost. Every day that passed brought a crisis closer.

In St. Mary parish, events unfolded very quickly. Evicted strikers took refuge in Pattersonville, where they found themselves isolated from the union leadership in Morgan City because of the military control of the railroads.[32] A sheriff's posse, including both planters and local residents, was assembled and moved to confront a crowd of "negro strikers." Accounts of the events varied widely, but at least four, and possibly as many as twenty, strikers were killed.[33] The local planter Donelson Caffery took a leading role in the repression and obtained support from individual members of the Knights of Labor who had opposed the strike from the beginning.[34] Caffery wrote bluntly to his son on November 11: "The strike is effectually squelched. It was necessary to apply a

[29] Hall, "Labor Struggles."

[30] This observation on the distinction between upper and lower Lafourche is developed by Jeffrey Gould in "Sugar War" and "'Heroic and Vigorous Action.'"

[31] See the *Thibodaux Weekly Sentinel* for mid-November 1887.

[32] The name of the town is variously reported as Patterson, Pattersonville, and Pattersville.

[33] Gould, "Strike," p. 51, describes the posse as being led by A. J. Frere, a Knights of Labor member. Hall reports that the posse was initially reported to be led by "Don Caffery, a prominent planter and politician of St. Mary's," who denied such leadership, attributing it to another planter, Col. E. M. Dubroca. Caffery did say that he had assumed command of part of the posse to round up "rioters" (Hall, "Labor Struggles").

[34] A. G. Frere appears both as a signatory of the declaration dissociating Local 6295 in Franklin, St. Mary's Parish, from the strike call, and among the posse that fired on workers in Pattersonville. See *Daily Picayune* (New Orleans), October 31, 1887, and Gould, "Sugar War," p. 51. (Gould lists him as "K of L white delegate A. J. Frere," but I am presuming that this is the same person.)

strong remedy—and it has been done. The negroes are quiet and have with few exceptions gone to work."[35]

Planters in upper Lafourche continued to carry out large-scale evictions, forcing strikers to move with their families into the town of Thibodaux. Militia units were periodically deployed to estates where there were rumors of violence or of the imminent arrival of strikebreakers. But the militia was of little use in actually obliging strikers to work. Tension mounted and General Pierce continued to emphasize the need for local initiative. Although he believed that the presence of the militia had a salutary effect on the laborers, he emphasized that the time had come for planters to take responsibility for self-defense. Most of the militia forces were withdrawn during the third week of November, and Pierce himself returned to New Orleans on November 20.[36]

By then there were numerous evicted strikers in the town of Thibodaux, and the local press began calling for strong and confident action. With the departure of all but one of the militia units, a paramilitary group under planter leadership was formed and set up pickets at the exits from town.[37] As in the 1870s, the "insolence" of black women was again invoked as evidence of how much the proper order of things had been disturbed. Mary W. Pugh, from a planter family, wrote to her son that on her way home from church she met "negro men singly or two or three together with guns on their shoulders going down town & negro women on each side telling them to 'fight-yes-fight we'll be there' (you know what big mouths these Thib. negro women have. I wish they all had been shot-off) they are at the bottom of more than half the devilment."[38]

At this point, the story takes on some of the characteristics of a Greek tragedy. From the point of view of workers, planters were aiming to drive them into complete submission. Their dream of land division was still thwarted, their hopes of higher wages were being met with intransigence. Unity under the Knights of Labor seemed to promise some recourse. From the point of view of planters, the battle for supremacy was imminent. Mary Pugh wrote in retrospect: "I had seen for three weeks it had to come or else white people could live in this country no longer."[39] A labor struggle was being continually reinterpreted as a racial struggle, and planters were able to draw white townspeople into an alliance in anticipation of trouble from the evicted strikers.

The stage was set for an open confrontation. The vigilantes held the preponderance of force, and exercised it. On November 22, unknown persons shot at

[35] Letter from D. Caffery, Franklin, Louisiana, to "my dear son," November 11, 1887, in vol. 6, Donelson Caffery and Family Papers, LLMVC.

[36] See Pierce, *Report*, pp. 22–30.

[37] See *Thibodaux Weekly Sentinel*, French section, November 19, 1887.

[38] Mary W. Pugh to Edward F. Pugh, November 25, 1887, in folder 1, Mrs. Mary W. Pugh Papers, LLMVC.

[39] Ibid.

two white men guarding the edge of town, and the posse went into action.[40] In Mary Pugh's words, "they began then hunting up the leaders and every one that was found or any suspicious character was shot. Before Allen got back the rifles on St. Charles Street sounded like a battle. . . ." She witnessed the capture of one hidden striker:

> they brought them by our side gate. I thought [they] were taking them to jail instead they walked with one over to the lumber yard where they told him to 'run for his life' [and] gave the order to fire. All raised their rifles and shot him dead. This was the worst sight I saw but I tell you we have had a horrible three days & Wednesday excelled any thing I ever saw even during the war. I am sick with the horror of it. but I know it had to be else we would all have been murdered before a great while. I think this will settle the question of who is to rule the nigger or the white man? for the next 50 years but it has been well done & I hope all trouble is ended. The niggers are as humble as pie today. Very different from last week.[41]

When one is faced with a narrative of this kind, it is easy to see these events as a continuation of the drama of black and white in Reconstruction, and of the irrepressible rise of white supremacist ideology and action. And when we note that unions did not organize again in the cane fields of Louisiana until the 1950s, racial repression and class repression seem to converge quite neatly. In his very fine analysis of the 1887 strike, Jeffery Gould comes to the conclusion that racist repression constituted in some sense the final solution to the long-standing problem of a resistant and mobilized labor force.[42]

But one could also shift the perspective by a quarter turn and see the violence and vituperation in somewhat different terms—not as a process that simply drew upon a black/white gap, but as one partly responsible for defining the struggle as a binary contest between "black" and "white," radically simplifying complex social and racial categories. The analysis of racial categories as socially constructed is an important accomplishment of recent scholarship on race and racial ideology, sharply distinguishing it from the "race relations" literature of earlier decades, which tended to take the categories of black and

[40] The description in *The Weekly Pelican* (New Orleans), November 26, 1887, emphasized the presence of armed white men, said to be "Shreveport guerrillas," and charged that the shooting of the two sentries was actually carried out by others on patrol. Scattered evidence suggests that one last militia unit—from Shreveport—may indeed have been in town at the time. For a detailed discussion of events in the 1870s and 1880s, see Rebecca J. Scott, "'Stubborn and Disposed to Stand their Ground': Black Militias, Sugar Workers, and the Dynamics of Race and Labor in the Louisiana Sugar Bowl, 1863–1887," presented at the Tulane-Cambridge Atlantic World Studies Group Inaugural Conference, Tulane University, November 21–23, 1996, and forthcoming in *Slavery and Abolition* (London).

[41] Pugh to Pugh, November 25, 1887.

[42] See Gould, "Strike of 1887," and "'Heroic and Vigorous Action.'"

white as given. Indeed, some nineteenth-century Louisianans were already well aware that the process of construction of identity was social and relational. In 1869 there took place the following exchange between a congressman and J.B. Esnard, a delegate to the 1867–68 constitutional convention in New Orleans.

> Question: Are you colored?
> Answer: I cannot answer that; I do not know exactly whether I am or not.
> Question: Do you rank and acknowledge yourself as a colored man?
> Answer: I do.
> Question: But if you have any colored blood you don't know it?
> Answer: No, sir.
> Question: It is charged and you don't deny it?
> Answer: Yes, sir.[43]

Governor McEnery declared in 1887 that "God Almighty has himself drawn the color line."[44] But the compression of socioracial categories and the eliding of class identity and racial identity in the identification of "black" with "strikers" was very much the work of men and women. The repression that occurred in Thibodaux and Pattersonville was more than either racist violence or class war. It was a selective combination of the two, synthesized in such a way as to assist in the construction of whiteness as privileged and blackness as dangerous.

Covington Hall observed in passing that "during the whole period only one white man, a picket in Thibodaux, was reported as seriously wounded. All dead were colored and unionmen, though many whites were active members of the Knights."[45] The reality of a workforce containing individuals categorized as white, mulatto, and black was redefined in the theater of repression as white order versus black disorder.

This construction of a binary and highly politicized color line, of course, was not simply a discursive act. The refusal to rent sugar lands to former slaves; the reconstruction of gang labor; the recruitment of African-American seasonal workers from Virginia and northern Louisiana: all of these combined to create a reality in which wage work in the cane was strongly associated with blackness. The process of building the color line might be seen as a reciprocal one, in which racial ideology shaped class relations (as in the reluctance to rent sugar lands to black workers), and class relations in turn shaped the construction of race and politics.

[43] House Miscellaneous Documents, 41st Congress, 2d sess., no. 154, pt. I, pp. 698–99, as cited in Tunnell, *Crucible*, p. 114.
[44] Quoted in *The Weekly Pelican* (New Orleans), October 15, 1887.
[45] Hall, "Labor Struggles."

A comparison with Cuba provides an example of a sugar region in which race, labor, and politics were equally contested and intertwined, but in strikingly different ways. The presence of similar elements, and very different outcomes, may help to highlight the contingent nature of white supremacy as a dominating ideology.

Cuba

Slavery had been destroyed in Cuba in a prolonged struggle, one in which parliamentary initiatives from Spain both responded to and provoked slave initiatives in Cuba, in the context of repeated rebellions against Spanish domination. Throughout this process, Spanish policymakers improvised and compromised on the organization of labor, while attempting to manipulate the issue of race through invocations of the danger of "race war." Like later white supremacists in Louisiana, Cuban colonial officials tried to modify reality to substantiate this discourse, selectively arresting Afro-Cuban conspirators and allowing whites to go free, in order to reinforce an image of the conflict as "racial."[46]

Cuban nationalists of the 1860s and 1870s had repeatedly stumbled in the face of this maneuver, with conservative white reformists and insurgents portraying themselves as the "civilized" alternative to black domination—and in the process helping to fracture the nationalist movement.[47] By 1880 anticolonial rebels had been defeated. But abolition could not be removed from the agenda. Slaves and their allies continued to challenge planters' authority and posed a continuing threat to the maintenance of colonial power.

The Spanish parliament voted to abolish slavery in 1880, placing former slaves under a thinly disguised "apprenticeship" designed to last until 1888. Their strategy postponed the definitive end of slavery, but apprentices themselves provided an accelerating counterforce, pursuing legal and illegal avenues for more rapid emancipation. By 1886, only 25,000 former slaves remained under the "apprenticeship," and the government finally liquidated the institution.[48]

Though Cuban planters had generally stalled the ending of slavery, the more prosperous among them adapted quickly to free labor. Eager to expand production for the growing North American market, they invested or borrowed to purchase new equipment and contracted with small-scale growers (*colonos*)

---

[46] This process is highlighted in Ada Ferrer, "Social Aspects of Cuban Nationalism: Race, Slavery, and the Guerra Chiquita, 1879–1880," *Cuban Studies* 121 (1991): 37–56, and developed further in her dissertation, "To Make a Free Nation: Race and the Struggle for Independence in Cuba, 1868–1898" (Ph.D. diss., University of Michigan, 1995).

[47] See Ferrer, "To Make a Free Nation."

[48] See Scott, *Slave Emancipation in Cuba*.

to provide yet more cane. The expanded central mills thus drew cane from nearby renters and owners as well as plantation fields worked by wage laborers. Planters sought wage workers among former slaves, former smallholders, and the thousands of immigrant workers who came from Spain, some to work seasonally, others to become cane farmers.[49] Within a few years the field workforce was unmistakably multiethnic and multiracial. By the early 1890s sugar production on the island had broken the one-million-ton mark.

This seeming success story, however, did not resolve the question of the place of workers in Cuban society, nor of Cubans in an island ruled by Spain. Rural employment was highly seasonal, and estate workers were dependent for much of the year on the product of small plots elsewhere, at a time when access to land was becoming more difficult. The health of the entire sugar industry depended on exports to the United States, which in turn were vulnerable to the same tariffs that were a godsend to the planters of Louisiana. The weight of Spanish colonialism—embodied among other things in restrictive legislation and in sporadic and intrusive campaigns against banditry—rested heavily on many rural communities.

Throughout the early 1890s exiled nationalist leaders, including José Martí, a Cuban of Spanish descent, Antonio Maceo, from a free family of color in eastern Cuba, and Máximo Gómez, who was from the Dominican Republic, sought to lay the groundwork for a new rebellion. In part this represented the reactivation of struggles begun in the 1860s. But the movement of the 1890s was animated by a far more inclusive vision of Cuban nationality, and by an ideology in which social transformation and national liberation were tightly linked.[50]

In February 1895, insurgents rose up in the eastern end of the island and with time drew together small-scale cultivators, sugar workers, urban artisans, and some landowners in a massive challenge to Spanish rule. Within rebel lines officers categorized as white, black, or *pardo* (mulatto) commanded troops from every socioracial category. The official goal of the rebellion was Cuba Libre, a free Cuba in which racial and ethnic privilege would be rejected. Different groups of insurgents, however, interpreted this goal differently. Some white insurgents appear to have been worried about the possibility of black predominance, while some insurgents of color were adamant that all racial privileges should be eliminated immediately, which meant challenging the distribution of power within the rebel forces themselves.[51]

[49] On Spanish immigration to Cuba see Jordi Maluquer de Motes, *Nación e inmigración: Los españoles en Cuba (ss. xix y xx)* (Gijón: Ediciones Jucar, 1992).
[50] See Gerald E. Poyo, *"With All, and for the Good of All": The Emergence of Popular Nationalism in the Cuban Communities of the United States, 1848–1898* (Durham, N.C.: Duke University Press, 1989), and Ferrer, "To Make a Free Nation."
[51] For a more detailed discussion, see Ada Ferrer, "The Black Insurgent and Cuban National

Cuba's population in 1895 probably contained approximately half a million people categorized as black or mulatto.[52] Questions of race and slavery had long divided nationalist politicians in the island, insurgents as well as reformists, and the invocation of a potential "race war" was one of the staples of colonial manipulation. An effective anticolonial movement would have to circumvent this tactic and appeal to some of those who had owned slaves or had benefitted from the privileges of whiteness in a slave society, as well as many of those who had been slaves. It is thus not altogether surprising that nationalist leaders sought to overcome racial divisions as they attempted to organize a movement that could succeed where earlier ones had failed. What is more striking is that this strategy apparently worked—at least initially—at the level of recruitment and mobilization.

Mobilization itself, however, was not a simple matter of responding to an ideology. The large-scale recruitment of rural workers to the insurrection seems to have taken place in waves, as the position of noncombatants became more and more precarious. Initially, rebels sought supplies and recruits from sympathizers within working plantations, addressing themselves to the mixed population of black, mulatto, and white laborers, artisans, and colonos. Then, as cane fires and orders to halt grinding brought production to a standstill, plantation residents and employees had to choose between taking to the hills to join the rebellion or resigning themselves to internment in Spanish concentration camps, which had been established precisely to prevent them from making contact with rebel forces. The perception that rebels were people like oneself, while Spanish soldiers were trigger-happy interlopers, tended to predetermine the outcome. It is hardly surprising that, given the choice, many went with the rebels.[53]

The mechanism by which rural dwellers identified with the rebels owed something to shared economic status, to regional identity, and to deep-seated local loyalties to rebel *cabecillas* (chieftains) in the countryside. Though sociracial categories may have entered at various points, other elements of perceived sameness could override them. As one man, the nephew of a cane farmer, commented when asked to describe the arrival of a band of insurgents on the estate where he worked: "I saw them and we were even drinking beer with some of them, and . . . I knew that nothing could happen to me as I was

---

Identity, 1895–1898," and Rebecca J. Scott, "Mobilizing across the Color Line: Race, Class, and Anti-Colonial Insurgency in Cuba, 1895–98," both presented at the Seminario de Historia de Cuba, Universitat Autònoma de Barcelona, March 25–26, 1993.

[52] See Scott, *Slave Emancipation*, p. 248.

[53] The case files of the U.S. Spanish Treaty Claims Commission (entry 352, record group 76, U.S. National Archives), provide repeated glimpses of this process of recruitment. See Scott, "Mobilizing across the Color Line," for examples.

like them."[54] The near absence of racial labels in the primary documents makes it difficult to prove that this man from a cane farming family was categorized as "white," or that many of the insurgents with whom he was drinking beer were categorized as "black" or "mulatto." But the odds are in favor of both guesses.

Several of the most admired insurgent leaders were Afro-Cuban, and their troops came from virtually all ethnic and socioracial groups. The rebel general Antonio Maceo, a *pardo,* had as his chief of staff Jose Miró y Argenter, a Catalan, and numbered among his followers white mechanics and professionals, as well as hundreds of black, white, and mulatto peasants and wage workers. The staff officers who served his brother José Maceo included the sons of elite white families from Oriente. Together they harassed, confronted, and helped to undermine the Spanish forces.

Spanish colonial authorities still tried to play the theme of "race war," claiming that the rebellion would lead to "another Haiti." But this ideological maneuver was a perilous one, and making it explicit would accelerate the alienation of most Cubans of color. Moreover, the rebel leaders were prepared for this claim and could point to abundant evidence of the multiracial character of their own leadership and followers. José Martí also tried to counteract the idea of "race war" by proposing a different image of black and mulatto officers. He employed a language of honor, gentility, and strength to describe General José Maceo, celebrating not only Maceo's leadership, but also the fact that he treated his white staff officers like sons. This image of a mulatto officer commanding white troops would not gratify a dyed-in-the-wool white supremacist, but for Martí it was a stirring picture of social inversion carried out with restraint and "civilization."[55]

Within the first years of the war the nationalists succeeded in gaining control of a large fraction of the countryside. But the Spanish forces held on in the cities. They deployed large numbers of conscript troops from the peninsula and recruited irregular forces among Spanish immigrants and poor urban Cubans, including, it seems, some unemployed Cubans of color.[56] The war thus became a bloody stalemate, a ghastly struggle of attrition between city and country in which thousands of noncombatants died from hunger and disease. In effect, by 1898, the Cuban nationalists had won. Spain could not sustain colonial power in this fashion indefinitely. But the final military blow, of

54 Deposition of Eduardo Vilar, August 12, 1904, claim 97 (Central Teresa), pt. 1, Entry 352, RG76, USNA.

55 See Abelardo Padrón Valdés, *El general José: Apuntes biográficos* (Havana: Editorial de Ciencias Sociales, 1975), sec. 7, Iconografía.

56 I am grateful to Louis A. Pérez, Jr., for sharing with me some of his preliminary findings on the socioracial composition of the pro-Spanish guerrillas. Pérez, personal communication, February 1992.

course, came with the uninvited intervention of United States forces, who arrogated to themselves the authority relinquished by Spain.[57]

With the U.S. occupation of Cuba in 1899, the narratives of Louisiana and Cuba in some sense intersect. Many among the U.S. occupying forces brought with them a new and rigorous set of racial distinctions and invidious stereotypes, drawn from the post-emancipation and post-Reconstruction contest over the meanings of race in the United States. Cuba had never lacked expressions of racism, and some Cuban liberals were among the most vocal proponents of all-white immigration. But an obsession with whiteness and with the degenerative powers of "mongrelization" was a relatively novel element in a society that had long utilized multiple color categories. While for some purposes the dominant racial ideology in Cuba had at times employed a white/black dichotomy, socioracial categories were more often defined along a hypothetical color gradient, including *blanco* (white), *trigueño* or *mestizo* (dark), *mulato* or *pardo* (brown), and *negro* or *moreno* (black), each defined both phenotypically and contextually. In certain settings, such terms were used as descriptors of appearance; in others, they could be constituted as social categories.[58]

During and immediately following the years of U.S. occupation, "whiteness" and "blackness" took on new and contested public meanings in Cuba. U.S. authorities initially sought to limit the voting rights of Cubans of color through the imposition of literacy or property requirements, but they were thwarted in that goal by the intense commitment of many Cuban nationalists to suffrage for those who had fought in the war. Then in organizing a new force for order in the countryside, the Rural Guard, North American officials were able to use networks of patronage to create an institution that was largely under the control of those denominated "white." The implications were ominous counterpoising a "white" force of repression to an increasingly active multiracial rural labor movement. Although American troops departed in 1902, the Rural Guard remained in place.[59]

Like the Knights of Labor in the United States, the Spanish anarchists and Cuban veterans who took up the task of labor organizing in the cane fields in 1902 championed interethnic and interracial solidarity. But they carried it an important step further, building up their unions through explicit appeal to existing Afro-Cuban groups, and insisting on an aggressive antiracism in their

[57] See Louis A. Pérez, Jr., *Cuba Between Empires, 1878–1902* (Pittsburgh: University of Pittsburgh Press, 1983).

[58] On Cuban racial ideology see Verena Martinez-Alier, *Marriage, Class, and Colour in Nineteenth-Century Cuba* (Cambridge: Cambridge University Press, 1974), and Ferrer, "To Make a Free Nation." On the complexities of the relationship between phenotype and "racial" categories, see Peter Wade, *Blackness and Race Mixture: The Dynamics of Racial Identity in Colombia* (Baltimore: Johns Hopkins University Press, 1993).

[59] See Pérez, *Cuba Between Empires.*

writings. One of the earliest sugar workers' unions emerged in the towns of Cruces and Lajas, in the expanding sugar-producing region of Cienfuegos. Evaristo Landa, a mulatto veteran of the 1895 conflict, was one of the group's leaders; meetings were called in the old Centro Africano, established a decade earlier by former slaves; and the movement welcomed Spanish workers, who constituted about a quarter of the wage labor force. Indeed, Spanish-born anarchists were vigorous contributors of manifestos and declarations.[60]

The structure of the labor force on sugar plantations tended to subordinate rather than elevate racial distinctions. Within the wage labor force former slaves, long-free Cubans, and immigrants from the peninsula worked side by side. The rural smallholding population, which provided some seasonal workers to the plantations, included many descendants of free persons of color, as well as Cubans who categorized themselves as white. This is not to say that distinctions of "color" did not map onto distinctions of class. There were certainly sharp differences in the degree of access to productive resources, and "colored" renters and owners controlled only a small fraction of the island's land. But the daily working experience of most of those who labored in cane was not one of strict segregation. When the members of the Workers' Guild of Cruces called for an alliance of all those who sweated to earn a paltry wage, without distinction of nationality, some workers responded readily.[61]

But to stop the story here would be to create something of a romantic myth. For while the memories of the nationalist struggle helped to forge a multiracial Cuban identity, and the ongoing organization of the labor movement reinforced cross-ethnic alliances, there was in Cuba the possibility of bitter division. Planters and property owners in Cuba, whatever their previous nationalist credentials, were as unwilling as their counterparts in Louisiana to see the development of an assertive working-class movement. Two organizers involved in the 1902 sugar strikes in Cruces were "disappeared," their bodies found more than a year later. At that point, the repression seems not to have had definite racial overtones, though planters did speak with particular hostility about groups of "men of color" who had tried to stop work on the plantations.[62] But in the years that followed, the language of race exploded onto the scene.

A small group of veterans, distressed at, among other things, the exclusion of Cubans of color from many public offices, founded in 1908 an "Agrupación Independiente de Color." Their self-identification as a racially based political group met with tremendous hostility from mainstream politicians and the

[60] The pioneering work on this movement is John Dumoulin, "El primer desarrollo del movimiento obrero y la formación del proletariado en el sector azucarero. Cruces 1886–1902," *Islas* 48 (May-August 1974): 3–66.

[61] See Dumoulin, "El primer desarrollo," p. 18.

[62] Dumoulin, "El primer desarrollo."

press, though their denunciations of racism were well founded and their platform was a relatively familiar reformist one.

In 1912 the group, now denominated the Partido Independiente de Color, attempted the classic tactic of an armed protest in pursuit of recognition and negotiations. The consequences seem to have gone well beyond the intentions of their leaders. The army was called out to defend property, and hard-pressed rural dwellers in Oriente attacked plantation buildings and repositories of land titles, symbols of the expulsions and indignities they had suffered from local and foreign landowners.[63]

The national government responded aggressively. Constitutional guarantees were suspended; noncombatants were ordered out of the area; and a pitiless repression began. In scenes reminiscent of rural Louisiana, patrols roamed the back roads of Oriente and hanged or macheted any black male whom they found. The army suppressed the protest through what was in effect assassination, and the conflict was retroactively characterized as a "race war." One observer reported that the army "was cutting off heads, pretty much without discrimination, of all negroes found outside the town limits."[64] The estimates of the number of victims of the repression are entirely conjectural, but range into the thousands.[65] As in Louisiana, the moment of repression called forth a categorical white/black dichotomy and the selection of victims according to that division.

The events of 1912 sent a terrible chill through the rural population of color and became an unspoken—and nearly unstudied—chapter in Cuban history. But at the same time, the labor movement continued to grow as an interracial movement, and widespread strikes in 1917 brought dozens of mills to a halt.[66] Moreover, the enfranchisement of former slaves and their descendants had led to an electoral structure in which no party was likely to identify openly with blatant white supremacy.

The killings of 1912 make it clear that a single color line could be drawn in Cuba, and that it took on powerful meanings in fear and in memory. But those fears and memories were not a permanent obstacle to the mobilization of

---

[63] See Aline Helg, *Our Rightful Share: The Afro-Cuban Struggle for Equality, 1886–1912* (Chapel Hill: University of North Carolina Press, 1995), and Louis A. Pérez, Jr., "Politics, Peasants, and People of Color: The 1912 'Race War' in Cuba Reconsidered," *Hispanic American Historical Review* 66 (1986): 510–38.

[64] Cited in Pérez, "Politics, Peasants, and People of Color," p. 537.

[65] Louis A. Pérez, *Cuba Under the Platt Amendment* (Pittsburgh: University of Pittsburgh Press, 1986), p. 151, cites a figure of 3,000 Afro-Cubans "slain in the field."

[66] See John Dumoulin, "El movimiento obrero en Cruces, 1902–1925: Corrientes ideológicas y formas de organización en la industria azucarera," in *Las clases y la lucha de clases en la sociedad neocolonial cubana* (Havana: Editorial de Ciencias Sociales, 1981), and Dumoulin, *Azúcar y lucha de clases 1917* (Havana: Editorial de Ciencias Sociales, 1980). Further work is needed, however, to trace the role of Afro-Cuban field workers in the 1917 strike, which was initiated largely by mechanics who worked in the mills.

workers. In the long run the realities of labor and electoral politics helped to keep the public meanings of racial identity highly unstable.[67]

Race and Politics in Cross-National Perspective

It would be foolhardy to try to draw extensive conclusions about social relations in Louisiana and Cuba from this very brief discussion of selected incidents. But there is an intriguing structure to the comparison that emerges. Both cases remind one of the complexity of racial identities; both show instances of cross-racial alliance and of white racist repression. But the balance is different. In Louisiana, the fragile solidarity briefly displayed in the strikes of the 1880s showed glimpses of an alternative future, one quickly buried in the triumph of the "white line" strategy and of white supremacist ideology. In Cuba, a pattern of uneasy but effective cross-racial alliances was interrupted by a ferocious repressive episode in 1912, but continued to hold force in a growing labor movement.

Clearly the paths taken out of slavery conditioned a different set of outcomes in the two cases. The structuring of the rural labor force in Cuba, which included a multiethnic corps of sugar workers embedded within a multiethnic peasantry, helped to open up possibilities that were effectively foreclosed in Louisiana. At the same time, the history and precepts of Cuban nationalism provided a matrix within which to envision cross-racial cooperation. It cannot be proven, but one might hazard the observation that neither the specific pattern of class relations, nor the inherited language of nationalist unity, could *alone* have brought about the kind of cooperation that marked the sugar workers' movement for decades.

In Louisiana, the construction and politicization of a single color line was encouraged by a specific strategy adopted by the Democratic party and its allies throughout the South. Even after "redemption" from federal rule was achieved, planters could draw on the demonology of Reconstruction by invoking the image of large groups of black workers challenging their white employers. But that the groups of strikers should have been composed primarily of workers defined as black was itself the direct result of a specific path taken out of slavery: the large-scale reimposition of gang labor on former slaves.

---

[67] For a more detailed discussion of race and party politics in the twentieth century, see Rebecca J. Scott, "'The Lower Class of Whites' and 'The Negro Element': Race, Social Identity, and Politics in Central Cuba, 1899–1909," in Consuelo Naranjo, Miguel A. Puig-Samper, and Luis Miguel García, eds., *La Nación Soñada: Cuba, Puerto Rico, y Filipinas ante el 1898,* (Aranjuez: Editorial Doce Calles, 1996) pp. 179–91. See also Alejandro de la Fuente, "With All and For All: Race, Inequality and Politics in Cuba, 1899–1930" (Ph.D. diss., University of Pittsburgh, 1996).

In those few areas in southern Louisiana where the rural workforce comprised significant numbers of members of several socioracial groups, the picture was somewhat different. In Terrebonne and lower Lafourche parish, where estates with a multiracial workforce coexisted with a network of small farms, some of them operated by people of color, cross-racial alliances fared somewhat better and repression was less severe.[68] But everywhere the sharp distinctions of citizenship imposed under Democratic rule helped to reinforce the color line during strikes, for only whites were eligible for militia service.

In Cuba broad rights to formal citizenship coexisted with various forms of discrimination, and racism coexisted with antiracism.[69] In the light of the Louisiana experience, it is perhaps the explicit antiracism that stands out as in need of historical explanation. José Martí argued that divisions between black and white Cubans would begin to be overcome "where all that is just and difficult begins, among the humble folk."[70] This assertion can be seen as a romantic—and somewhat patronizing—populist gesture. But there was some evidence to support such a picture of potential working-class unity. In the formation of the nation, "race" had been provisionally subordinated to *cubanidad*—Cubanness—both at the level of ideology and in the field of battle. After the war, the reality of life in the cane fields reinforced the perception that workers' interests were not divided along the lines of "racial" groupings. But at the same time, veterans of color who sought mobility through public office did encounter obstacles, giving rise to an increasing sense of betrayal.

In the decades after emancipation a self-conscious concept of whiteness emerged at important moments in Cuba, urged on by the confident supremacist thought of the U.S. occupation government, and reinforced by planters seeking "superior" European immigrant workers. Within the plantations, however, the effect of that immigration, in conjunction with the rapid overall growth of the workforce in sugar, was to eliminate the segregationist alternative. It was a nice irony that Spanish anarchists joined Cuban veterans to challenge planters, some of whom no doubt imagined themselves to be Cuban nationalists.

---

[68] A logical urban comparison would be the New Orleans waterfront, where fragile cross-racial alliances survived for decades. See Eric Arnesen, *Waterfront Workers of New Orleans: Race, Class, and Politics, 1863–1923* (New York: Oxford University Press, 1991).

[69] For the most recent general overview of the early twentieth century, see Tomás Fernández Robaina, *El negro en Cuba, 1902–1958: Apuntes para la historia de la lucha contra la discriminación racial* (Havana: Editorial de Ciencias Sociales, 1990).

[70] He was referring specifically to intermarriage. "Por dónde empezará la fusión? Por donde empieza todo lo justo y difícil, por la gente humilde. Los matrimonios comenzarán entre las dos razas entre aquellos a quienes el trabajo mantiene juntos." These sentences are from an undated manuscript by Martí, reproduced in the *Anuario del Centro de Estudios Martianos* 1 (1978), p.34. I am very grateful to Ramón de Armas for calling this document to my attention, and I have used the transcription of the text cited in his essay, "José Martí: La verdadera i única abolición de la esclavitud," unpublished, December 1986.

These alliances would be repeatedly strained, however, during periods of scarce employment, when Cuban workers lobbied for legislation that would give Cubans priority over Spaniards in seeking jobs. Moreover, the events of 1912 in the East reactivated the imagery of "race war" and may have affected sugar workers as well as the peasants who were its immediate victims. But while ethnic and racial categories posed potential lines of division, they did not overwhelm the growing movement of sugar workers. The color line could on occasion be drawn, but it was not, in the long run, explicitly politicized.[71]

The very effective politicization of the color line in Louisiana seems in this light to be a more contingent phenomenon. One could argue that the salience of whiteness as a component of identity in Louisiana needed no elaboration, that it was a predictable consequence of defeat in war, compounded by black assertiveness after the war. But white supremacy as an ideology was not simply the "natural" ideology of Louisianans defined as white. White Unionists had opposed secession, and a mixed crew of Louisianans, including free people of color, white unionists, and former slaves, had fought in the Union army. White Republicans had participated—however opportunistically—in many of the processes of African-American political assertion in the state, and some native whites were stronger supporters of black rights in the constitutional convention of 1867–68 than were northern carpetbaggers.[72] These actions did not necessarily imply egalitarianism, but neither did they prefigure white supremacy.

The construction of events in the Louisiana "sugar bowl" from the 1860s through the 1890s as racially encoded encounters of civilization and barbarism was an act of interpretation, not an automatic reflex. A newspaper editorial from St. Mary's, written in support of the White League, made the metaphor explicit, declaring that civilization was the birthright of the white race, "and it is ours, and ours alone."[73] The editors of the *Caucasian,* published in Alexandria in 1874, called for the formation of a "white man's party" to make the next election a "fair, square fight, Caucasian versus African."[74] These publicists were not simply reflecting existing lines of cleavage. They were attempting to give specific political content to a particular, binary construction of race and racial identity.

Having made these comparative observations, it may be appropriate to conclude by confessing that there are many aspects of the events that I have described that remain deeply puzzling. It is difficult to understand the goals of

[71] Nationality, however, was politicized, and legislation to establish preferential quotas for Cuban workers was introduced repeatedly between 1910 and 1925. Employers, backed by the United States, thwarted its passage in order to maintain their freedom of action. See Pérez, *Cuba Under the Platt Amendment,* pp. 153–64.

[72] On the Constitutional Convention, see Tunnell, *Crucible,* esp. p. 150.

[73] Quoted in ibid., p. 173.

[74] Ibid., pp. 193–94.

the Cuban army members, some of whom must have been veterans of the independence struggle, who turned on black and mulatto peasants, also veterans of the struggle, in Oriente in 1912. And while it is not difficult to see the interests that were served by formation of the sheriff's posse that fired on striking workers in St. Mary's Parish, Louisiana, in 1887, it is more difficult to envision what was in the mind of A. Frere, a white Knights of Labor member who joined in leading the posse.[75] However carefully we trace class relations and social constructions, there is within racism a kind of vicious "excess," as Thomas Holt has put it, that often defies our attempts to analyze the forces involved.[76]

Recognizing this analytic residuum, however, need not drive one back to the notion that the most murderous forms of racism can only be understood as psychopathology. The more difficult challenge is to historicize the concept of racism itself, in order to understand how at one moment behaviors which under other circumstances would appear pathological came to seem normal to many of those involved, while at other moments the racial divisions emerging from slavery were effectively overcome in pursuit of shared goals. Some of the same people were involved in both processes, and it is well to remember that neither antiracism nor racism is necessarily a more "basic" or "essential" characteristic of people who may indeed express them both.

The very complexity of these two stories should make their most virulent incidents look more contingent, less inevitable, and therefore, in a sense, even more troubling. Division and conflict between poor whites and former slaves thus appear not as necessary legacies of slavery, but rather as the result of the changing circumstances in which these groups were constituted and in which they encountered each other, and as the result of specific political decisions and initiatives taken by leaders. A substrate of tension, stereotypes, and prejudice may well be the universal legacy of systems of slavery defined as racial. But the systematic construction of a single color line, and the subordination of those on one side of it, is a much more historically specific development. In both Louisiana and Cuba the racial categories were not ready-made, and their political meanings were repeatedly contested, as those who worked in the countryside developed multiple alliances in pursuit of resources, security, and citizenship.

[75] See the notes 33 and 34 above on Frere. Perhaps his involvement was made more likely by family connections. The papers of the planter Donelson Caffery (in LLMVC) include an invitation to a wedding in which a Caffery weds a Frere.

[76] The phrase is from an unpublished paper by Thomas C. Holt, and I am grateful to him for allowing me to quote from his work in progress. See also his "Marking: Race, Race-Making, and the Writing of History," *American Historical Review* 100 (February 1995): 1–20.

CHAPTER 8

Religious Toleration and Jewish Emancipation in France and in Germany

JUDITH EISENBERG VICHNIAC

In "Notes and Queries on the Theory and Practice of Legitimate Opposition," an unpublished essay distributed to his students, Barrington Moore, Jr., discusses the social underpinnings of legitimate opposition. He argues that free speech, a key element of the complex network of liberal institutions and practices, is intimately connected with the growth of religious toleration. He specifies that there are two significant aspects to the emergence of such toleration. First, religious groups come to a realization that they "can agree to disagree." This usually comes after lengthy and protracted fights between those concerned. Second, secularism becomes more prevalent as the growth of scientific knowledge helps to unravel many of the mysteries of the world. Moore writes, "Perhaps the key to the whole process lies in the fact that some secular matters came to take priority over religious ones, making it possible and indeed necessary to agree to disagree about religious ones."[1] Those "secular" matters include the achievement of national unification and the enhancement of economic development. Indeed, the growing commercialization of the economy meant that religious affiliation was relegated to the background as "men learned to disregard and bracket the secondary issues."[2]

When he penned these words, Barrington Moore clearly was thinking about the religious wars of the seventeenth century between Catholics and Protestants. John Locke also had these conflicts in mind when he wrote his *Letter*

---

[1] Barrington Moore, Jr., "Notes and Queries on the Theory and Practice of Legitimate Opposition," mimeograph, Harvard University, n.d. p. 18.

[2] Ibid., p. 19. Jacob Katz also emphasizes the secular basis of the state in *Tradition and Crisis: Jewish Society at the End of the Middle Ages* (New York: Free Press, 1961), p. 38.

Concerning Toleration in 1689. This led Locke, however, to note that "neither Pagan, nor Mahometan nor Jew ought to be excluded from the civil rights of the commonwealth because of his religion."[3] This paper will focus on the emergence of religious toleration and the emancipation of one non-Christian religious minority, the Jews in France and Germany. Moore's emphasis on the consolidation of the nation-state and the emergence of capitalism goes a long way in explaining the changing fortunes of French and German Jews in the modern period of European history. But there are other insights from *Social Origins of Dictatorship and Democracy* that are less useful in understanding the changing plight of these Jewish communities.[4] What will become clear from this paper is that when one includes Jewish history in an understanding of European political development, the story that one can construct takes on quite a different form.

The *Encyclopedia of Religion and Ethics* tells us that religious toleration "connotes a refraining from prohibition and persecution. Nevertheless it suggests a latent disapproval, and it usually refers to a condition in which the freedom which it permits is both limited and conditional." It involves tolerating the presence of a religious minority in one's midst that is no longer persecuted relentlessly. The openness with which a minority group can practice its religion, however, is often limited. The rights of religious minorities to own property, to testify in court, and to gain access to certain occupations also reflect different levels of religious toleration. Toleration is different from religious liberty or equality.[5]

"Jewish emancipation" is religious toleration in a much more positive sense. It connotes religious liberty and equality. What do I mean by Jewish emancipation? Ira Katznelson and Pierre Birnbaum underline three aspects.

(1) whether broadly liberal and republican doctrines and institutional arrangements grounded in the Enlightenment values would come to govern transactions between the state and civil society to provide fresh potential bases for Jewish citizenship; (2) whether such innovative formulas for political participation, once in place, would prove sufficiently encompassing to include the Jews; and (3) whether the terms of admission to the polity these arrangements countenanced would permit a far-reaching or narrowly gauged pluralism for Jews

[3] Jacob Katz, *Out of the Ghetto: The Social Background of Jewish Emancipation, 1770–1870* (Cambridge: Cambridge University Press, 1973), p. 1.

[4] Barrington Moore, Jr., *Social Origins of Dictatorship and Democracy: Lord and Peasant in the Making of the Modern World* (Boston: Beacon Press, 1966).

[5] James Hastings, ed., *Encyclopedia of Religion and Ethics,* vol. 12 (New York: Charles Scribner's and Sons, 1961), p. 360.

seeking both to take up the offer of citizenship and remain meaningfully Jewish.[6]

Jacob Katz has a broader definition. He characterizes it as a process by which Jewish communities in Western Europe from roughly 1760 until 1870 "underwent a transformation that changed their legal status, their occupational distribution, their cultural habits, as well as their religious outlook and behavior."[7] Jews, who were formerly considered a national minority living in western Europe, were accorded legal equality as well as political rights while losing community control over significant aspects of Jewish life. Concurrently, Jews were able to intermingle and become part of the larger national societies in which they lived.

The era of religious toleration of French and German Jews began in the early modern period of European history. At that time, there were broad similarities between the experience of the Jewish communities in both countries. The economic and political forces that allowed Jews to return to and settle in French and German villages and towns between the sixteenth and the eighteenth centuries were at work across western Europe. It was the French Revolution and its aftermath that separated the trajectories of the Jewish communities in both countries. In France, Jewish emancipation took an enormous step forward when, during the French Revolution, Jews became French citizens. No longer did they suffer from specific legal disabilities that had stigmatized the community before. After the revolution, except for a short period under Napoleon when certain restrictions were imposed on the Jewish community, Jews came to view themselves as French men and women *de confession Israélite* rather than an alien group living in a foreign country. This was a radical transformation that occurred very rapidly. While anti-Semitism was certainly a factor in France during the nineteenth century, Jews made steady gains in many spheres of French life, including political, academic, and judicial appointments of significant stature and took advantage of many new opportunities in business and commerce.

In Germany, however, the process took much longer, stretching out over the greater part of the nineteenth century. The question of German unification complicated the issue of Jewish emancipation. Each duchy and principality had different rules. Emancipation was "partial" and "selective" in Prussia, Bavaria, Baden, and Württemberg.[8] The "Jewish Question" preoccupied certain seg-

[6] Pierre Birnbaum and Ira Katznelson, "Emancipation and the Liberal Offer," in Birnbaum and Katznelson, eds., *Paths of Emancipation: Jews, States and Citizenship* (Princeton: Princeton University Press, 1995), p. 5.

[7] Katz, *Out of the Ghetto*, p. 1.

[8] Peter Pulzer, *Jews and the German State: The Political History of a Minority, 1848–1933* (Oxford: Blackwell, 1992), p. 79.

ments of German society, generating an extraordinary debate, of which Marx's essay "On the Jewish Question" is only one famous example.[9] It was not until 1871 that Jews were accorded equal rights. This formal equality did not mean, however, that Jews were welcome into many spheres of civil society. Restricted access to appointments in government and military circles continued to be an issue. A Dreyfus Affair, for example, could not have occurred in Germany because Jews were excluded from achieving this level of appointment within the German Army.

What distinguished the German case from the French then is not that anti-Semitism was rampant in one society and not the other. Both had significant pockets of anti-Semites, and the tragic history of the late nineteenth and twentieth centuries underlines this fact. As Pierre Birnbaum has pointed out, both France and Germany had major political movements that defined themselves as anti-Semitic.[10] Rather, the French Revolution was a watershed event in the history of French Jewry, providing the vocabulary for the integration of the Jewish community within French society. In Germany, in contrast, the process was slower and more fitful with more pervasive restrictions on access to important spheres within German society continuing into the twentieth century. How do we account for this difference?

By looking at these two cases, I hope to accomplish two things. First, I want to consider the applicability of standard interpretations that view the centralization of political power as inimical to the development of toleration and liberty. Second, I want to distinguish between the trajectories of these two communities. While it is clear that similar forces encouraged the development of religious toleration in both societies, when it came to Jewish emancipation, however, their paths diverged. In the final analysis, as Jacob Katz emphasizes, the fates of different West European Jewish communities were bound up with the general histories of the countries in which they resided and less with the internal developments of the communities themselves.

The Growth of Toleration

Our story begins with the expulsion of the Jews from Spain and Portugal at the end of the fifteenth century. Such expulsions took place all over Europe, including France and Germany. In urban centers throughout this area, Jews were driven from their homes by urban mobs aroused by religious fervor and economic pressures. Jews found protection only in two geographical regions in the Holy Roman Empire: first, in areas where the Emperor, as protector of German

---

[9] Ibid., pp. 14–18. See also Karl Marx, "On the Jewish Question," in Robert C. Tucker, ed., *The Marx-Engels Reader*, 2d ed. (New York: W. W. Norton, 1978), pp. 26–52.

[10] Pierre Birnbaum *Anti-Semitism in France: A Political History from Léon Blum to the Present* (Oxford: Blackwell, 1992).

Jewry, was in direct control, and second, where Catholic prince-bishops were looking to counter the growing power of a Protestant bourgeoisie.[11] But, by the end of the sixteenth century, the situation began to improve. The wars generated by the Reformation and the Counter-Reformation broke the control of the Catholic Church over Europe. Rulers searched for ways to raise the cash and supplies needed to wage the wars unleashed by dynastic and religious rivalries. Jews were a major beneficiary of this quest. They were allowed to settle in previously restricted areas in France and parts of Germany by invitation of the rulers.

In France, the Bordeaux region became one of the first important areas of settlement. Small numbers of Sephardic Jews came to the Bordeaux area after 1472, when Louis XI allowed foreigners to reside in Bordeaux and guaranteed their right to own property and to sell goods without letters of naturalization.[12] Interested in rebuilding commercial activity in the city after the occupation of the English, Louis insisted on these changes despite local protests. When the ordinances were adopted by both the Paris and Bordeaux *parlements* and thus became law, Jews slowly began to immigrate. At first they kept up the guise of being Christians; they were, therefore, known as *nouveaux Chrétiens*. The prevailing climate made it impossible to be open about their commitment to Jewish religious practices.

The other main area of French Jewish settlement was Lorraine. German Jews were allowed to settle in Metz after France conquered the city in 1552. This was done against the wishes of local ecclesiastical, commercial, and guild interests within the city. Metz and the surrounding region were under the control of the Ministry of War, which looked to the Jews to supply their troops. In other instances in the East, Jews were invited by municipalities and *seigneuries* to settle in a number of other towns. As opposed to the Bordeaux region, where Jews were expressly invited by the crown, here in the east, local decisions often were paramount. France until the Revolution was not united administratively, and local regions and towns had different prerogatives and limitations. For towns and noblemen, allowing Jews to settle could be a quick way of raising capital since they could charge new arrivals a settlement tax. They could continue filling their coffers by charging Jews special taxes to marry, have children, do business, and most important, to continue to reside in the area. Only a few were afforded this opportunity. There were no more than five thousand Jews in all of France by the year 1700.[13]

[11] Jonathan Israel, *European Jewry in the Age of Mercantilism* (Oxford: Clarendon Press, 1989) pp. 8–13.

[12] Frances Malino, *The Sephardic Jews of Bordeaux: Assimilation and Emancipation in Revolutionary and Napoleonic France* (Birmingham: University of Alabama Press, 1978), p. 2. See also Arthur Hertzberg, *The French Enlightenment and the Jews* (New York: Columbia University Press, 1968), pp. 16–17.

[13] Hertzberg, *French Enlightenment*, pp. 18–19.

In Germany, because the Holy Roman Emperor was the protector of the Jews, one does see growth in the number of cities and towns in which Jews were permitted to settle. But the Emperor and other princes were constantly balancing their need for the business acumen of the Jewish community and the hostility of the urban populations to Jewish settlement. In the south and west, ecclesiastical princes opened their bishoprics to Jews in the hopes of improving trade with South Germany. Often the numbers allowed in were minuscule, but even these changes provoked latent anti-Jewish feelings. Jews were not allowed to live in the Imperial Free Cities except for Frankfurt, where, by 1613, one seventh of the population of 20,000 was Jewish. What happened in Frankfurt is instructive. It was the arrival of Calvinists from the Netherlands that broke open the traditional guild structures. This allowed Jews to participate in the growing trade with South Germany.[14] Religious fragmentation provided an opening wedge for the Jews. They were not, however, invited to return to Prussia. At this time, the Elector was too beholden to the wishes of the Estates to challenge them on this issue.

It was during the Thirty Years' War (1618–1648) that many of these trends intensified. Within the complicated web of religious, dynastic, and class divisions, Jews found the authorities willing to be more flexible in granting protection and certain rights to the Jewish community because Jews had skills and resources that were in even higher demand in wartime than in time of peace. The Holy Roman Emperor and the princes who were always short on cash depended on interest-free loans that Jews were "persuaded" to give them to fight the Protestant forces. In return, "Jews . . . could be repaid in a different form, in concessions and privileges of which they alone had need and which were within the Emperor's power to grant."[15] In fact, the Emperor instructed his troops to extend special protection to the Jewish communities.

Even the Lutheran armies of the King of Sweden, which invaded Germany in the 1630s, came to depend on Jewish suppliers, and this despite the fact that the Swedish crown excluded Jews from residence in the Baltic provinces under their control as well as in Sweden. They were also the champions of the German Lutherans, who were staunchly anti-Jewish. Again, the same dynamic came into play. Jews traditionally facilitated trade between town and country, specialized in the horse and grain trades, and were willing to give the changing occupiers extremely good terms in return for intangible rewards. Each side in the conflict had their own Jewish suppliers, who were paid, in return, through a loosening of restrictions on residence, protection from the ravages of war, and a broadening of economic opportunities. In fact, one historian has gone so far as to say that the Swedes favored the Jews over the rest of the population.[16]

14 Israel, *European Jewry*, pp. 40–42.
15 Ibid., p. 88.
16 Ibid., pp. 93–97.

In France, the Thirty Years' War solidified the position of new groups of nouveaux Chrétiens. Richelieu, for reasons of state, allowed a new wave to settle in the French ports of Rouen and Nantes and in other towns in the southwest of France. The embargo of the Spanish by the Dutch meant that a large contraband trade developed between Amsterdam and Madrid via France. The nouveaux Chrétiens were crucial for the expansion of this trade. *Raison d'état* guided the decision in one famous legal case in which Richelieu protected a group of crypto-Jews from charges brought against them. Knowing full well that they were in fact practicing Jews, he cynically had the case set aside, using the technicality that the accusers' testimony could not be trusted because they were converts themselves. From that time onward, the nouveaux Chrétiens felt freer to practice their religion more openly. This policy of tacit tolerance continued under Colbert.[17]

In the northeast of France, Jews in Lorraine continued to supply the French garrisons. The Treaty of Westphalia, which ended the Thirty Years' War, changed the composition of French Jewry dramatically by incorporating the Yiddish speaking Jews of Alsace into France. Unlike their Sephardic counterparts in the Bordeaux region and in the ports in the west of France, they had always and openly practiced their religion.

The key economic role that Jewish purveyors and financiers played during the Thirty Years' War continued to expand after the Peace of Westphalia. Jews furthered the mercantilist agendas of rulers all over Europe. Supplying the troops was only one role. In Germany, the Court Jews, with their dense net of ethnic ties in the Sephardic and Ashkenazic communities, were able to mobilize relatively large amounts of capital quickly, and many heads of state came to depend on Court Jews to consolidate their political power.[18] They were connected with the European gold and silver bullion trade which was dominated by Jews. In France, Jews were important as purveyors but played a much less significant role in aspects of finance. This second role would come later.

The desire of local groups in Germany to renew the expulsion of the Jews after the Thirty Years' War was blocked in most instances by state authorities. In Prussia, for instance, not only did Frederick William, the great elector, stop the attempt by tradesmen to expel Jewish competitors in newly acquired territories, but for the first time bucked the estates and towns and insisted on the right of small numbers of Jews to settle in Brandenburg, Berlin included, and East Prussia. As he told the estates, "the Jews and their businesses seem not harmful but rather useful to us and the country."[19] In fact, Jewish businessmen were part of the elector's strategy of bringing the estates and towns to heel. This happened in Königsberg, when Jews were settled in nearby Memel

[17] Israel, *European Jewry,* pp. 116–17.
[18] Ibid., pp. 123–24; Katz, *Out of the Ghetto,* pp. 29–30.
[19] Pulzer, *Jews and the German State,* p. 72.

in an attempt by the elector to rob its neighbor of its trade. Other princes in Germany followed similar policies of protecting Jewish tradesmen from local hostility.

In France, after the Thirty Years' War, the fortunes of the Jewish communities depended on the whim of state policy makers. As we have seen, Colbert followed Richelieu's lead and allowed many New Christians to settle and practice their Judaism almost in the open. Colbert described the usefulness of the Jewish businessmen bluntly. In 1673, he wrote,

> There is nothing as advantageous for the general estate of commerce as the increase of the number of those engaging in it. What might not be of advantage to the particular inhabitants of Marseilles is of great importance to the kingdom as a whole. The establishment of the Jews has never been forbidden by commercial considerations, because business generally increases wherever they are, but only by religion. Since, at this moment, commerce is the only issue, there is no reason to pay any attention to the arguments which have been advanced to you against the Jews.[20]

Colbert's policy of opening France up to commercial groups, whatever their religious persuasion, did not always carry the day. During Louis XIV's more Catholic phase, after 1680, Jews who had come to play an important role in France's American colonies as well as those residing in Marseilles were expelled. This was the period of the Revocation of the Edict of Nantes (1685). It appears, however, that the flight of the Huguenots prevented Louis XIV from continuing his crusade against the Jewish communities of the southwest of France, where a few families, but certainly not all were forced to leave. The economic loss would have been too great.[21]

By the beginning of the eighteenth century, the fortunes of the Jewish communities in France and the German states had taken a decided turn for the better. With the consolidation of political power by the French monarchy and Prussian Hohenzollerns, the economic value of the Jewish community forced both states to tolerate a continued Jewish presence. This meant that Jews could practice their religion more openly. In the southwest of France, Jews, who were still considered New Christians, felt comfortable enough to congregate for Jewish prayer and acquire a cemetery for burials, while in cities in Prussia and other German principalities, Jews won the right to build synagogues. This growing tolerance came about against the express hostility of most local groups and without much enthusiasm by those who accorded Jews these privileges. And it took place within the context of an almost complete social separation of the Jewish communities from the gentile universe around

---

[20] Hertzberg, *French Enlightenment*, pp. 23–24.
[21] Israel, *European Jewry*, pp. 160–63.

them. But, the process was under way whereby "men learned to disregard and bracket the secondary issues."[22]

Religious toleration of the Jewish communities in France and Germany, then, was bound up with the consolidation of power by the French and Prussian monarchies. Military considerations played a crucial role in state building in early modern Europe, and Jews were often crucial to this effort.[23] The skills and networks of the Jewish businessmen became an important resource for the monarchs to tap. Not only would they lend money at very advantageous rates to state authorities and supply their armies, but they stimulated economic growth. As the French government shifted towards free trade, Jews were often the agents for dissolving the old restrictions.

But these services were not free. Jews pressured for the right to practice their religion openly and for an end to civil and economic disabilities, and they became increasingly bold as time went on. The tempo of change varied, however, from region to region; the permission to construct synagogues and to purchase land for cemeteries, to settle in "new" areas, and to enter "new" trades and occupations, all depended on the balance of local and state interests.

These concessions, moreover, came against the express wishes of many important groups within the population. It goes without saying that ecclesiastical authorities tried to block an improvement of Jewish conditions. Not surprisingly, masters and artisans objected to interlopers as well. Furthermore, many peasants hated the Jew in their midst who was often the agent of the landholder or the lender of only resort. In addition, merchant and commercial classes were fearful and jealous of these new competitors.

This, too, comes as no surprise although it underlines the way in which taking Jewish history into consideration throws a different perspective on the role of the bourgeoisie in European political development. Local authorities in Alsace and in the principalities and bishoprics of Germany often tried to block Jewish inhabitants from moving in and opening shop. When these different groups came together in provincial assemblies, they were unyielding in their hostility to the Jews. In Prussia, when the estates maintained power, Jews were not allowed to settle. Similarly, at the last meeting of the Estates General in France, anti-Jewish sentiment was rife.[24] In case after case, the fate of the Jewish community depended on the good will of the state and not on support of local authorities or provincial bodies. As Hannah Arendt noted in *The Origins of Totalitarianism*, the Jews "had somehow drawn the conclusion that

22 Moore, "Notes," p. 19.
23 For a recent treatment of this subject, see Brian M. Downing, *The Military Revolution and Political Change: Origins of Democracy and Autocracy in Early Modern Europe* (Princeton: Princeton University Press, 1992), pp. 56–83. Downing does not address specifically the Jewish contribution to this process.
24 Israel, *European Jewry*, p. 67.

authority, especially high authority, was favorable to them, and that lower officials, and especially the common people, were dangerous."[25]

When that good will disappeared, restrictions and tighter controls would often reappear. Frederick William I, for instance, was much less sympathetic to the Jews in Prussia than his two predecessors. Immigration was restricted into Brandenberg-Prussia after 1713 and the quotas of Jews allowed in certain localities were reduced. This Prussian monarch also strengthened the guilds, excluding the Jews. Only in Berlin and Silesia did the population grow.[26]

Whether the emergence of liberalism in the West was linked with the development of strong city governments and provincial assemblies and the containing of royal absolutism has been subject to much debate. In this instance, however, minority rights were intimately connected with the checking of just these forces and the strengthening of the central powers. Groups concerned with the protection of local "liberties" did not often have a relatively progressive view on the toleration of Jews who lived around them. An improvement of the predicament of this "pariah people," to use Max Weber's term, depended on the consolidation of political power at the center and not on the strengthening of local authority.[27]

The Achievement of Emancipation

Religious toleration in western Europe allowed Jewish communities to grow and, some would argue, to thrive. These communities, however, had minimal contact with the outside world. Only when the Old Order began to crumble did other possibilities open up. Achieving civil equality and political freedom for Jews was intimately bound up with achieving civil equality and political freedom for everyone in their host countries. The question of Jewish emancipation as such did not present itself until the debates concerning civil and political equality dominated the political agendas of France and Germany. As Jacob Katz reminds us in *Out of the Ghetto*, Jewish emancipation ultimately depended on general trends within the larger society and relatively little on changes internal to the Jewish communities.[28] The French Revolution had its Jewish dimension because the discussions concerning liberty and equality of necessity spilled over into the debate about the status of Jews in France.

Even before the French Revolution, there was serious discussion of the

---

[25] Hannah Arendt, *The Origins of Totalitarianism* (New York: World Publishing, 1972), p. 23.

[26] Israel, *European Jewry*, p. 240.

[27] Max Weber, *The Protestant Ethic and the Spirit of Capitalism* (New York: Charles Scribner's and Sons, 1958), p. 270–71 n. 58.

[28] Katz, *Out of the Ghetto*, pp. 37, 198–99.

plight of the two major Jewish communities, in Alsace and the Bordeaux region. The Sephardim in the southwest of France continued to make gains. Jews in Bordeaux were already allowed to buy and sell property, could participate in public assemblies, paid taxes on the same footing as other French subjects, and were treated as members of the bourgeoisie of the city.[29]

The situation of Jews in Alsace was much more difficult. The last written documents promulgated by the French monarchy on the Jews were two *lettres patentes* of 1784 concerning their status in Alsace. In these, Louis XVI reiterated the French crown's commitment to the protection of the Jews and addressed them for the first and only time as French subjects. Any change in their status was dependent on the will of the crown. The *lettres patentes* went on to affirm the right of Jews to engage in a wider range of occupations.

This decree was a direct response to increasing tensions within the Alsatian countryside between Jews and indebted peasants. In 1777, a counterfeit ring had passed out forged receipts in the thousands, and the French government found itself in a difficult quandary, not to mention the Jewish lenders, who could not collect on debts. Weakening the economic situation of the Jewish community meant that they were less able to pay taxes. Without debt relief, however, there might be widespread rioting.[30] Jewish lenders were forced to accept a reduction in the overall debt and to agree to longer periods for repayment.

The controversy, however, made the crown more open to arguments for broadening the economic opportunities for Jewish businessmen. The edict emphasized the importance of removing obstacles to the growth of commerce. To this end, Jews were allowed to open workshops and engage in banking. They could rent (not own) farms and vineyards but could not employ non-Jewish laborers to work them. The crown removed the so-called body tax, stating clearly that such a tax was unacceptable because it put Jews in the same class as animals. Critics feared that this change foreshadowed a broader reform of the status of Jews in Alsace. Jews could buy only their own homes, but no other properties, and then only in the areas open to them. Once a region or community had accepted Jewish settlement, Jews could not be expelled at will by a town or a nobleman except when the courts concurred.

The autonomy of the Jewish community's corporate institutions, known as the *kehillah*, was reaffirmed, including the jurisdiction of Jewish courts in cases involving only Jews. All other cases were to be heard in French courts.[31] The community's syndics were responsible for collecting taxes for the state. The

---

[29] Malino, *Sephardic Jews*, p. 50.

[30] Hertzberg, *French Enlightenment*, p. 120. See also Paula E. Hyman, *The Emancipation of the Jews of Alsace: Acculturation and Tradition in the Nineteenth Century* (New Haven: Yale University Press, 1991), p. 14.

[31] Hertzberg, *French Enlightenment*, pp. 317–20; Katz, *Out of the Ghetto*, p. 167.

lettres patentes made it clear, however, that the institutions of the *kehillah* were not to be used for self-defense purposes, unless a clear collective issue was at stake. By the end of the Old Regime, cracks were clearly appearing in the autonomous control exercised by the community. Even before the Revolution, the controls of the state were tightening.

The French Revolution dramatically changed the status of Jews within French society. The story of these changes has been documented by many historians.[32] Civil rights for the Jewish communities of France came only after a long process of debate within the National Assembly. Shortly after the Revolution, it became clear that Protestants and Jews were not covered by the Declaration of the Rights of Man of August 26, 1789. Jews were still considered by many as unable or unwilling to assimilate. Others feared violence in the east of France if Jews were accorded equal rights.

Faced with these divisions, the Jewish communities of France adopted different lobbying strategies. The Sephardim in the southwest of France were already much more assimilated than their counterparts in the northeast. Recognizing the merits of the case, on January 28, 1790, the Assembly by a vote of 374 to 224 accorded them "the rights of active citizens." They had become what one writer has called "the prototype of the assimilated and therefore acceptable Jews."[33]

For the Alsatian Jewish community, the road was more difficult. Initially, the Alsatian leadership's primary interest was to broaden the economic possibilities open to the community and remove the unfair tax burden. Simultaneously, they sought to maintain the corporate structures that supported Jewish education and religious and charitable institutions by taxing the community. Because of the force of events, they modified their position and asked for citizenship, dropping the demand for communal control over issues that related only to Jews. They joined the communities of Paris and others in Lorraine in asking that they too be accorded the "Rights of Man." They framed their request by acknowledging that the Jewish community needed to be reformed but said that that could only take place once the disabilities had been removed. Then, the leaders argued, Jews could become good Frenchmen. The non-Jewish defense of the request for emancipation centered around the notions of reason and the fact that Jews were human beings.[34] These arguments

---

[32] See Herzberg, *French Enlightenment;* and Malino, *Sephardic Jews.* See also Bernhard Blumenkranz and Albert Soboul, *Les Juifs et la révolution Française: Problèmes et aspirations* (Paris: Edouard Privat, 1976); David Feuerwerker, *L'Emancipation des juifs en France de l'ancien régime à la fin du Second Empire* (Paris: Editions Albin Michel, 1976); Zosa Szajkowski, *Jews and the French Revolutions of 1789, 1830, and 1848* (New York: Ktav Publishers, 1970).

[33] Malino, *Sephardic Jews,* pp. 50–53.

[34] Katz, *Out of the Ghetto,* p. 74.

were finally accepted after a long and tortuous debate, and on September 27, 1791, Jews were granted citizenship.[35] As the Revolution moved leftward, Jewish religious institutions suffered the same treatment as churches. Synagogues were destroyed and turned into Temples of Reason during the Reign of Terror. As the revolutionary fever dissipated, the community structures were left in shambles.

Arthur Hertzberg, in his *The French Enlightenment and the Jews,* asks the interesting question of why emancipation occurred during the Revolution. He argues in effect that the revolutionaries really had no other choices but to accord the Jews equality or to expel them. The logic of the "Declaration of the Rights of Man" made it impossible to maintain discrete categories of individuals who were excluded from French society, just as the logic of the emerging capitalist economy made it unthinkable to limit Jews to specific professions. Enlightenment thought, moreover, reinforced the notion that even the Jews could be reformed. "Regeneration" was the operative notion of the day. "It was simply unthinkable, as the framers of the first constitution had to remind themselves in the closing days of their deliberation, that they could extend this principle to all of France and leave only the Jews to be born into the status of exclusion."[36] Jewish emancipation, accorded during the French Revolution, transformed the situation of Jews in France and had a dramatic impact far beyond the borders of France.

Throughout the nineteenth century, French Jews found the opportunities open to them steadily increasing. That Jews were citizens like any other Frenchmen meant that they could share the expanding possibilities that came with the growth of capitalism and a society now open to talent. But this all took time. There was a brief hiatus during the reign of Napoleon when certain civil restrictions were reinstituted on the community (in certain departments). They included limitations on settlement, close monitoring of business affairs, and the refusal to allow Jews to find substitutes for the French army, an option open to other Frenchmen. These, however, were allowed to lapse in 1818.[37]

It was during Napoleon's reign that the French government and the Jewish leadership agreed to the creation of the consistory system of governance. This was a set of quasi-governmental institutions composed of laymen and rabbis that reported to the Ministry of Cults and brokered the relationship between the Jewish community and the state. The consistory's twin goals were to maintain the integrity of Judaism as a religion while promoting integration within French society. Its success on this level is subject to much controversy.

[35] Hertzberg, *French Enlightenment,* pp. 343–49.
[36] Ibid., p. 338.
[37] Hyman, *Emancipation,* pp. 17–20.

It did, however, mold "trustworthy and patriotic citizens, and it afforded the population a sense of security as a recognized religious group."[38]

Civil equality did not mean that prejudice disappeared. In fact, anti-Semitic riots continued to erupt in the Alsatian countryside during periods of economic downturn and revolutionary activity, and they were fairly common until the Second Empire. Agrarian life remained relatively unchanged in the rural areas of Alsace, and Jews continued to lend money to French peasants who often found themselves caught between market forces that they did not understand. Local authorities lobbied for a reimposition of the restrictions that had been placed on Jews in 1808 but to no avail. State authorities steadfastly insisted on equal protection for Jews and tried to nip any threats of civil disobedience in the bud as a threat to public order. Alsatian Jews came to count on the central government as "guarantor of their rights."[39] The socioeconomic structure of the Jewish communities in Alsace and elsewhere in France did change somewhat. The vast majority of Jews still dealt in commerce, but as time progressed, they left behind the moneylending, peddling, and secondhand dealing that carried such opprobrium as new opportunities presented themselves.[40]

During the Second Empire and the Third Republic, Jews began to make considerable strides in all walks of life. Whereas before the Revolution it had been difficult for Jews to become skilled craftsmen, increasing numbers of workers took advantage of apprenticeship programs sponsored by Jewish schools and supported by government money. This was part of the "regeneration" of the Jewish community after Emancipation.[41] Such work was considered to be worthy in contrast to those "Jewish" occupations that were deemed unworthy. But, even the economic role of middleman came to be seen in a new light as France modernized. A commission studying agriculture in Alsace noted in 1866 that

> One cannot fail to recognize the important role which the Jews played in the upward mobility displayed among day laborers and rural workers. . . . It is their intervention, without doubt, which has facilitated for many of them the access to property. . . . It is thanks to these brokers that cultivators large and small can make their purchases and sales at home, dispense with running to fairs and markets while losing much time and much money, and devote all their time and care to their cultivation. It is difficult to admit that such spirit of business, if it

[38] Phyllis Cohen Albert, *The Modernization of French Jewry: Consistory and Community in the Nineteenth Century* (Hanover: Brandeis University Press, 1977), p. 314.

[39] Hyman, *Emancipation*, p. 20.

[40] Albert, *Modernization of French Jewry*, p. 20.

[41] Jay R. Berkovitz, *The Shaping of Jewish Identity in Nineteenth-Century France* (Detroit: Wayne State University Press, 1989).

has had unfortunate consequences, has also brought advantages and has rendered real services to the country.[42]

Jews also joined the professions in increasing numbers and were accepted into universities and even into the officer corps. Still, during the Second Empire, Jews were barred from the higher reaches of government administration.

This changed during the Third Republic. It was during this period, when French liberal institutions were being consolidated, that significant elements of the Jewish community came to identify with the values and the policies of the Third Republic in the most enthusiastic of terms.[43] The number of Jewish state officials who held important positions was greater in France than in any other country at that time, according to Pierre Birnbaum.[44] In fact, he argues that the Third Republic explicitly used such officials to implement policies that were anathema to the Christian right, thereby focusing the attention of the anti-Semitic right on Jewish officials as scapegoats. He writes, "It was as if the State voluntarily gave them the responsibility of performing the ungrateful task of shaking things up while taking the risk of polarizing attention on them."[45]

It is during this time that Franco-Judaism flourished, which one author defined as the "identification of Jewish values with republican values constructed around a worshipping of the homeland and an abandonment of the idea of the Jewish people."[46] Even the Dreyfus Affair did not shake the confidence of Jews in the Republic, because the anti-Dreyfusards were antirepublican as well.[47] And, this, despite, the virulent anti-Semitic eruptions that characterized the affair which were unparalleled in western Europe at the time. The belief in the Republic made the vast majority of French Jews resistant to the pull of Zionism even though it was this affair that started Theodore Herzl's quest for a Jewish homeland.

French Jews struggled to maintain a sense of ethnic identity while simultaneously integrating themselves into French society and political life. They succeeded in balancing the particularistic claims of their Jewish identity with

[42] Hyman, *Emancipation*, p. 20.
[43] In Philippe Landau, "'La Patrie en danger': D'une guerre à l'autre," and Catherine Nicault, "La Réceptivité au sionisme, de la fin du XIXe siècle à l'aube de la seconde guerre mondiale," in Pierre Birnbaum, ed., *Histoire politique des juifs de France: Entre universalisme et particularisme* (Paris: Presses de la Fondation Nationale des Sciences Politiques, 1990).
[44] Pierre Birnbaum, "The History of Jews in France," in Birnbaum and Katznelson, eds., *Paths of Emancipation*, p. 115.
[45] Pierre Birnbaum, *Les Fous de la république: Histoire politique des juifs d'etat de Gambetta à Vichy* (Paris: Fayard, 1992), pp. 489–90.
[46] Landau, "La Patrie," pp. 76–77.
[47] Pierre Birnbaum, ed., *La France de l'Affair Dreyfus* (Paris: Gallimard, 1994). See also Michael Marrus, *The Politics of Assimilation: The French Community at the Time of Dreyfus* (Oxford: Clarendon Press, 1971).

the universalistic claims of the Republic. This can best be seen within the Alsatian Jewish community. While maintaining their "droit à la différence," their identification with France led one quarter of the community to emigrate to Paris and other French cities after the Franco-Prussian War.[48] This group clearly voted with its feet and uprooted itself, thus demonstrating its own sense of where it was preferable to live.

Policies related to mercantilism and state building solidified the position of Jews in both France and Germany during this early modern period. Religious toleration for Jews and centralization of political power went hand in hand in France and in Germany. Local authorities, in contrast, were much less sympathetic to allowing Jews to settle in their midst. Full equality, however, only came when royal absolutism was destroyed by the French Revolution. In France, the fate of Jewish emancipation was bound up with the undermining of the Old Regime and the creation of a political system where legal and civil distinctions could no longer be tolerated. Once this legal basis was established, many different avenues for talent opened up, including the political and military spheres, which in many other countries were closed to Jews well into the twentieth century. Again, this does not suggest that anti-Semitism disappeared or that it was not an important force in French society. It definitely was. But the institutions of the Third Republic provided a defense for this community, and when it was dismantled, Jews living in France and Jews with French nationality found themselves at risk again.

The granting of Jewish emancipation in Germany was a much longer and more tortuous process. The French Revolution put this issue squarely on the German political agenda. Even before, the Jewish community was being transformed by changes taking place within it and around it. First, the German state's bureaucratic hold was strengthened over the *kehillah* structure of the community itself. During the eighteenth century, the state demanded that the financial accounts of the community be kept in German to facilitate auditing. The government set up procedures for electing leaders and restricted the prerogative of Jewish courts to the religious sphere while placing civil cases in the hands of German courts. Population controls were maintained through the issuance of residential permits. State policy controlled Jewish population growth in the cities while allowing greater numbers to take up residence in the countryside. Government restrictions kept the city of Berlin at roughly 2,000 Jews in 1743, up from over 1,000 in 1713.[49] Again the Prussian monarchy was crucial in determining the pace of change. Unlike his predecessors, Frederick William I restricted Jewish settlement by reducing the quotas allowed except for Berlin and Silesia, which was annexed in 1740. For the time being, how-

---

[48] Landau, "La Patrie," p. 74.
[49] Israel, *European Jewry*, p. 240.

ever, the *kehillah* was not totally dismantled because it continued to be the most effective way for the Prussian state to tax the Jewish community.[50]

Despite the tightening of controls, the community pushed for reform. In the eighteenth century, only a very small group at the top, those bankers, purveyors, and administrators of state monopolies who were integrated in German society, called for change. This economic elite comprised roughly 2 percent of the Jewish population.[51] The majority of Jews were too busy eking out a living within the tiny range of occupations that were available to them, while a few were economically secure but not wealthy. Those calling for civil equality saw no conflict between royal absolutism and the achievement of this goal. Indeed, the elite of the community recognized that the princes and electors of Germany had expanded the possibilities for Jews in their jurisdictions, while free cities, with a constitutional form of government, had often expelled Jews from their midst.[52]

During the second half of the eighteenth century, the German enlightenment sparked a Jewish *Haskalah* (the word itself meaning "enlightenment" in Hebrew), which combined Enlightenment categories of thought with specific Jewish sources.[53] It was centered around the figure of Moses Mendelssohn who stressed the rationalist tradition in Jewish thought while rejecting the more messianic and mystical elements. From Berlin, the Haskalah spread throughout western Europe and later on into the large communities of Eastern Europe. The *Maskilim*, a Hebrew term which means "the carriers of Enlightenment thought," called for the separation of church and state, the dismantling of the communal control over Jewish life, the removal of restrictions on Jewish participation in the economy, and the granting of citizenship to Jews. They exhorted their followers to open themselves up to the majority culture through the creation of new schools while maintaining a commitment to religious values.[54] In short, the first generation of Maskilim sought to break the control that the rabbinical establishment had on the Jewish community and allow for the modernization of the community within the context of Jewish tradition. In return, they asked that Jews be granted the rights of citizenship by a secular state.

[50] Michael Graetz, "Jewry in the Modern Period: The Role of the 'Rising Class' in the Politicization of Jews in Europe," in Jonathan Frankel and Steven J. Zipperstein, eds., *Assimilation and Community: The Jews in Nineteenth-Century Europe* (Cambridge: Cambridge University Press, 1992), p. 72.

[51] David Sorkin, "The Impact of Emancipation on German Jewry: A Reconsideration," in Frankel and Zipperstein, *Assimilation*, p. 179.

[52] Pulzer, *Jews and the German State*, p. 73.

[53] David Sorkin, "Preacher, Teacher, Publicist: Joseph Wolf and the Ideology of Emancipation," in Frances Malino and David Sorkin, eds. *From East to West: Jews in a Changing Europe, 1750-1870* (Oxford: Blackwell, 1991), p. 108.

[54] Katz, *Out of the Ghetto*, pp. 57–66, 126–33.

In Mendelssohn's view, Jews had a natural right to be treated equally. This was not the view of many Jewish and Christian thinkers. For them, Jewish emancipation must be preceded by a reforming of the Jewish community. The assumption was that Jews were not as civilized as their Christian counterparts. Only profound moral, political, and occupational change would allow Jews to become worthy of being considered equal.[55] The 1809 emancipation edict of the Grand Duchy of Baden put it succinctly: "This legal equality can become fully operative when [the Jews] in general exert themselves to match the Christians in political and moral formation."[56]

Events in Austria and France provided the international context for change in Germany. Joseph II of Austria led the way "convinced on the one hand of the perniciousness of all religious intolerance, and on the other hand of the great advantage of a true Christian tolerance to religion and the state."[57] The Edict of Tolerance issued by him in 1781 and 1782 called for compulsory education of Jewish children in Christian schools when Jewish ones were unavailable. Occupational restrictions, separate dress codes, and the body tax were abolished. Civil equality, however, remained a distant goal because Jews still could not purchase land, and limitations on population were maintained.

The French Revolution and the Napoleonic Wars had a more profound influence on the Jewish question in Germany. In those areas annexed by France after Napoleon's invasion, Jews were accorded equal rights. And, in the Grand Duchy of Baden, Jews became full citizens between 1807 and 1809, albeit with certain restrictions. While there was an extension of rights in Bavaria, in Saxony and Hanover there was no change.[58] Only in Hesse-Kassel were Jews accorded full unconditional equality.[59]

The Prussian reforms that were provoked by Prussia's military defeats provided for partial emancipation. The Prussian municipal reform of 1808 made the right to vote and stand for office independent of religious affiliation; and after this reform Jews did run for municipal office in the western and eastern parts of Prussia.[60] Similarly the elimination of the requirements of noble status to purchase landed estates meant that the market was open to Jews also. The old order was horrified at the prospect that "merchants, Jews, petty shopkeepers, tailors, bankers, tenant farmers, peasants or others who in a different capacity had come into possession of the necessary amount of money," could now become landowners.[61] These reforms, however, were only partial and did

55 Sorkin, "Preacher," pp. 118–19.
56 Pulzer, *Jews and the German State*, p. 73.
57 Ibid., p. 71.
58 Katz, *Out of the Ghetto*, p. 69.
59 Pulzer, *Jews and the German State*, p. 75.
60 Ibid., pp. 71–78.
61 Hans Rosenberg, *Bureaucracy, Aristocracy and Autocracy: The Prussian Experience, 1660–1815* (Boston: Beacon Press, 1958), p. 219.

not apply in those territories acquired by Prussia after Napoleon's defeat in 1815. In Prussia alone, nineteen different codes applied to Jews, and these were unified only in 1847.

The French Revolution and the Napoleonic Wars not only fostered legal reform but they underlined the need for political change. One part of the liberal camp, the so-called liberal nationalists, sought to transform Germany into a unified and liberal state.[62] The liberal movement's push for reform culminated in the Revolution of 1848, when a series of revolutionary upheavals forced the German state governments to lift restrictions on the press and associations and to promise further reform.[63] Divisions among the reformers and the strength of the conservative opposition slowed or reversed the process of reform, and national unification was not achieved.

Whether one considers 1848 a failure or not is subject to debate.[64] For the Jewish community, however, this period was a watershed for many reasons. For the first time, Jewish activists of many different political stripes played important roles in the events in Parliament and on the streets. Seven Jewish and seven baptized representatives were elected to the Frankfurt Parliament as full or substitute members. Further, as part of the Basic Rights of the German people, the Parliament went on record specifying that "the enjoyment of civic and citizens' rights is neither conditioned nor restricted by religious belief." This attempt to provide for Jewish emancipation wedded the Jewish community to the liberal camp in German politics.[65]

Jews were drawn to liberalism not only for political reasons. Their political views also reflected a change in their economic fortunes. During the nineteenth century, German Jewry became solidly middle class. Whereas in 1750, a majority of the community was very poor, in 1870, according to tax records, 60 percent were in the upper middle class. Jewish businessmen reaped the benefits of an expanding economy in Germany, especially during the second part of the nineteenth century. They tended to be concentrated in commerce and trade. In Prussia, for example, in 1861, a majority of Jews were in commerce, as compared with a small minority of Christians.[66] With this change, of course, came increased urbanization. Whereas before, Jews had been scattered

[62] Michael Hughes, *Nationalism and Society: Germany 1800–1945* (London: Edward Arnold, 1988), pp. 22–24.

[63] James J. Sheehan, *German History: 1770–1866* (Oxford: Oxford University Press, 1989), pp. 656–62.

[64] For the older view emphasizing failure see Theodore S. Hamerow, *Restoration, Revolution, Reaction: Economics and Politics in Germany, 1815–1871* (Princeton: Princeton University Press, 1958), pp. 95–195. This view is shared by Pulzer, *Jews and the German State*, p. 85, and Hughes, *Nationalism and society*, pp. 93–98. For a different view, see David Blackbourn, "The German Bourgeoisie: An Introduction," in David Blackbourn and Richard J. Evans, eds., *The German Bourgeoisie* (London: Routledge, 1993), p. 19.

[65] Pulzer, *Jews and the German State*, p. 84.

[66] Sorkin, "The Impact," p. 179–80.

around the countryside, now, they tended to live in cities. Approximately two-thirds of the community lived in Prussia.[67]

The Jewish community came to understand its success as a by-product of the gradual achievement of political emancipation. As one historian has noted, however, the transformation of the German economy had more to do with it: "Emancipation lifted barriers, but it was the modernization of society, the sudden possibilities of attaining eminence through education and wealth (*Bildung* and *Besitz*) that gave the Jews the unanticipated chance of leaping ahead."[68] Their interest in dismantling trade barriers, unifying the market, and removing restrictions on the access to jobs, as well as their concern for civil and political equality, placed them squarely in the liberal camp.

Complete Jewish emancipation was not legislated until 1866 and 1871, when German unification was achieved and religious affiliation no longer affected one's right to acquire citizenship. Bismarck, who in 1847 had argued that Jews were not eligible to become judges because of the Christian nature of the state, ultimately embraced a secular view of the state.[69]

A new type of anti-semitic movement, political in nature, that was used by a section of the right in its war against liberalism, developed shortly thereafter. Associations were formed, and parties organized, that were explicitly anti-Semitic. Race rather than religion became the defining characteristic of the Jew for many anti-Semites. How can we understand this new phenomenon? Most scholars working on this more recent form of anti-Semitism attribute it to the tensions experienced by European societies undergoing rapid modernization. The Jew, who had benefited from political and socioeconomic change, symbolized all that was wrong for those who were disconcerted or displaced by these changes. Starting in the mid-1870s, the anti-Semite identified the Jew with capitalism and liberalism. While Germany was not the only country to see such a movement take root, anti-Semitism became one of the main pillars of what Fritz Stern has termed "illiberal nationalism." He writes of its "aggressive and xenophobic character; it was even more intolerant of pluralism or of minorities that were at once cohesive at home and had special ties abroad than was illiberal nationalism elsewhere. Other countries had similar prophets of illiberal nationalism, but their resonance among the leading classes of society was greater in Germany than elsewhere."[70]

At first, the Jewish community looked to the liberal parties and associations to defend their interests. In this respect, they differed from the Catholics, who developed sectarian organizations when they too came under attack. Later on,

---

[67] Fritz Stern, *Gold and Iron: Bismarck, Bleichröder and the Building of the German Empire* (New York: Vintage Books, 1979), p. 464.

[68] Ibid., p. 462.

[69] Katz, *Out of the Ghetto*, p. 198.

[70] Stern, *Gold and Iron*, p. 462.

however, Jews would form similar organizations. After 1878, the Empire took a more authoritarian direction: Bismarck allied himself with the Conservatives, and the hopes for a liberal breakthrough did not materialize. It became clear "[t]hat the kind of open society in which merit, not status, earned rewards, half-achieved by the 1870s, would remain as distant a goal as it was then."[71] For the most part, Jews found themselves in the liberal and social democratic opposition. Avenues that had only begun to open up now closed down again—in the academic world, in the judiciary, in the armed forces, and in the state bureaucracy.[72] And, this despite the rather dramatic improvement in the economic fortunes of the Jewish community and the feeling of many German Jews that the future of German Jewry was bright.[73]

If in France, opportunities expanded during the last quarter of the nineteenth century, important spheres of German life remained closed to Jews. Although Jewish Emanicipation was finally granted, the political turn of the German Empire made Germany an increasingly inhospitable place. The growing anti-Semitism of public opinion and the overt discriminatory practices by state and local authorities led Walter Rathenau, when describing conditions in Imperial Germany, to observe that "[i]n the days of every German Jew's youth there is a painful moment which he remembers for the whole of his life: when he becomes fully conscious for the first time that he has entered the world as a second-class citizen and that no skill or merit can ever free him from this situation."[74]

These sentiments differed dramatically from the Franco-Judaism that flourished during the Third Republic. While French Jews had to contend with their own version of political anti-Semitism, they depended on the institutions of the state to defend them from prejudice. For the most part, their faith in the Republic was justified.

In *Social Origins of Dictatorship and Democracy,* Barrington Moore writes that a "vigorous and independent class of town dwellers has been an indispensable element in the growth of parliamentary democracy."[75] Yes, this is certainly true, and the political trajectories of Germany and England highlight the importance of this observation. But not in all instances and not for all people. Without the support of royal absolutism, the early modern period of European history would not have seen growing religious toleration for the Jews. Indeed,

[71] Pulzer, *Jews and the German State,* pp. 101–2.
[72] Ibid., p. 108.
[73] For an article emphasizing the optimism of this generation, see Hans J. Morgenthau, "The Tragedy of German-Jewish Liberalism, " in Max Kreutzberger, ed., *Studies of the Leo Baeck Institute* (New York: Frederick Ungar, 1967), pp. 49–51.
[74] Pulzer, *Jews and the German State,* p. 191.
[75] Moore, *Social Origins,* p. 418.

religious toleration for this minority went hand in hand with the centralization of political power and not the limiting of that power.

It was only starting with the Enlightenment period, when liberal and democratic politics became part of the political agenda, that we can say Jewish interests became wedded to the emergence of parliamentary forms of government and the checking of royal absolutism. The ultimate protection for a minority such as the Jews was to become citizens like everyone else, and that change certainly depended on liberal outcomes over the long run.

The comparison of French and German Jewish history demonstrates this dynamic. The age of mercantilism and state building created a convergence of interests between royal authorities and the Jews. Jewish businessmen allowed French and German monarchs to fight their wars, expand their trade, and fill their coffers. And, in return, Jewish leaders asked that they and their fellows be allowed to settle and practice their faith. With time, they became more daring in their demands. Not only did they seek religious freedom but also the right to be treated like other subjects.

The chances for Jewish emancipation, however, were embedded in the larger fabric of change in each country. Liberty and equality for Frenchmen *de confession Israélite* was connected to the achievement of these goals of liberty and equality for all French citizens. The logic of universal categories of liberty and equality came to encompass French Jews as well, however grudgingly. Once civil and political equality was accorded, it was only a matter of time before social mores changed and Jews were able to enjoy real success in many aspects of French life. Again, I repeat, this did not mean that Jewish upward mobility met widespread approval or that anti-semitism ever stopped rearing its ugly head. French authorities, nevertheless, provided a bulwark against discrimination until the end of the Third Republic. When that regime unraveled, the bulwark disappeared.

In Germany, the question of Jewish emancipation festered. Jews were not granted complete equality until the issues of unification and the constitutional arrangements of a unified Germany had been resolved. But by that time, Jews had given their political allegiance for the most part to liberalism and social democracy, only to find themselves increasingly isolated in an empire defined by "illiberal nationalism." While many Jews contributed to the economic modernization of German society, they were kept from occupying important positions in the judiciary, higher education, or the government. Just at the time when formal Jewish equality was finally achieved, the political complexion of German society veered to the right, undercutting this achievement. The future of German Jewry was linked to the consolidation of democratic institutions in Germany. And when Weimar unraveled, the downward spiral began in earnest.

PART III

GLOBAL AND
NATIONAL POLITICS
SINCE MID-CENTURY

CHAPTER 9

The International Origins of Democracy: The American Occupation of Japan and Germany

Tony Smith

In *Social Origins of Dictatorship and Democracy*, Barrington Moore, Jr. plots the different trajectories of three paths of political and economic modernization: fascism, communism, and democracy. Of course, these three distinct ways of industrializing and incorporating the masses into politics were not only alternatives to one another; they were also in deadly competition, as the record of our century, the most murderous in human history, so grimly attests. This essay reviews the 1940s, the century's most critical decade, when the fascist powers were not only defeated by the combined determination of communist and democratic forces, but the groundwork was also laid for the ensuing struggle between communism and democracy. In that contest, the democratic forces led by the United States were mightily aided in their competition with the Soviet Union by the conversion of the former fascist powers to democracy. To date, no systematic comparative analysis of American Occupation policy has been published, and the importance of this episode in American foreign policy has correspondingly gone unnoticed. It is my hope that this essay will encourage more research into the comparative analysis of the international origins and repercussions of the transition from dictatorship to democracy. In these efforts, Barrington Moore's work will long remain central for its concern with the socioeconomic underpinnings of political order.

For World War II to matter so decisively in the ensuing contest between the United States and the Soviet Union, America had to shape from the peace a world order suitable to its interests. The question, of course, was whether Japan and Germany could be converted to "liberalism," a set of institutions and practices that may be defined as democratic in terms of domestic politics;

nondiscriminatory, antimercantilist, and open in terms of international economic policy; and anti-imperialist in terms of foreign political policy (and thus open to the negotiation of conflicts among nations through established international institutions). It was not enough to contain the Soviet Union to secure a world order congruent with American purposes. The basis for a liberal democratic international system needed to be laid as well, and in this enterprise the cooperation of Germany and Japan was deemed essential.

Though Japan and Germany both were utterly defeated, their modern character as industrial societies had already been established. One might wonder how the Americans could hope to succeed here when their record at fostering basic developmental changes had been so poor in seemingly more malleable countries like the Philippines and the Dominican Republic. To the extent that the success of liberalism in either Germany or Japan depended on a favorable international environment, how could Washington expect the victims of these countries' rapacious aggression ever to trust the aggressors enough to cooperate with them in consolidating a liberal world order? Indeed, how did a consensus in favor of promoting such a transformation in these two countries win out after 1945 in the United States when other proposals existed: either attempting permanently to cripple these militaristic countries, or, alternately, allowing them to regain a healthy measure of economic vitality as dependents of the United States without insisting on their liberalization.

Americans' greatest reservations over the likelihood of transforming these countries stemmed from a consideration of the deeply authoritarian character of their historical development. Despite their great differences culturally, Germany and Japan were remarkably similar in the reasons for their historical aversion to liberalism. Possessed of a sense of weakness and worried about the encroachments of western powers, each country had unified and set up a strong central government supported by a resolute military at about the same time—Japan in 1868, Germany in 1871. Driven by a powerful current of nationalism, the tenets of which served to extol the superiority of Japanese ways to those of a dangerously liberal West, the Japanese soon launched a program of rapid industrialization. In addition, by the late 1870s, German industrialization (which had begun twenty years earlier) took a protectionist turn that could eventually be labeled neo-mercantilist.[1]

---

[1] A seminal comparative perspective on conservative authoritarian versus liberal democratic modernization is Barrington Moore, Jr., *Social Origins of Dictatorship an Democracy: Lord and Peasant in the Making of the Modern World* (Boston: Beacon Press, 1966), chaps. 5, 7, and 8. The following discussion draws from a variety of sources. On Japan, see Kentaro Hayashi, "Japan and Germany in the Interwar Period," R. P. Dore and Tsutomu Ouchi, "Rural Origins of Japanese Fascism," and Edwin O. Reischauer, "What Went Wrong?" all in James William Morley, ed., *Dilemmas of Growth in Prewar Japan* (Princeton: Princeton University Press, 1971); and John W. Dower, "E. H. Norman, Japan and the Uses of History," in E. H. Norman, *Origins of the Modern Japanese State: Selected Writings of E. H. Norman* (New York: Pantheon

While economic modernization necessarily involves substantial changes in social structure and activity—such as proliferation of types of specialized, interdependent work; urbanization; an expanded educational system; and increased state bureaucratic capabilities—the process does not necessarily involve a convergence of political types. In a word, democratic political institutions—characterized by popular control of parties and party control of government, a preference for an open world economic order, and a relatively weak military establishment, such as that which typified the United States and Great Britain in the nineteenth century—need not be the automatic consequence of the industrial revolution.

Indeed, the contrary was often the case. When other governments began to consider how they might duplicate the British achievement, they naturally looked forward to an accelerated process controlled by their traditionally dominant elites, who were necessarily backed by an authoritarian state. In some cases, as in the Ottoman Empire, such "defensive modernization" failed. Elsewhere, however, resolute states were indeed able to industrialize their economies without becoming liberal democracies in the process.

Germany and Japan constitute cases in point. Here, conservative, authoritarian states survived the transition to economic modernization by a variety of procedures which at once preserved the allegiance of traditional groups, gained the loyalty of new economic elites, and effectively excluded from power the workers, peasants, and new middle class. In the process, the social and intellectual forces that had brought about democracy in the United States and Great Britain found themselves stunted.

Thus, while some of the traditional social elites in Germany and Japan were dispossessed in the process of change—a good part of the samurai, or warrior class, in Japan fell on hard times, for example—others maintained a firm grip on power. Both the land-owning Junkers in Germany and the oligarchs in Japan manned the bureaucracies and the highest levels of the military. The power at their disposal allowed them to keep at bay the forces struggling for parliamentary government.

Moreover, new economic elites—big business interests in both countries or the new class of landlords in Japan-also identified with a strong state. Beginning in the late nineteenth century, the state provided emerging big business with subsidies and protection and so guaranteed its wealth. By the twentieth

Books, 1975). On Germany, see David Blackbourn and Geoff Eley, *The Peculiarities of German History: Bourgeois Society and Politics in Nineteenth-Century Germany* (Oxford: Oxford University Press, 1984); Richard J. Evans, *Rethinkning German History: Nineteenth-Century Germany and the Origins of the Third Reich* (New York: Allen and Unwin, 1987); and Konrad H. Jarausch and Larry Eugene Jones, "German Liberalism Reconsidered," in Jarausch and Jones, eds., *In Search of a Liberal Germany: Studies in the History of German Liberalism from 1789 to the Present* (New York: Berg Publishing, 1990). This essay was written with the generous support of the Twentieth Century Fund.

century, with an increase in peasant discontent and the beginning of labor organization, big business (joined in Japan by a new landed elite) looked for an authoritarian state to protect its interests against popular discontent. Although the new capitalist class in both countries may have consisted of what the aristocracy would call parvenus, this "new money" elite deferred in interest and attitude to a repressive political order. To be sure, there were significant differences between these countries. Business and landed elites had their serious differences in Japan; they did not combine as they did in Germany (the "marriage of iron and rye") to repress popular forces. Nevertheless, each country, in its pursuit of foreign markets and raw materials, developed an integrated industrial and financial network (cartels in Germany, zaibatsu in Japan) supported by a range of state initiatives, developments that may be properly termed neo-mercantilist. Given the success of these undertakings as measured in the economic performance, authoritarian governments found new ways to claim legitimacy for their rule.

The extent to which such developments in Germany were distinctly different from events in Britain or France has been debated hotly in recent years (the case of Japan is scarcely ever mentioned). Critics of the notion of a German "special way" (*Sonderweg*) have demonstrated the survival of traditional forces in political life elsewhere in western Europe while pointing to the substantial strength of the German bourgeoisie at home. However, it is impossible to accept the notion that Germany (much less Japan) on balance experienced a form of political development similar to that of Britain or France (much less the United States, which these critics do not mention).

To be sure, there were democratic developments in both Germany and Japan. Both countries came to have constitutions which allowed popularly elected parliaments to have some control over the executive. In Germany, democratic forces actually came into power in 1919. Here an unstable coalition of democratic parties managed to rule the country's first democratic regime, the Weimar Republic, for fourteen years. However, authoritarian forces rooted in the state bureaucracy, military, big business and land-owning circles never accepted democracy's mandate. Meanwhile, new authoritarian groups on the left and the right—the communists as well as the Nazis—began to sap democracy's strength as well. Finally in 1933, parliamentary government collapsed under the weight of these continuing divisions, the depression, and Hitler's demagoguery.

There are historians who feel that Weimar democracy might have survived had, for example, it taken more aggressive action to purge the bureaucracy and military of its authoritarian leaders in 1919, yet commentators are noticeably more pessimistic on the likelihood that Japanese liberals might have expanded their hold on power in the 1920s. Factions that soon became parties appeared in Japan in the early 1880s, and after the promulgation of a constitution creating a Diet in 1889, these parties increasingly gained power over decisions made by the state. The emergence of a stronger parliament could not be but at the expense of the throne and the military. During the 1920s, reacting favorably to Wilsonian proposals for reducing armaments and increasing international cooperation of economic and political matters, the Diet cut military budgets, and prominent ministers opposed the military's expansionist designs, often at the price of their lives. Indeed, as late as 1936, one party received a plurality in national elections campaigning under the motto "Will it be parliamentary government or fascism?"[2]

Yet despite progress toward becoming better representatives of popular opinion and wielding effective influence in government, Japanese political parties were weak by even German standards, both in their ability to organize popular opinion and relative to the power wielded by the state and the military. Beginning in 1931, when it engineered the Manchurian crisis so as to take over that part of China, the Army started to displace parties and parliament in domestic politics just as it began to eclipse the throne. In the course of its move to take power, the military could point to its earlier role in defending the state before the Meiji Restoration of 1868, to its contribution to imperial authority thereafter, and to its victories in the name of national security in wars with China (1894–95), and Russia (1904–5), and to its part in the annexation of Korea in 1910. With the invasion of China proper in 1937, and the moves against Indochina in 194–41, the military finally became the undisputed center of power in Japan.

As the role of the Army in promoting fascism in Japan indicates, Germany and Japan had their important differences. In Japan, the position of the throne, the role of Shintoism in political life, and the evolution of the military's role in politics meant that there was no mass fascist party like the Nazis, and no demagogue of Hitler's sort. In Japan, constitutional forms could be kept, traditional values honored. Whatever the wanton ruthlessness of its leaders, Japan perpetrated no Holocaust.[3]

Despite these differences, the three prime elements of liberalism were lacking in both countries: except in Weimar Germany, parliaments did not control

[2] Robert A. Scalpino, *Democracy and the Party Movement in Prewar Japan* (Berkeley: University of California Press, 1953), and Scalpino "Elections and Political Modernization in Prewar Japan," in Robert E. Ward, ed., *Political Developement in Modern Japan* (Princeton: Princeton University Press, 1978); Harry Wray and Hillary Conroy, eds., *Japan Examined: Perspectives on Modern Japanese History* (Honolulu: University of Hawaii Press, 1983), pts. 7 and 9; Edwin O. Reischauer, *The Japanese Today: Change and Continuity* (Cambridge, Mass.: Harvard University Press, 2d ed., 1988), chaps. 7–9; Akira Iriya, *Power and Culture: The Japanese-American War, 1941–1945* (Cambridge, Mass.: Harvard University Press, 1981), Chap. 1.

[3] Two comparisons that point to the differences between Japan and Germany are Richard J. Smethhurst, *A Social Basis for Prewar Japanese Militarism: The Army and the Rural Community* (Berkeley: University of California Press, 1974), pp.18ff, and Kentaro, "Japan and Germany."

governments (that is, democracy was weak); mercantilist policies of national economic development were pursued (capitalists tended to think in competitive, nationalistic terms, a condition which remained true also under Weimar); and militarism was the primary instrument of foreign policy (that is, imperialist expansion was a deliberate policy of the state). With the triumph of fascism (in 1931 in Japan; in 1933 in Germany), both countries became thoroughly antiliberal, and they were proud to trumpet the distinction.

Given the deep-seated authoritarian character of German and Japanese life, it appeared to some people another misbegotten example of Wilsonianism for Americans to think these countries could be remade in a liberal image. And, indeed, other possibilities were mooted. One was simply to destroy the war-making ability of these defeated nations once and for all, making them into agrarian-pastoral nations, as Secretary of the Treasury Henry Morgenthau proposed for Germany (and less directly for Japan), a warning to others who might follow their example. Yet another possibility was to use their enormous potential power in world affairs to contain the Soviet Union without making much effort to reconstruct them as liberal democracies, an option favored early on by the prominent State Department official George Kennan. (Kennan found much to respect in Salazar's authoritarian regime in Portugal, wasted no time lamenting the failure of self-determination in Eastern Europe, and felt that General Douglas MacArthur was being far too liberal in Japan.)

Others who looked forward to the reconstruction of Germany and Japan were more sanguinely liberal, men like Secretary of State Cordell Hull or General Lucius Clay, the commander of the American zone in Germany. These men were committed to reworking the domestic structures of the defeated enemy countries in the direction of democracy and economic liberalism in the expectation that their militarism could thereby be controlled. Unlike Kennan, they also believed that fostering democracy was an instrument in the containment of the Soviet Union.[4] Like MacArthur, they might be called liberal realists, men who championed both causes at once; they were determined that Germany, like Japan, should be liberalized and join the struggle against communism but were unwilling to subordinate either goal to the other.

Rather than dealing in any detail with the intellectual provenance of American liberal thinking with respect to Germany and Japan, let us rather establish its character by looking at what it set out to accomplish in the first years after the war. The record is one of an astonishing variety of initiatives over a wide range of issues. American behavior bears comparison with what we find in the

4 Godfrey Hodgson, *The Colonel: The Life and the Wars of Henry Stimson, 1867–1950* (New York: Knopf, 1990); Jean Edward Smith, *Lucius D. Clay: An American Life* (New York: Holt, 1990); Thomas Alan Schwartz, *America's Germany: John C. McCloy and the Federal Republic of Germany* (Cambridge, Mass.: Harvard University Press, 1991). In contrast, see George F. Kennan, *Memoirs, 1925–1950* (Boston: Little Brown, 1967).

North's reconstruction of the defeated Confederacy, from 1866 to 1877, an undertaking done with the purpose of reintegrating these defeated states into the Union on a basis that would make national unity forever stable thereafter. So now, in analogous fashion, the Americans who set out to democratize Germany and Japan in the wake of their defeats sought to change those lands so that they would be more reliable partners in world affairs.

The process of imposed political reorganization differed in important respects in Japan and Germany. In the case of Germany, the Nazi regime simply collapsed. Allied military commanders took over control of the country, which had previously been divided into four separate zones (American, British, Soviet, and French), in each of which the military governor had final authority, working through his own bureaucracies (with extensive German help, to be sure). By contrast, in Japan, MacArthur had final authority that he did not have to divide with other allied officials, and he exercised it primarily through the maintenance of the established Japanese throne, Diet, and bureaucracy.

Although their situations were different, occupation authorities had much the same understanding of what democratization entailed: political reform was the heart of the process. Such had been standard American practice from the end of the nineteenth century onwards, whether in the Philippines, Latin America, or Central and Eastern Europe. Fundamentally, Americans conceived of legitimate, stable government as a process in democratic self-determination. organized civic interest groups, usually of a class, ethnic, or religious kind were the backbone of the project. A party system would then organize these groups and establish competitive elections for effective control of government. A wide range of civil liberties would allow citizens to assemble, articulate their interests, and elect their candidates. Constitutionally established checks designed to keep state officials monitored in the exercise of their functions were mandated.

In April 1945, JCS 1067 set out official American policy for Clay in Germany in terms that would find a ringing endorsement at Potsdam three months later:

> The principal Allied objective is to prevent Germany from ever again becoming a threat to the peace of the world. Essential steps in the accomplishment of this objective are the elimination of Nazism and militarism in all their forms, the immediate apprehension of war criminals for punishment, the industrial disarmament and demilitarization of Germany, with continuing control over Germany's capacity to make war, and the preparation for an eventual reconstruction of German political life on a democratic basis.[5]

[5] U.S. Department of State, *Foreign Relations of the United States* (hereafter *FRUS*), 1945, vol. 3, p. 487.

Again in July 1947, when JCS 1067 was replaced by JCS 1779 as the document stating basic American policy, the United States once more defined its political objective as "fundamentally that of helping to lay the economic and educational bases of a sound German democracy, of encouraging bona fide democratic efforts and of prohibiting those activities which would jeopardize genuinely democratic developments."[6]

With respect to Japan, the Allies at Potsdam declared that they looked forward to:

> a peacefully inclined and responsible government . . . established in accordance with the freely expressed will of the Japanese people. . . . The Japanese government shall remove all obstacles to the revival and strengthening of democratic tendencies among the Japanese people. Freedom of speech, of religion, and of thought, as well as respect for the fundamental human rights shall be established.[7]

Similarly, the American "Initial Post-Surrender Policy for Japan," dated August 29, 1945, and intended as MacArthur's charter for governing, declared the country's "ultimate objectives" to be as follows:

> a) to insure that Japan will not again become a menace to the United States or to the peace and security of the world; b) to bring about the eventual establishment of a peaceful and responsible government which will respect the rights of other states and will support the objectives of the United States as reflected in the ideals and principles of the Charter of the United Nations. The United States desires that this government should conform as closely as may be to principles of democratic self-government, but it is not the responsibility of the Allied powers to impose upon Japan any form of government not supported by the freely expressed will of the people.[8]

In the process of passing from principle to practice, the Americans engaged in a panoply of activities aimed at creating the conditions for democratic organizations to flourish. In both countries, individuals (including communists) who had been political prisoners under the former regimes were released, civil liberties necessary for a functioning democracy were proclaimed, and parties were invited to organize in a democratic manner. Once occupation

6 JCS 1779 is reprinted in the U.S. State Department, *Documents on Germany, 1944–1985* (Washington, D.C.: United States Government Printing Office, 1985), 124.

7 FRUS, Potsdam, 1945, vol. 2, p. 1476.

8 "United States Initial Post-Surrender Policy for Japan, August 29, 1945," reprinted in *Political Reorientation of Japan, September 1945-September 1948,* vol. 2 (Westport: Scholarly Press, 1968), p. 423.

officials authorized parties to function, election schedules were announced and honest elections were held following a full and free deliberation of the issues (with, however, an allowance made for the exclusion of right-wing forces as discussed below).[9]

In Germany and Japan, the Americans made no effort to impose their own style of presidential or party system as they had in places like the Philippines and Central America. Instead, both countries were permitted to develop more in line with their own democratic traditions, which resembled British far more than American ways. Thus, parties had fixed programmatic concerns and substantial powers to insure internal discipline; for example, they could appoint members to run in specific electoral districts and expel them when they broke ranks in parliamentary voting. Similarly, the Americans did not insist on a presidential system, but instead endorsed an executive selected by parliamentary procedures. Not only did this correspond more closely to German and Japanese prewar practices, but it also presumably made for a somewhat weaker executive, which is what the Americans preferred.

In the process of organizing a political framework for democratic expression, the Americans explicitly banned from political and bureaucratic life, as well as high corporate position, those individuals who had played an active role in wartime affairs in Germany and Japan. JCS 1067, for example, ordered that "all members of the Nazi party who have been more than nominal participants in its activities, all active supporters of Nazism or militarism and all other persons hostile to Allied purposes will be removed and excluded from public office and from positions of importance in quasi-public and private enterprises."[10]

Initial estimates were that at least two million Germans would be subject to these strictures (in all four zones), while in Japan (which had no equivalent to the Nazi party) the purge would fall most directly on the military. War crimes trials (at Nuremberg and Tokyo most prominently) resulted in nearly 500 execution in Germany and nearly 900 in Japan. Thousands more were imprisoned. Tens of thousands more were barred from high public or private office. In both countries, state debts were repudiated so impoverishing those individuals or firms which had supported the War. In Germany, property belonging to Nazis convicted of personal complicity in the prosecution of the war was confiscated, while in Japan the profits of firms and families which had bene-

---

[9] John Gimbel, *The American Occupation of Germany: Politics and the Military, 1945–1953* (Stanford: Stanford Univeristy Press, 1973); Hans W. Gatzke, *Germany and the United States: A Special Relationship?* (Cambridge, Mass.: Harvard University Press, 1980); John H. Backer, *Winds of History: The German Years of Lucius Dubignon Clay* (New York: Van Nostrand Rheinhold, 1983). On Japan, see Michael Schaller, *The American Occupation of Japan: The Origins of the Cold War in Asia* (Oxford: Oxford University Press, 1985).

[10] *FRUS, 1945*, vol. 3, p. 488.

fited exorbitantly during the war were likewise seized. Parties and societies that had supported the wartime governments were banned from political participation. American rules mandated a party system "constituted by voluntary associations of citizens in which leaders are responsible to the members." But it specified to Clay that if "an authorized party is adopting or advocating undemocratic practices or ideas, you may restrict or withdraw its rights and privileges."[11]

Despite these efforts, scholars who have studied the purges are nearly unanimous in criticizing their failures (with respect to Germany more so than to Japan). Except for the cases conducted before the highest tribunals, punishments were inconsistent or nonexistent. Those purged often later returned to power (especially after the occupations ended), apparently little chastened by the experience.[12]

Many people see little reason to lament these facts. To them, the purges were obstacles to rebuilding these countries, which they felt was a more important goal than weakening the countries by decapitating their leadership. But even for those who deplore the failure to conduct the purges more thoroughly, there nevertheless remains the fact that barring individuals from political and economic life, like preventing the organization of parties championing the old regime, contributed more than marginally to the promotion of democracy in both countries. It allowed new elites to arise and new parties on the democratic right to woo away otherwise extremist voters from their wartime sympathies. Certainly by dissolving the military in Japan, disbanding the ministries of the army and the navy, and barring some 117,000 of its officers from high public or private office, the United States effectively broke the power of that institution which was most responsible for fascism in Japan.

In the case of Germany, the emergence of a newly constituted national government proved a laborious project. Elections were held in the American zone in January 1946 for local governments, and thereafter throughout the year for constituent assemblies to write the constitutions of the three states (Laender) the Americans controlled. During the process, the Americans insisted that the Germans themselves write their constitutions. When later it

---

11 Quotation is from JCS 1779 as found in U.S. State Department, Documents on Germany, p. 126. See also FRUS, 1945, vol. 3, pp. 488ff.

12 An early account is still among the most vivid: John D, Montgomery, Forced to be Free: The Artificial Revolution In Germany and Japan (Chicago: University of Chicago Press, 1957). See also, on Germany, Dennis L. Bark and David R. Gress, From Shadow to Substance, 1945–1963 (Cambridge: Blackwell, 1989), chaps. 8–9; and John H. Herz, "Denazification and Related Policies," in Herz, ed., From Dictatorship to Democracy: Coping With the Legacies of Authoritarian and Totalitarianism (Westport: Greenwood Press, 1982). On Japan, see Edwin O. Reischauer, The United States and Japan (Cambridge, Mass.: Harvard University Press, 3d ed., 1965), chap. 10; and the official American report in Political Reorientation of Japan, 1:8ff;2:479ff.

became time to establish a federal constitution, the Germans, working from domestic tradition, decided to keep the parliamentary system characteristic of Weimar, diminishing, however, the powers of the president and amending such matters as the character of proportional representation so as to reduce the number of parties in the Bundestag. Thanks in good measure to American influence, federalism was introduced (with an eye to eliminating the power of Prussia and limiting the national government), and Supreme Judicial Courts were established as an additional check on the power of the central government.

Moving to integrate the four zones was far more difficult than providing a political structure for the American zone alone; first the French, then the Soviets raised objections to the reconstitution of a German state. But by May 1949, after endless difficulties that involved debates over both the economic integration of Europe under the auspices of the Marshall Plan as well as over the nature of the response to the Soviet threat in Europe, the three Western zones were finally politically merged under the terms of a new constitution. Bundestag elections were held in August, and on September 20, 1949, Konrad Adenauer of the Christian Democratic party was elected the first chancellor of the Federal Republic of Germany.

In Japan, by contrast, the process of forming a new national government could move more quickly. A Japanese government remained in place, federalism was not contemplated (though the Americans replaced the appointed heads of the prefectures by elected governors), and, most importantly, MacArthur did not have to work with other Allied commanders to come to an agreement on how the new system should be organized.

On the other hand, Japan's weak democratic tradition meant that far more American intervention was called for than had taken place in Germany. The Cabinet committee first designated to rewrite the country's constitution failed to comply. With the assistance of an able staff, MacArthur himself drafted a text, one which the Japanese finally adopted with few revisions. The new constitution converted the emperor into a constitutional monarch and abolished the peerage. It vested supreme power in the Diet, now made wholly responsible to the people organized by competitive party elections. A Bill of Rights was formulated, whose assumptions of individual and group freedom clashed with basic collectivist values enshrined in Japanese tradition. Indeed, with its measures to provide equality for women and collective bargaining for labor, the civil liberties promised the Japanese were more advanced than American domestic legislation at the time. Finally, MacArthur insisted on the famous Article IX of the new constitution, by which Japan pledged itself never again to go to war: "Aspiring sincerely to an international peace based on justice and order, the Japanese people forever renounce war as a sovereign right of the nation. . . . Land, sea and air forces, as well as other war potential, will never be maintained. The right of belligerence of the State will not be recognized."[13]

National parliamentary elections were first held in April 1946. As in Germany, the Americans were reassured that few votes were cast for the communists or groups that could be construed as representing the extreme right (a combined total for the far left and far right of less than 20 percent in each country). Also as in Germany, although with a far stronger mandate, the conservatives dominated the Diet. (The Liberals and the Progressives—renamed the Democrats in 1947—won just over 50 percent of the vote in 1946; in 1955, they united in the Liberal Democratic party, which ruled Japan until the early 1990s).

Scholars who have studied these new political systems in ensuing years have been nearly universal in their praise for the American accomplishment. Of course, some problems were not faced (for example, the organization of electoral districts that favored rural districts in Japan might have been handled better). And one should not minimize the contributions of Japanese and, more especially, German leaders to the success of the undertaking. The powerful roles of leaders such as Konrad Adenauer, Kurt Schumacher, Yoshida Shigeru, and Emperor Hirohito were of fundamental importance from the first days of the occupations. Finally, democratization occurred through a framework sanctioned by tradition; the choice of a party and parliamentary system more like those of the prewar order in Japan and Germany clearly represented a return to a national type of liberal political organization. That said, the American contribution to German democratic political organization was substantial; to the new Japanese order, it was fundamental.

In three critical respects Washington also reformed the character of economic practices in these countries in ways that greatly reinforced democracy. First, the Americans insisted on the right of labor to organize freely and to enter into collective bargaining agreements with management. In Germany, business finally accepted unequivocally the right of labor to organize and be represented both in domestic politics and at the work place. In Japan, the gains were even greater. Whereas unionism had a long history in Germany, in Japan it had always been weak. But by the end of 1946, Japanese unions had eleven times as many members as they had had at their high point before the war. As in Germany, labor's rights politically and with respect to management were broader and more secure.[14]

---

[13] Arthur E. Tiedemann, "Japan Sheds Dictatorship," in Herz, Dictatorship to Democracy; Reischauer, The United States and Japan, chap. 10; D. Clayton James, The Years of MacArthur, vol. 3, Triumph and Disaster, 1945–1964 (Boston: Houghton Mifflin, 1985), chap. 4; and for copies of the constitution at its various stages, see Political Reorientation of Japan, 1:82ff, 2:586ff.

[14] Lucius D. Clay, Decision in Germany (New York: Doubleday, 1950), p. 281.

A second basic transformation engendered by the American occupation was enforced only in Japan: a thorough-going land reform program. This program altered the pattern of ownership in the countryside and, at one stroke, removed the major social pillar of traditional authoritarianism and militarism. Japanese village life had been one of the chief bases of the romantic conservatism of modern fascism; its economic poverty had been an obstacle to the creation of a larger national market; and the sons of its landlords and well-to-do peasants had formed the bulk of the junior officer corps while the peasants themselves constituted the better part of the conscripts. An analogous charge could be made against the landholding system of prewar Germany, where the landed elite, the Junkers of Prussia, had comprised the core of the state bureaucracy and the military. Soviet power had conquered this area, however, and had speedily expropriated of the 7,000 large estates there, taking without compensation all properties over one hundred hectares, converting them to smallholdings or state-owned collectives.[15]

The Americans proceeded with an equally radical reform in Japan. In MacArthur's words, the intent was to "remove economic obstacles to the revival and strengthening of democratic tendencies, establish respect for the dignity of man, and destroy the economic bondage which has enslaved the Japanese farmer to centuries of feudal oppression . . . to exterminate those pernicious ills which have long blighted the agrarian structure of land."[16]

In Japan almost half the population lived on the land, with some two-thirds being either wholly or partially tenant farmers. The land reform law of October 21, 1946, placed limits on the maximum amount of land a family could own. Long-term government bonds paid for the expropriated land, which in effect meant they were seized without adequate compensation. The tenants-turned-owners were thereupon provided with sufficient credit to take over the land they were awarded. In short order, the rate of tenancy fell from perhaps 70 percent to 10 percent of the rural population, and the rents on the let land which remained were lowered. Most importantly, the new farmers were mobilized into politics under the auspices of their own interest groups and the conservative parties. MacArthur was correct when he counted this reform one of the two greatest accomplishments of his administration (the other being the constitution) and remarked, "The redistribution formed a strong barrier against any introduction of communism in rural Japan. Every farmer in the country was now a capitalist in his own right." He might have added that by the same token, he had also destroyed the most important social base for a relaunching of fascism.[17]

---

[15] See Moore, Social Origins, chap. 5; Dore, Land Reform, pt. 2.

[16] MacArthur's statement on land reform is in Political Reorientation of Japan, 2:752.

[17] W. I. Ladejinsky, "Agriculture," in Hugh Borton, ed., Japan (Ithaca: Cornell University Press, 1951); Douglas MacArthur, Reminiscences (New York: McGraw-Hill, 1964), pp. 313–

The third major contribution of the American occupation to liberalism in Japan and Germany from a socioeconomic point of view was the effort to break down their nation-centered, neo-mercantilist form of economic organization. In its place, Washington proposed a world economy sustained by actors respecting general principles of economic openness and interdependence. Such an ambitious undertaking required not simply reworking the thinking and organization of the German and Japanese economic establishment but also actually providing a world order capable of meeting the needs and new expectations of these two countries.

The importance of American liberal initiatives in this respect should be emphasized. While international trade is as old as world history, the energy of the industrial revolution had forced countries out onto the world market with particular force, so that they inevitably risked clashes over preferential access to materials and markets. Since the early nineteenth century, Great Britain sought to regulate this competition through international practices of free trade or, if this were not obtainable, through nondiscriminatory practices where commerce moved without the need of governmental protection. The core idea was the hope that mercantilism, or state sponsorship of a country's economic growth through aggressive moves in world affairs, would be replaced by a system of economic interdependence which encouraged peace through mutually beneficial ties. But as the "new imperialism" of the late nineteenth century seemed to have demonstrated—when Africa was partitioned, the Ottoman and Chinese Empires weakened—establishing such an order was a large, if not impossible, undertaking.[18]

It was not difficult to see that Britain's ideas were largely self-serving. As the first industrial country, its goods could flood foreign markets, threatening to create a situation which retarded the industrial growth of other lands while ensuring Britain's continued paramount position. Indeed, with the depression of the 1930s, Britain itself abandoned its century-old ways and retreated within an imperial preference system. By the time of the Roosevelt Administration, however, the United States had come to champion much the same the international economic system that the British had earlier favored, and for many of the same reasons.

With respect to West Germany, the American ambitions to convert the country to a more liberal orientation ultimately bore fruit in the 1950s, thanks largely to the tremendous innovations in regional and world economic integration prepared by the Bretton Woods Agreements of 1944 and even more especially by the direct aid and planning contained in the Marshall Plan in

---

14; MacArthur's statement of February 1, 1948, in Political Reorientation of Japan, 2:780.

[18] Tony Smith, The Pattern of Imperialism: The United States, Great Britain, and the Late-Industrializing World Since 1815 (Cambridge: Cambridge University Press, 1981), chap. 1.

1947. Thereafter, the initiative was seized (as the Americans had hoped) by the Europeans themselves. In 1949, Western powers negotiated the entry of the Federal Republic into the Council of Europe and the Organization of European Economic Cooperation in return for a German agreement to relax exclusive sovereign control over its economic policy. In 1950, with the Schuman Plan to integrate French and German industry through the creation of a joint High Commission in charge of coal and steel production, and in 1957, with the signing of the Declaration of Rome creating the European Economic Community, Europe entered formally into what must be considered one of the greatest economic undertakings in history. This effort (still not achieved) sought to overcome national rivalries and divisions through the creation of an economic structure so interdependent that the interest of each of its members could only be pursued in ways commensurate with general agreement among partners.[19]

It was equally important to provide Japan access to the markets and resources of the world. Since the 1890s, Japanese militarism had depended on the feeling that the country must expand abroad economically or die. Part of the problem was obtaining raw materials when the Japanese islands themselves were so deficient. Part of the problem was felt to be population pressure: the number of Japanese had increased from about 30 million to some 65 million between 1868 and 1930. Thus, the conquest of Manchuria in 1931 had been part of a plan to settle some five million Japanese there over a twenty year period, where they would farm and oversee the export to the homeland of abundant, critical raw materials (iron and coal especially). The pressures were so acute that Akira Iriye sees the failure of Japan to obtain adequate assurance of equal access to world markets as the principal cause of its belligerence from 1931 to 1941:

[Militarism was) the antithesis not of pacifism but of peaceful expansion. Militarism triumphed not as a goal but as a means for obtaining the same ends which the diplomacy of the preceding era had unsuccessfully sought. . . . What united the military, the nationalistic groups, and the bulk of the intellectuals was the shared perception of the 1920s as a decade of futile attempts at peaceful expansion through international cooperation. . . . The dilemmas of modern Japan were the world's as well as Japan's. They were an expression not only of the

[19] John Gillingham, *Coal, Steel, and the Rebirth of Europe, 1945–1955: The German and the French from Ruhr Conflict to Economic Community* (Cambridge: Cambridge University Press, 1991); Volker Berghahn, *The Americanization of West German Industry, 1945–1973* (Leamington Spa, Warwickshire: Berg, 1986); and Charles S. Maier, "The Two Postwar Eras and the Conditions for Stability in Twentieth-Century Western Europe," *American Historical Review*, 86, no. 2 (April 1981).

pathology of the modern Japanese mind but also of the inherent contradictions and irrationalities of the modern world.[20]

Japan's sense of economic encirclement may have been exaggerated, but it was real. Its desperate search for markets and resources abroad had led to a bid for direct control over Asia from Indonesia to Korea, including China. Unlike the case in Europe, where the German threat manifested itself in every form imaginable, American diplomacy in Asia before the war consisted largely in trying to accommodate Japan's perceived economic interests abroad without permitting rampant imperialism.[21]

For the Americans after 1945 the job appeared much as it had before 1941: to persuade the Japanese that their interests would be served by a liberal, nondiscriminatory international commercial system. And there was good reason to think the Japanese would accept with alacrity a renewal of the prewar offer. Important business interests before the war had favored the Anglo-American approach to an open global economic system. Hence, in August 1945, according to the report of a former president of the Japanese National Chamber of Commerce and Industry, leading business leaders contemplating the forthcoming American victory "uncorked their champagne bottles and toasted the coming of a new 'industrialist' era."[22]

The question was whether the Americans could deliver on their program. The promises of economic liberalism with respect to Japan were necessarily more limited by virtue of the fact that Japan's neighbors could not be anticipated to work with it as Germany's neighbors might work with Germany. Nevertheless, the promise of the Bretton Woods Agreements was an effort to create a liberal world economic order where Japan's needs would be met. As FDR put it in his February 1945 message to Congress asking that it approve these accords, "The point in history at which we stand is full of promise and of danger. The world will either move toward unity and widely shared prosperity or it will move into necessarily competing economic blocs."[23]

Japan's economic recovery began in earnest in 1950, largely on the rush of orders from the United States after the Korean War broke out. Thereafter, Japan has found its need for foreign markets and raw materials amply satisfied by the Pax Americana. Nearly half a century later, although there are signs on every side that the system may not hold, the liberal postwar world economic system has functioned admirably so far as Japanese interests are concerned.

[20] Akira Iriye, "The Failure of Military Expansionism," in Morley, *Dilemmas,* pp. 107, 138.
[21] Cordell Hull, *Memoirs,* (New York: Macmillan, 1948), chap. 71, 78–79.
[22] Montgomery, *Forced to be Free,* pp. 106–7.
[23] Samuel I. Rosenman, *The Republic Papers and Addresses of Franklin D. Roosevelt* vol. 13 (New York: Random House, 1950), p. 554.

The problem nonetheless remains that despite this success, Japan's economy continues to be at once self-reliant and yet dependent in a way that
contrasts with the contemporary German economy. Japan is self-reliant in that
its constant primary concern must be the strength of its own economy seen in
narrow national terms; and it is dependent to the extent that it must rely on a
high level of foreign trade for markets and raw materials with countries over
whom its influence is relatively minor. While the Americans obtained a limited
restructuring of German and Japanese capitalism from state-protected cartels
to competitive oligopolies (thereby making them more efficient), the critical
differences lie in the extent of German economic integration with the rest of
Western Europe and the closeness of this association, in turn, with the United
States. Of course, Japan remains the second most important trading partner of
the United States (after Canada). And one may hope that Japan's problems
will be amenable to handling by domestic reform or continued international
cooperation. Yet it remains true that the place of Japan in the world economic
system is not so secure as that of Germany, and that many observers with a
memory of the past find this lack of a firmer resting place most disquieting.

While a final balance is impossible to draw as to the extent direct American
involvement mattered in bringing democracy to Japan and Germany, it was far
from negligible. It is difficult to believe that left to its own devices Japan would
have undertaken comprehensive land reform, abolished its military ministries,
or reworked its constitution either to provide the range of civil liberties dictated by the Americans or to restrict the throne so completely to ceremonial
duties. These policies were of the utmost importance in determining the
character of postwar Japan. Whatever the failures or shortcomings of the
purges, or of the efforts to deconcentrate economic holdings, the impact of
American restructuring has until today, over four decades after the end of the
Occupation in April 1952, continued to mark Japanese political life profoundly. So far as Germany is concerned, American influence included its
preference for the Christian Democrats, its support for European economic
integration, and the creation.of NATO. If the first of these three matters is
probably of no more than marginal importance, by contrast, the second and
third—America's general policies in Western Europe—appear to have been
critical in overcoming the German problem.

In late 1944, a State Department planning document had phrased the
American hope clearly:

In the long run, the best guarantee of security, and the least expensive, would be
the assimilation of the German people into the world society of peace-loving
nations. These considerations urge the search for a continuing policy which will
prevent a renewal of German aggression and, at the same time, pave the way for

the German people in the course of time to join willingly in the common enterprises of peace.[24]

While European economic integration might be one means to this end, the State Department insisted especially on the force of democracy:

> Germany's repudiation of militaristic and ultranationalistic ideologies will in the long-run depend on the psychological disarmament of the German people, tolerable economic conditions, and the development of stable political conditions. The most plausible hope for lasting political reconstruction and orderly development lies in the establishment of democratic government despite the fact that serious difficulties will beset such an attempt.[25]

From today's perspective, the self-congratulatory words of John McCloy, America's High Commissioner in Germany, seem vindicated: "We made unthinkable another European civil war. We ended one of history's longest threats to peace."[26]

By contrast, with respect to Japan the conclusions to be drawn are less clear. While democracy seems firmly established and the military tradition a memory of the past, contemporary commentators worry ceaselessly about Japan's relationship to the international economic order. There are persuasive arguments to the effect that Japan does not play by the rules; that it acts in a neomercantilist manner which favors its commerce while discriminating against those of its neighbors. Nor is there full confidence that the Pacific Rim markets (which include the United States) will continue to provide Japan with the economic exchanges it requires. Given the nationalism of the country's conservative leaders (complete with racist pronouncements and unconvincing apologies for past aggressions), it is understandable that so many observers express their skepticism both as to Japan's future and to that of liberalism in the Pacific.[27] Perhaps these concerns about Japan are exaggerated. However, it is notable that in all these respects, parallel concerns about Germany are practically nonexistent. If McCloy's words on America's successful role in solving the German Question would be widely accepted, MacArthur's declaration on Japan would be sure to meet with more skepticism: "History records no other instance wherein the military occupation of a conquered people has been

---

24 *FRUS, Yalta,* 1945, pp. 185–86.
25 Ibid.
26 McCloy cited in Schwartz, *America's Germany,* pp. 306–7.
27 For example, see George Friedman and Merideth LeBard, *The Coming War With Japan* (New York: St. Martin's Press, 1991); Steven R. Weisman, "Pearl Harbor in the Mind of Japan," *New York Times,* November 11, 1991; and the three essays that appeared in the *New York Times* to commemorate Pearl Harbor, entitled "Fifty Years Later," December 3, 4, and 5, 1991.

conducted with the emphasis placed, as it has been here, upon the moral values involved between victor and vanquished. Right rather than might has been the criterion. The fruits of this policy are now self-evident."[28]

And yet should such reservations blind us to the substantial victory which liberalism has already won? For by the conversion of Germany and Japan to democracy and into willing participants in liberal economic internationalism, the United States achieved the world historical power to face down the Soviet Union and to promote the eventual collapse of the communist world. The liberal consequences of the peace have already fulfilled enough of their promise to be worthy of respect.

[28] MacArthur on September 2, 1947, in *Political Reorientation of Japan*, 2:775.

CHAPTER 10

The Political Sources of Democracy: The Macropolitics of Microeconomic Policy Disputes

PETER A. GOUREVITCH

Does capitalism require democracy? Are capitalists leaders in the demand for democracy? Barrington Moore's *Social Origins of Dictatorship and Democracy* is deservedly one of the canonical texts in a discussion of these questions.[1] Moore's answer—"no bourgeoisie, no democracy"—is often misunderstood. He did not mean that all bourgeoisies demand democracy and that capitalism cannot work without it. Moore shows quite clearly the opposite: in some contexts bourgeois elements are quite content to live with authoritarian systems that respect property rights. Moore's argument is that the major champions of constitutional government during its historical evolution were market-oriented actors, largely, though not exclusively bourgeois. Where such bourgeois champions of change did not exist, there was little demand for democratization. Aristocrats might develop an interest in constitutional procedures to limit the powers of the crown. Increasing suffrage required bourgeois who wanted to limit the power of the crown in order to promote active policies in their interest (harbors, roads, water systems, banks, a standardized tax system, the elimination of guild restrictions, and so on).

The linkage between democracy and the market remains as vital a question as it was when Moore published his book three decades ago, though the context has changed. At that time, Moore sought to grasp the divergent roads into the twentieth century: the contrasting systems that had fought in a

---

[1] Barrington Moore, Jr., *Social Origins of Dictatorship and Democracy* (Boston: Beacon Press, 1966). Many thanks for comments on an earlier draft from Miles Kahler, John McMillan, Victor Perez-Diaz, and Harvey Rishikof.

cataclysmic global war—fascism, communism and bourgeois democracy. Why had some systems escaped the trap of totalitarian fascism and communism, while others had not? Now, history has changed the terms of the question: fascism in its mid-century form was defeated in Germany, Italy, and Japan; communism in the Soviet empire collapsed of its own internal incompetence. Both have fallen into the ash can of history, at least under the formal names they had in this century; either could revive in different guises.

If communism and fascism have disintegrated, authoritarianism has not. There are more democracies in the world than there were in the beginning of the twentieth century, but most of the world's regimes remain nondemocratic, or more precisely, nonconstitutionalist. Some democracies are young, untested, and possibly quite fragile; and even in the old established ones, there exist discontented elements, critical of what they see. Can democracy work? Can it manage change, meet aspirations? What forces propel societies toward democracy, and what forces undermine it? The questions remain as pertinent as they did when Moore wrote his book, even if the context has changed.

In our period, the connection between political institutions and economic system surfaces in the context of three broad developments occurring around the world: reform processes in the formerly planned economies of the communist system; economic rationalization and restructuring in the advanced industrial economies experiencing stress in new conditions of global competition; and economic development choices faced by countries seeking to move up the ladder of the global division of labor.

The countries of the former Soviet bloc face substantial challenges in developing market economies able to sustain constitutional political processes. As of this writing, the outcome of these challenges is not yet known, but the difficulties being confronted are obviously substantial. Democracy and economic reform both seem quite shaky in many or even most of these countries.

The advanced industrial countries confront an epochal transformation of their economic structures: technology, global competition, deregulation, and new forms of market institutions are causing massive stress on existing systems of employment, organization, and social services. It is perhaps too extreme to see the democracies of western Europe, North America and Japan at grave risk, but they are all experiencing considerable stress and, at a minimum, substantial challenges to the political alignments and allegiances created in the historical compromise of the post–World War II period.

The developing countries confront a major debate about the proper paths to growth: shall they adopt industrial policy Japanese style or, instead, free market approaches associated with the prescriptions propounded by the World Bank and the IMF? This debate burst forth recently with the publication of the World Bank's *East Asian Miracle* report which tried to reconcile in one volume sharply contrasting analyses and prescriptions.[2] Avoided in that report is the political question: Whichever policy is chosen, is it best carried out by authoritarian regimes like Singapore and China, or democratizing ones like Taiwan and South Korea?[3]

In each of these regions of the world, which is facing difficult economic policy choices, the linkage among economic policy alternatives, economic cleavages in society, and political institutions is of vital importance. This linkage is central to Moore's *Social Origins,* and we can benefit by applying his approach to its contemporary manifestations. Moore sees social actors fighting over political institutions for instrumental reasons. Actors have interests rooted in their economic situation. These actors come into conflict with each other when they have contrasting interests. Each side realizes that institutions will affect the outcome of their policy disagreements. Therefore they seek to change or preserve political institutions in order to acquire the power to change or preserve economic arrangements.

Social Origins explores these kinds of conflicts over political institutions by tracing two broad policy disputes: first, the conflicts generated by the commercialization of agriculture, and second, the conflicts generated by industrialization.[4] In each country Moore examines, the fight between constitutionalism and absolutism, and between democracy and the two modern forms of populist authoritarianism, expresses the desire of agents of social change to create the political institutions that help them reach their goals. In England, commercial interests sought political power in the seventeenth century so as to prevent the crown from interfering with the transformation of English economic relationships. In late-nineteenth-century Germany, the iron and rye coalition hindered democratization in order to preserve economic arrangements that benefited them substantially.

The logic of Moore's reasoning, then, tells us to look for the axes of economic cleavage—the fault lines along which political life is organized—and

[2] World Bank, *East Asian Miracle* (New York: Oxford University Press, 1993).

[3] Robert Wade, *Governing the Market: Economic Theory and the Role of Government in East Asian Industrialization* (Princeton: Princeton University Press, 1990); Stephan Haggard, *Pathways from the Periphery: The Politics of Growth in the Newly Industrializing Countries* (Ithaca: Cornell University Press, 1990); Tun-Jen Cheng and Stephan Haggard, *Newly Industrializing Asia in Transition* (Berkeley: Institute for International Studies, 1987); Peter Gourevitch, ed., *The Pacific Region: Challenges to Policy and Theory,* Annals of the Society, vol. 505 (Philadelphia: The American Academy of Arts and Sciences, September 1989), pp. 8–161.

[4] Moore deliberately pushed the starting point for analyzing political development back from comparative industrialization models, the dominant "common experience" attracting attention when he began the book, because he noted prior choices that influenced what happened when industrialization occurred. Perry Anderson pushes the referent point back even farther with *Passages from Feudalism to Antiquity* (London: New Left Review, 1974) and *Lineages of the Absolutist State* (London: New Left Review, 1974).

then to seek the conflict over political institutions to which the economic cleavages are linked. Groups fight over political institutions, Moore suggests, because the political institutions influence the outcomes of their struggles over economic issues. They want institutional change in order to attain broader goals.

Applying Moore's reasoning to contemporary settings requires that we explore the cleavage lines of current political economy. Here we may explore one important shift that alters or places under stress historical cleavage structures: a movement from macroeconomic lines of conflict toward microeconomic ones. This shift expresses intellectual change—a greater appreciation in economics and politics, as well as in other fields, of the micro foundations of behavior and a "deconstruction" of broader macro categories. But it also expresses important changes in reality, as a number of micro issues have developed growing significance in the context of macroeconomic coordination and harmonization.

The shift from macro to micro issues fragments political life in various important ways.[5] Much of the partisan conflict that links economic actors to political disputes has been constructed around a macro conception of policy alternatives: workers versus owners or managers, employment versus inflation, savings versus spending. Unions and worker-allied parties try to form large solidarities across a wide spectrum of employees in quite diverse situations. To do so, they need an understanding of policy alternatives which stresses solidarities and conceals the divergence.

Micro issues, by contrast, are fragmenting in their nature, or, more precisely, different from the traditional macro issues in the solidarities and conflicts they promote or discourage. Rules of accounting, bank regulation, insider trading, conflict of interest, corporate governance, antitrust, cross-shareholding, and the like, all lie at the core of important economic differences among countries. They have a substantial affect on the way individuals and countries respond to competitive pressures in the world economy. They enter politics quite differently from the way the macro issues do.

The link between macro and micro issues and macro- and micropolitics is an important one for understanding democracy. Applying Moore's ideas and methods, we may look, first, at the debate around macro versus micro policies so as to determine what are the most effective policies for international competition and, second, at a consideration of the political dynamics of micro policies by national political systems. As observers, we need to understand the macropolitics of micro policy.

[5] Some of these themes are explored in Peter Gourevitch, "Democracy and Economic Policy: Elective Affinities and Circumstantial Conjunctures," *World Development* 21, no. 8 (August 1993): 1271–80.

Macro Orthodoxy

The law of comparative advantage tells us that to raise their living standards, countries must trade. In the macro perspective, the task of government is "to get prices right" through proper management of monetary and fiscal policy. Fiscal policy balances taxation and spending; monetary policy shapes the size of the money supply and interest rates. Trade policy encourages open borders. Under the right set of macroeconomic conditions, individual private actors are free to calculate efficient action. Economic health derives from the proper mix of macro policies.[6]

From the macro perspective, divergence in national economic performance can be located in the content of macroeconomic policy. In the 1980s, the United States ran massive budget deficits with very low savings rates. In Japan, by contrast, despite recurrent budget deficits, policies encouraged savings and depressed consumption. As a result, the Japanese economy grew faster than the American, and Japan exported a substantial part of its production, while the United States, spending more than it made or saved, imported a great deal to make up the gap.

Macroeconomic definitions of policy choices define political cleavages around the costs and benefits of various ways of attaining the macro goals. Improving growth in the U.S. economy requires that someone pay the costs: less spending on defense or social services, fewer tax breaks for real estate or other special interests, greater spending on infrastructure and education.[7] Because each method involves cost, the battle over these alternatives is intense. Developing countries and reforming Soviet economies face similar conflicts over budget deficits, risking acute unemployment in the interests of macrostability.

Advocates of a macroeconomics approach generally favor free trade. The more you import, the more the exporter can buy from you; the more you export, the more you can buy from them. All the industrial powers signed the GATT agreement after World War II; by and large, it has done a better job in promoting trade than the anarchy of the prewar years. Formally, most countries comply with the requirement to lower tariff barriers. The European Com-

---

[6] For a very clear analysis of macroeconomics policies, see Ben Friedman, *The Day of Reckoning: The Consequences of American Economic Policy under Reagan and After* (New York: Random House, 1988). The classical view was that governments could do little to manage an economy. Governments actually did intervene quite a bit. Keynes provided one important strand of theoretical justification. Nationalism, security interests, and special interest lobbying provided another.

[7] The macro view assumes that macro policy will elicit the desired micro response—for example, that savings rates really will respond to policy incentives, though this turns out to be hard to prove. See Miles Kahler, "The Politics of Impatience: Savings, Investment, and the International Political Economy" (Paper presented at the 15th World Congress of the International Political Science Association, July 21–25, 1991, Buenos Aires, Argentina).

munity has produced substantial gains in doing so among its members. On the dimension of tariffs, Japan ranks as one of the least protectionist countries in the world. The United States has rejected the high tariff posture typical of the years between the Civil War and World War II.

In the macro approach, then, the route to economic vitality lies in a balanced macro policy and low tariff barriers. This mix is appropriate not only for the advanced industrial countries facing economic rationalization of "rust belt" industries, but for the other two sets of countries facing major policy challenges: the transition countries, moving from planning to market, and the developing countries, moving from traditional precapitalist socioeconomic forms to integration in the world economy. For both these categories, macroeconomic champions have proposed the same prescriptions that are applied to advanced industrial countries: tight money, low fiscal deficits, limited government, and free trade. In their travels to countries seeking financial assistance, representatives of the World Bank, the IMF and other international lending agencies, use these kinds of considerations as their yardstick for deciding on aid.

This approach has dominated American thinking and public policy as well as that of international financial institutions. It has at the same time provoked considerable controversy. For the Soviet bloc countries, the "big bang" approach of rapid deregulation has been criticized for neglecting microlevel property relations and the learning curve for realistic pricing and market behavior.[8] For the developing countries, the macro approach is seen as neglecting institutional issues in economic development and the linkages of industries to growth-promoting policies of central government using techniques other than macroeconomic orthodoxy. For the developed countries facing economic competition and rationalization issues, the macro approach neglects issues of governance, subcontracting, and industrial policy, which can have a substantial effect on efficiency. In all cases, micro institutions are central to the critique and the issues.

In trade relations, it has become clear that despite the lowering of tariff barriers, it is obvious that protectionism has not gone away. Instead, it is has found new forms: voluntary export restraints, taxes, inspection systems, and countless rules and procedures which do not violate formal agreements but which do restrict trade.[9] Domestic regulatory structures used be understood in

---

[8] On the reform of Soviet economies, contrasting "big bang" versus gradualist models, see John McMillan and Barry Naughton, "How to Reform a Planned Economy: Lessons from China," *Oxford Review of Economic Policy* 8, no. 1 (Spring, 1992): 130–43.

[9] Trade barriers of this kind are not new. In the late nineteenth century, health inspection was used in agricultural trade wars; the American Food and Drug Administration was created partly in response to European prohibitions on American products. W. A. Williams, *Roots of the Modern American Empire* (New York: Random House, 1969) and Gabriel Kolko, *The Triumph of Conservatism* (New York: Free Press, 1963).

purely domestic terms, expressing national preferences in various areas.[10] As these regulatory structures have acquired "dual usage" in their ability to restrain foreign competition as well as manage domestic affairs, they become objects of controversy between countries.[11] In all these issue areas, microeconomic institutions have acquired considerable importance and attention.

Micro Institutions

The microeconomic view stresses the organization of markets and the internal organization of firms. The way factors of production are used is not a simple direct response to macro conditions. For micro theorists, factors of production can be assembled in different ways, with distinctive properties. Firms may vary in the distribution of authority, the delegation of power, the relationship with subcontractors, the social relations among managers and workers—the various elements of hierarchy that operate in markets. These arrangements may have a very substantial impact upon effectiveness.[12] Macro analyses treat firms as a black box, whose interior workings require no particular analysis; under the right conditions, firms adapt structures to fit the logic of market pressures. Micro theorists give independent causal status to the interior of the black box. The micro approach puts issues, property relations, contracting, governance, and market structure at the center of policy debate and programming.

That firm and industry organization can have an impact upon economic efficiency is not a new idea to economic historians. Moore and Alexander Gerschenkron noted the distinctive features of late industrializers.[13] Furthermore, the role of cartels, banking systems, industrial concentration, corporatism, union incorporation, job training, welfare and other elements of capitalist organization has attracted the attention of researchers for many years.

These micro institutional issues have attracted renewed interest in recent years because of the rapid growth of the Japanese economy in the 1980s and

[10] These debates can be examined through the literature on "creating comparative advantage." See the writings of John Zysman and Stephen S. Cohen, *Manufacturing Matters: The Myth of the Post-Industrial Economy* (New York: Basic Books, 1987); Laura Tyson, *Who's Bashing Whom* (Washington, D.C.: Institute for International Economics, 1992); Michael Dertouzos et al., *Made in America* (Cambridge, Mass.: MIT Press, 1989); Paul Krugman, *Rethinking International Trade* (Cambridge, Mass.: MIT Press, 1990); and idem, ed., *Strategic Trade Policy and the New International Economics* (Cambridge, Mass.: MIT Press, 1986).

[11] My thanks to Miles Kahler for drawing this point out.

[12] See Oliver Williamson, *Markets and Hierarchies* (New York: Free Press, 1975); Herbert Kitchelt, "Industrial Governance Structures," *International Organization* 45, no. 4 (Autumn 1991): 453–94; John McMillan, "Dango: Japan's Price-Fixing Conspiracies," *Economics and Politics* 3 (November 1991): 201–18.

[13] Alexander Gerschenkron, *Economic Backwardness in Historical Perspective* (Cambridge, Mass.: The Belknap Press, 1962).

difficulties with the American one. Analysts note distinctive organizational forms in the Japanese economy: the "just-in-time" inventory system (*kanban*), assembler-supplier relations, the *keiretsu* system (a pattern of firm linkages usually built around a bank), lifetime employment, a flatter income hierarchy between supervisors and workers, more fraternization between supervisor and worker—these are some of the most striking and well-known features. So significant are these features that some analysts see the combination as a distinctive form—"lean production"—itself an innovation as significant, in the view of the MIT Auto Project authors, as Henry Ford's change from craft production to mass production of standardized interchangeable parts.[14]

The core of these process innovations lies in the microorganizational structures within firms, as well as between firms and their upwardly and downwardly linked allies. In support of this system, Japan developed a complex regulatory system linking firms, government and the market into a network of managed competition. This system of administrative guidance helped to structure cartels, shelter imports, and promote exports. Firms competed in patterned ways with each other. Government regulatory policy toward stocks, real estate, money supply, and bank regulation channeled funds to industry. Technology policy provided public support to specific industries. Regulatory and government procurement policies set standards and approval processes in ways which stabilized markets and provided shelter from foreign competition. Tax policies discouraged consumption and rewarded savings. Antitrust and bank policy encouraged interlocking ownership patterns. This system of administrative guidance lacked "transparency"—that is, a set of clear rules known to all ahead of time. The cloudiness of the system allowed interventions, which people accustomed to a legalistic complaint system typical of American practice have trouble identifying and controlling. The overall affect has been a system which excludes newcomers, foreign and domestic.[15]

The dynamism of Japan's economic performance has compelled appreciation for its production methods and efforts to learn from them. Other countries have adopted versions of it with similarly spectacular effects: notably, Korea, Taiwan, Singapore, and Hong Kong. Products from these countries have flooded markets, driving out American and European producers. At the same time, troubles in the Japanese economy since the bursting of the bubble in the early 1990s have drawn criticism of its system and admiration for American practices such as venture capital, vigorous markets for governance, and substantial job creation. Turbulence in Asian financial markets during the

[14] Publications from the MIT Auto Project include James Womack et al., *The Machine That Changed the World* (New York: Rawson, 1990), and John F. Krafcik, "The Triumph of the Lean Production System," *MIT Sloan Management Review* 29, no. 1 (Fall 1988): 41–52. See also Michael Piore and Charles Sabel, *The Second Industrial Divide* (New York: Basic Books, 1984).
[15] Tyson, *Who's Bashing Whom.*

summer and fall of 1997 have broadened the critique to the "Asian model" itself.

As micro-institutional innovations develop in one country, how do they spread to others? In a macro view, Japanese innovation should lead via market forces to organizational change among its competitors, in the United States and Europe. If a better organizational practice develops in one country, the market should transmit that information to other companies, which then adopt them. Has this happened? To some degree, but perhaps less rapidly than one might imagine. U.S. companies are learning and adapting lean production methods. But there appears also to be a lot of resistance to doing so. The MIT Auto Project's Book notes fascinating differences in the response of executives in the United States and Europe to better Japanese practices and the length of time it took many firms to learn and absorb these innovations. Just how plastic and transferable are organizational process innovations, from one economy to another? Perfect market theory sees no obstacles; the black box changes its internal features as market forces compel them. In practice, however, there are obstacles to micro-organizational adaptation. What are they?

Answers may be sought in three areas: cultural influences on organizational forms, the distribution of power within the firm, and public policy that shapes firm organization. Works in the sociology of culture find the sources of lean production in Japanese values, traditions, psychology, and modes of interpersonal relations. Ronald Dore, pioneer in the comparison of Japanese and British economic organization, contrasts two models of the firm, the community model found in Japan and the company law model found in the United Kingdom and the United States.[16] In the community model the firm is defined as "a social unit made of all the people working full-time in it ('in' rather than 'for')," the shareholders are but one of the constituent elements requiring satisfaction, and the participants in the system feel a common purpose and obtain a fair distribution of rewards. In the company law model the firm is defined as "the property of shareholders whose rights are paramount, the management are the trusted agents of the shareholders," and all other claims against management (those of workers, community, and so forth) are adversarial and/or secondary. Japanese firms were able to develop these institutional arrangements because they resonated well with the value systems and the socializing institutions of Japanese culture.[17]

If culture influenced the invention of the community model, Japanese "lean

---

[16] Ronald P. Dore, *British Factory/Japanese Factory* (Berkeley and Los Angeles: University of California Press, 1973).

[17] Ronald P. Dore, *Taking Japan Seriously* (London: Athelone Press, 1987), p. 54. See C. W. Kester's contrast of corporate governance versus contractual governance systems in "Industrial Groups as Systems of Contractual Governance," *Oxford Review of Economic Policy* 8, no. 3 (Fall 1992): 24–44.

production," does culture prevent its adoption elsewhere? The authors of the MIT Auto Project study, think not. What it takes to invent is not the same as what it takes to observe and adapt it to other settings. These authors note the diffusion of the lean system around the world.[18] But while culture may not prevent the diffusion of lean production, it may nonetheless inhibit it by blocking understanding and acceptance.

A second view of resistance to change looks at the distribution of power within the firm. The firm can be seen as a polity, having its own problems of governance. What may be good for a part of the firm, may not be good for the firm as a whole. The firm consists of a range of institutional offices, occupied by various actors, who have some interest in defending their positions. Firms differ in their governance systems: that is, the structures that define accountability, or incentives upon managers and other employees. German and Japanese firms, for example, have shares held for long periods by main banks and members of financial groups. In American firms, shareholders have less incentive to interact with managers and are prevented by insider-trading rules and other regulations from doing so. These differences in governance systems have a substantial impact on firm behavior.[19]

A third area of resistance to reorganization of production within firms lies in the economic ideology about public policy. For a large body of thought, both academic and business, the internal organization of firms and markets is not a valid external and public concern. What happens in the firm is the business of the firm and no one else. American business culture strongly supports this distancing, at least officially.

The macro view of policy reinforces this separation by discounting the policy relevance of micro issues. The macro view finds nothing in Japanese success which challenges its paradigm. American firms were lazy after years of market dominance. Market pressures did not force process innovation but rather encouraged squeezing greater profit from existing methods, exactly in the same way that innovation made sense for those seeking to catch up (i.e., the Japanese manufacturers). If other countries have become more efficient, then, according to the ideology, manufacturing should relocate, shifting workers from low- to high-value-added activities. Macro policy should help the process by encouraging investment. Micro policy should make it possible to cut wages and reduce environmental and other regulatory costs.

With this line of reasoning, macro ideas blunt arguments over deficiencies in micro institutions. The development of micro theory about firms and institutions in recent years provides an important source of ideas in countering the

[18] Womack et al., *Machine*.
[19] Michael C. Jensen, "The Modern Industrial Revolution, Exit, and the Failure of Internal Control Systems," *The Journal of Finance* 48, no. 3 (July 1993): 831–80.

macro view. Many if not most micro theorists accept the importance of sound macro policy, but argue for the importance of microinstitutional issues as well.

Public Policy on Micro Issues

If firms are resistant to change, is there anything public policy can do about it? If firm organization is an important element of efficiency, and if firms appear resistant to change, then it becomes a legitimate concern of public policy to explore what policies might induce change. A first step is to identify which rules and laws influence internal firm organization. The examples below are drawn mostly from American experience.

Antitrust Policy

Since the Sherman Act of 1890, American public policy has prohibited the linkages which appear to play a critical role in the coordination of Japanese units. Antitrust laws and their enforcement inhibit certain forms of firm coordination, such as the cross-ownership characteristic of Japanese *keiretsus:* Dupont, for example, was ordered to sell its stake in General Motors, breaking up an "American *keiretsu.*"

Financial Regulation

American law prohibits interstate banking and the mixture of commercial and industrial banking. This inhibits American banks from playing the role of their Japanese and German counterparts as key coordinators of industrial sectors. Different patterns of shareholder/manager relationships produce variance in the way managerial performances are evaluated.[20]

Retailing

American law favors competition among retailers. In Japan, as in much of Europe, various laws protect existing structures of distribution and inhibit competition. Large-scale supermarkets and retailers, discount pricing, and price competition of various kinds are restricted in many countries. These restrictions often express the influence of shopkeepers, small retailers, communities, and the desire of manufacturers for stability.[21]

[20] Alexander Gerschenkron's remarks on different banking systems is a classic source on this issue. See his *Economic Backwardness in Historical Perspective* (Cambridge, Mass.: Harvard University Press, 1962).

[21] Suzanne Berger and Michael Piore, *Dualism and Discontinuity in Industrial Societies* (New York: Cambridge University Press, 1980).

Small Producers

Many countries have rules which support small firms. Taxation, employee insurance, health and safety inspection, worker discharge and assignment, trade union regulation, and a host of other regulations encourage the existence of small enterprises. With fewer regulations, small firms can produce products at lower cost. This may encourage the subcontracting system in Japan; Toyota contributes 25 percent to the value added of a car, where American firms contribute 50 percent.

Labor Relations

Labor market regulation can have a substantial effect on firm incentives toward the employment of labor and the use of it. Laws on hiring and firing can raise costs of labor, thereby encouraging dualistic industry structure, and may change the way labor within the firm is used. Japanese company unions allow flexibility of job assignment, whereas European and American systems favor strict classification of job categories and graded pay scales.

Financial Regulations and Taxes

Financial systems provide different signals. A recent American study criticizes the American system for encouraging short-term concern with quarterly reports, a preoccupation with leveraged buyouts, an inadequate role for stakeholders (suppliers, workers, consumers, and communities) other than stockholders, and a neglect of functional skills like engineering and production.[22] European and Japanese systems are quite different in many of these items.

In a variety of ways, then, public policy influences the internal organization of firms. Change in public policy alters the international organization of productive systems. The question now becomes, what causes or prevents these changes in public policy?

The Politics of Micro Reform

If the micro issues are vital to effective economic policy, we must wonder what might be the politics that produce the "right" set of micro policies. The right policies are those that encourage the complex mixture of decentralization and coordination emphasized by "lean production." Policies arise out of politics. We need a way of thinking about politics that links micro policies to

[22] Michael Porter, "Capital Disadvantage: America's Failing Capital Investment System," *Harvard Business Review* 70, no. 5 (September/October 1992): 65–82.

222   Peter A. Gourevitch

macropolitics—that is, to the large political processes of the modern capitalist democracies that actually produce policy.[23]

At first blush it may appear that the two types of policy, macro and micro, sort out into a type of politics appropriate to their distinctive properties. Macro policies are large, chunky, and undifferentiated. They are not easily divisible and targetable. There is, more or less, one level of aggregate demand, one national inflation rate, one exchange rate, and so on. Micro policies, conversely, are precisely specific, focused, divisible, and targetable. There can be thousands and millions of rules, subsidies, and regulatory institutions.

Macro policies are thus likely to tap broad structures in mobilizing support. Macro clashes occur on crude class or broad sectoral lines. The Phillips curve posits a trade-off between employment and inflation. Social democratic parties with union ties prefer to fight unemployment; business affiliated parties prefer to prevent inflation.[24]

Micro policies conversely appear to be quite concentrated in their appeal. Their specificity rewards them in the political process. By providing measurable benefits to identifiable individuals or groups, micro policies are able to mobilize the support needed to thread their way through the complex blur of the modern polity. There is thus a "natural" tendency toward a de facto particularism in modern policy making. Policies are decentralized and delegated to the groups most intimately affected and connected. These groups are allowed to determine what shall happen in that area. Some larger interest or purpose generally fails to find political voice in this process. In virtually all constitutionalist capitalist countries, regardless of political institutions, farmers receive massive subsidies at the expense of the vast majority of the population, the consumers.

On closer examination, though, macro policies have micro tendencies, and micro policies have macro tendencies. Macro policies do not hit all "class-defined" segments uniformly. Export industries, for example, may prefer a low currency value in order to stimulate exports. Domestically oriented industries may prefer policies which stimulate domestic demand. These different views may link together workers and employers in a particular industry against those

23 Debates over trade politics explore an important distinction useful to the micro-macro debates: cleavages based on class, deriving from a Stolper-Samuelson conceptualization of perfect mobility of factors of production, and cleavages based on sectoral conflict, deriving from factor-specific ideas of immobile factors of production. See Ronald Rogowski, *Commerce and Coalitions* (Princeton: Princeton University Press, 1989); and Jeffrey Frieden, *Debt, Development and Democracy* (Princeton: Princeton University Press, 1991).
24 See Douglas Hibbs, "Political Parties and Macroeconomic Policy," *American Political Science Review* 71 (1977): 1467–87; Neal Beck, "Parties, Administrations and Macroeconomic Outcomes," *American Political Science Review* 76 (March 1982): 83–93; David Cameron, "The Politics and Economics of the Business Cycle," in Thomas Ferguson and Joel Rogers eds., *The Political Economy: Readings in the Politics and Economics of American Policy* (White Plains, N.Y.: Sharpe, 1984), pp. 237–62.

of another industry; if industries are physically concentrated, the splits could be geographical.[25]

Similarly, micro policies do have macro implications. The recent health care controversy in the United States is an example. As health care grows to 15 percent of the national GNP, compared to half or three-fourths of that figure in other industrial countries, many American businesses conclude that the system is pushing unacceptable costs on their competitive position. Business support for health care reform on cost grounds intersects with labor and other concerns about equality and other progressive goals. The micro issue becomes a macro one. In nineteenth-century America, railroad policy moved from a micro issue about the structure and pricing policy of a particular industry into a macro issue about antitrust when the concerns of farmers and many other producers coalesced into a general set of concerns about the power of business.

Micro issues do not become policies without becoming integrated into a macro balance of processes and forces. Micro regulations are the outputs of a process of coalition formation, powerfully influenced by institutional structures. Thus the micro regime of a particular country expresses the particular outcome of its macro processes.

This can be seen if we provide a political account over time of the different patterns we observe in Japan, the United States, and Germany. From about 1870 to 1910 we may say that the microeconomic systems of these countries had some rough similarities. In all, this is an era of gigantic combines, trusts, and cartels. A tremendous industrial expansion in Europe, North America, and Japan occurred in a framework of what some authors have called "organized capitalism" or "the search for order."[26] Large banks formed the core of great combinations of power in all aspects of industrial life.

Then politics produced divergence among market economies. In the United States, populism, the progressive movement, farmers and important business elements mobilized attacks on the great trusts—against railroads, as noted, but also against monopoly power in general, and in areas such as foods, health, and safety. Voices like this existed in other countries, including Japan and Germany, but only in the United States did they prevail.

Several factors account for the difference. The structure of interests, of society, and of property gave forth a different balance of preferences and numbers; America had the family farm, particularly in the Northeast, Midwest and Great Plains. America also had countless small independent proprietors scattered across the country. Its economy was diverse enough to spawn different clusters of interests with competing views and the need for allies in other social

[25] See Rogowski, *Commerce;* Peter Gourevitch, *Politics in Hard Times* (Ithaca, N.Y.: Cornell University Press, 1986).

[26] Robert Weibe, *The Search for Order* (New York: Hill and Wang, 1967); Heinrich Winkler, *Organisierte Kapitalismus* (Gottingen: Vanderhoeck & Ruprecht, 1974).

categories. At the same time, American institutional arrangements gave voice to these groups; federalism, universal suffrage, and competitive parties provided more leverage to farming populists and urban progressives than did the far more limited constitutions of Germany and Japan.

Because of these political differences, American policy pushed the structure of American industry down different tracks from its Japanese and continental European counterparts. The Interstate Commerce Act regulated transportation. The Sherman Antitrust Act demanded the breakup of the cartels and monopolies. In 1927, the McCarren Act prohibited interstate banking. In the early 1930s the Glass-Steagal Act severed the link between banking and industry. Not even Republican administrations could protect American business interests against these incursions. Indeed, many if not most Republicans did not believe that business should be shielded. The tense relations between business and government, so different from Japan and Germany, had strong roots in actual experience arising from politics.

The New Deal is held up by conservative publicists as a period of defeat for American business. In many ways, though, it marked a conversion between practices in the United States and those of other industrial countries. New Deal legislation developed structured competition in regulated markets. It created government sanctioned oligopolies, like those in Germany and Japan. Airlines, oil, trucking, retail trade, agriculture, labor relations, and many other aspects of life were structured by legislation that dove deep into prices, competitive structure, labor rules, standards, and other practices. Business interests were actively involved in working out a conceptualization of regulation that mixed business corporatism and social democracy.

But American politics left the U.S. system with a far weaker corporatist system of regulation than prevailed in Japan and continental Europe. In the 1970s and 1980s, as the New Deal consensus crumbled, deregulation and shifts in tax policy again widened the divergence between U.S. and foreign practices.

Japanese and German industrial development followed the pattern of microregulation for late developers observed by Gerschenkron[27]: a highly centralized pattern of market organization, with a substantial role for banks, with state funds, and with state regulations which allow or encourage cartels and trusts. No effective attacks were mobilized against this system in Japan prior to World War II. After the war, the occupation authorities proscribed the *zaibatsu,* compelled land reform, and promoted a more democratized constitutional process. But many old economic forms continued, in new form and in quite a different military context. The zaibatsu were replaced by keiretsu. Industries remained highly structured, with dense networks of interlocking

---

[27] Alexander Gerschenkron, *Economic Backwardness in Historical Perspective.*

companies. Government ministries helped sustain these structures, excluding newcomers, be they foreign or Japanese. The political foundations of this system lay in the coalition constructed by the Liberal Democratic Party: the internationally competitive great companies and keiretsu groups; the agricultural associations, quite inefficient in world terms; the small shopkeepers and retail stores, also inefficient; and many smaller producers and companies of various degrees of market efficiency. The system is bolstered by institutions: the electoral law which gives voice to well-organized interests and weakens urban consumers and institutional arrangements which facilitate the delegation of authority to well-trained bureaucrats in the ministries who manage the system.

The German system has some strong similarities to the Japanese one: it includes important banks that coordinate competition among industrial groups; giant companies astride dense networks; and policies that favor investment, export, monetary stability, savings, and reduced consumption. The substantial difference between Japan and Germany is the role of labor and the welfare state. German labor is far more strongly represented than its Japanese counterparts and has managed to obtain co-determination management policies and a substantially larger, more institutionalized support system of social insurance, worker training, and education.

In both countries, micro rules are thus deeply embedded into a broader system of power relationships and macro policies. Micro rules in Germany and Japan contribute to higher savings rates, management of competition, exclusion of foreigners, and export orientation. These create very different conditions for macroeconomic management.

In the 1990s, trends in the world economy and within countries have put these internal domestic details about micro arrangements at the forefront of public debate at both the national and international levels. National practices have become part of international trade disputes. Japanese, American, and German rules on micro policies are inseparable from macro and trade policies and politics. Trade flows—thus equity, fairness, wealth, and other goals—are not effectively covered by rules that deal only with tariffs and macro coordination. Countries can no longer argue that their internal rules are beyond the reach of foreigners. Micro coordination is part of the international trade dispute system.

The intrusion of microeconomic issues into the issue space defined by macroeconomics greatly complicates and confuses the ideological and political battles of our era. The macro side of these debates was already put into question when the Reagan administration ran massive deficits and the progressives called for more savings and investment—a rather considerable role reversal. Now, on micro policy issues, similar role reversals are at work concerning antitrust, finance, taxes, and foreign economic policy.

On antitrust, some progressives in the United States have wondered whether international competition has weakened the domestic necessity for these rules, putting the United States at some disadvantage.[28] In calling for the loosening of this kind of regulation, these thinkers join a branch of business conservatives. Against them are both conservatives and liberals who argue for the preservation of this historic feature of American capitalism.

Another area of conflict deals with financial institutions. The large banks have been campaigning for repeal of the McCarren and Glass-Steagal Acts. They have allies in progressive circles who are concerned that the financial system of the United States inhibits the provision of capital to manufacturing that is critical to jobs and industrial health.[29] Opposed to these reformers are traditional circles of American economic life, small banking interests located in small town America, drawing on populist traditions. The cleavage here, as with antitrust, cuts across the political parties and traditional left-right divisions.

Tax policy is a third area causing stress in traditional alliances. Progressive thought has always been torn over how to identify the interests of its popular base—as producers or consumers. In supporting the progressive tax structures, liberals stress the consumer element and have fought the consumption taxes preferred by conservatives. As progressives have shifted attention toward the preservation of jobs, they have become more concerned with the viability of industry and thus more interested in shifting resources from consumption to savings and investment. In that respect, they have paid increasing attention to value-added taxes, taxing social services benefits on the well-to-do, investment tax credits for the long term, and favoring manufacturing and technology industries over real estate and other forms of investment.

Foreign economic policy is yet another area of conflict within major political camps. When trading partners are found to engage in protective practices and there is little likelihood of agreement and enforcement on international rules, we must ask, what is the best policy—to acquiesce or to fight? And if the answer is to fight, then in what manner, with what instruments, and through what mechanisms? In the United States, protectionism has shifted its home from the Republican party to the Democratic party, but it is more accurate to say that both parties are internally divided on this issue.

Finally, the American debate on industrial policy shows interesting political cleavages. Since Hamilton and the founding of the Republic, American business groups have been divided over the importance of state activism in developing and maintaining the infrastructure and in other ways of aiding manufacturing. Today, this debate turns on arguments over the needs of different types of industry: high-technology manufacturing, for example,

---

[28] See Lester Thurow, *Head to Head* (New York: Morrow, 1992).
[29] See Michael Porter, "Capital Disadvantage."

which requires a well-developed "food chain" of public goods (education, research, investment, procurement, trade negotiation), in contrast to industries like real estate development, which focus on lower-factor costs and less regulation. The phrase "industrial policy" generates intense conflict in the United States; in the 1992 federal election, many Republican advocates of a more vigorous governmental role came from the ranks of high-technology industry, and many Democrats were associated with analysis of a more activist approach.[30]

European and Japanese debates differ from American ones, most notably the acceptance in those two countries by business conservatives of a different set of regulatory rules controlling competition and greater state activism. Japanese industry interacts with the state to administer de facto cartels or managed markets. On the European continent, to different degrees, corporatist arrangements institutionalize various forms of market management and restrictions and provide various forms of state assistance. In Europe, it is the progressives who have been divided on the role of the state. A reformist tradition there has challenged the highly centralized model of traditional socialism and communism, seeking greater responsiveness and accountability of bureaucracies (for which markets may be useful), stronger citizen participation in government through decentralization, worker participation managed through works councils, and attention to new issues concerning the environment and gender. Conservatives are concerned about state support for vital social investment in research and infrastructure and the use of state aid in international competition.

In Japan, economic policy debates center on consumer versus producer interests, on accommodation to international trade pressures, and on the price to be paid to inefficient sectors (agriculture and retail) in exchange for social and political stability. In the early 1990s, the Japanese economy experienced adjustment problems with a business cycle downturn and a fall in various asset prices (real estate and stocks). Some observers are convinced that this adjustment will entail the loosening of Japanese regulatory practices to make them more transparent and conform to "Western" practices. Other observers argue that regulatory practices can be used to manage the adjustment and make a strong economy based on the same processes and principles.[31] The conflicts among ministries and interest groups are more visible. The Japanese election of 1993 brought down the governing party. It is too soon to evaluate the

---

[30] See Tyson, *Who's Bashing Whom.*

[31] Japan specialists disagree sharply on how to interpret the interaction of societal actors and processes (elections, parties, legislatures, interest groups, social classes, and leaders) and the role of autonomous state institutions like the military and the bureaucracy. See, for example, Chalmers Johnson, *MITI and the Japanese Miracle* (Stanford: Stanford University Press, 1982), and Mark Ramseyer and Frances Rosenbluth, *The Market for Policy in Japan: A Rational Choice Approach* (Cambridge, Mass.: Harvard University Press, 1993).

effects of that election in changing the rules of the political game, shifting coalitions, and changing policy outcomes. It is also too soon to evaluate the impact of the Asian financial crisis of 1997 upon the patterns of micro institutional arrangements that have dominated the high growth economies of that region, but it is certain that those arrangements are now under challenge rather than uncritically accepted.

Fragmented Politics

The policy debates examined above reveal new trends in the international economy that challenge traditional analytic categories and historical political alignments. Macro and micro, national and international, public and private, domestic and foreign—these distinctions do not well capture the content of current policy alternatives. New issue cleavages challenge the older political structures that were built on traditional battle lines. Interest groups, societal actors, and individuals interact with political parties and governmental institutions through the prism of their various ideologies to produce policy outputs. Over the next years, under constant pressure of a highly competitive economic reality, the existing patterns will be open to change. Political entrepreneurs have opportunities to forge new coalitions and to alter existing institutional arrangements. Some of these political innovations may represent values of democracy, equality and constitutional procedures. Other innovations may be more destructive of those values.

The advanced industrial democracies have the prosperity, traditions, and institutions to sustain considerable shocks on their systems. In other parts of the world, such resilience is absent: Eastern Europe and the successor states of the Soviet Union, the developing countries of Africa and Asia, the newer democracies of Latin America—for these countries the relationship between economic policy battles and institutional change is quite open and pliable. In all these countries, democracy and constitutional government have still to compete with authoritarian forms in the struggle for legitimacy. It is far from agreed that democracy is the best instrument for attaining individual, group, or national objectives. Indeed, in many countries, governing elites and many groups in society believe that their economic success is inextricably linked to authoritarian processes, that democracy leads to fragmentation and chaos. Each moment of policy conflict puts into question the institutions that are used to manage the debate. In these countries, the bond between property and markets, on the one side, and constitutional government and democracy, on the other, has yet to be forged.[32]

---

[32] Victor Perez Diaz's discussion of the various meanings of civil society is quite helpful in

Written thirty years ago, *Social Origins* helps us prepare the ground for understanding the struggles over democracy and markets that occur around the world. That book covered several centuries to bring us to the Cold War era. Today, it provides not only historical context for understanding the current state of these issues, but both ideas and methods of handling them. Moore is thought of as a macro theorist focusing on domestic processes of political economy. In theoretical debates he is known largely as a champion of a "social forces" approach, looking at the pressure upon politics arising from society and its own divisions. Yet, Moore resisted typecasting. His writing and his teaching pay considerable attention to institutions, to ideology, to international competition, and to political entrepreneurship by leaders in fashioning coalitions and strategies out of the materials at hand (technology, geography, ethnicity, culture, and military elements). *Social Origins,* and the teaching Moore did in seminars, emphasized a way of asking questions more than a particular set of answers. Moore saw structured patterns framing trajectories of some indeterminacy. Moorean themes on the varieties of capitalism, the political economy of constitutionalism and authoritarianism, and the role of ideology and entrepreneurship are quite relevant to the problems of the new century. Our challenge is to use his methods and ideas about the past to decipher the signals of the present and future.[33]

---

understanding the link between political institutions and social ones. See his *The Return of Civil Society* (Cambridge, Mass.: Harvard University Press, 1993).

[33] Two contrasting views of comparative analysis, stages versus cycles, have been familiar to us since the classical theory of Greece and Rome. Most twentieth-century social science has had a stages approach, strongly permeated by an optimism of progress. The collapse of the USSR and the problem with political economy in the United States have brought renewed interest in cycle theory. See Gourevitch, "Democracy and Economic Policy."

CHAPTER 11

Fin de Siècle Globalization, Democratization, and the Moore Theses: A European Case Study

GEORGE ROSS

Social Origins of Dictatorship and Democracy is constructed around an elegantly simple argument. As of the mid-1960s, when the book was published, there seemed three significant models of political modernity—liberal democracy, fascism, and communism. To Moore, the origins of each were ultimately to be found in the different ways in which premodern agricultural social structures and capitalism came together. The values of premodern agrarian social classes and the manner in which these values either persisted or changed as capitalist processes evolved were central. If the largely authoritarian values lodged in earlier agrarian social settings were dissolved or drastically changed by the capitalization of agriculture, then there was a good chance that liberal democracy might emerge. However, if these values persisted and were reconfirmed in modified forms with the onset of capitalization, there was likely to be either "modernization from above," resistant to democratic forms, or little modernization at all. In the first case, fascist authoritarianism was a likely response when popular demands for participation had to be confronted. In the second, "modernization from above" by Communist elites was a strong possibility.

The explosive importance of this argument was no coincidence. It proposed an innovative response to the preoccupation of post-1945 social science with the causes of the murderous political pathologies of the first half of the twentieth century. Unlike most of his colleagues, who sought such causes in the shorter-run workings of politics, Moore claimed that the processes began far in the past. The consequences of agrarian modernization created a "path dependent" social class structure with characteristic political values which foreordained results in the twentieth century.[1]

There was another striking dimension to the argument. The long historical trajectories stressed by Moore were profoundly *national*. Wars and other transnational events could lead to change, but, other things being equal, these changes were likely to occur along the "path" that earlier change had set out for a particular nation. More generally, the nation was the generic envelope for capitalist and other forms of modernization. Not surprisingly, with this national focus, Moore was a realist about international matters. Nations pursued their own interests in international affairs and such interests would be constructed out of prior national "paths," largely by the classes that dominated their definition. Sometimes these national interests would promote peace, other times war, and still othertimes imperial conquest, but always they would constitute the primordial facts of international politics.

Three decades have elapsed since *Social Origins* was published. The formerly fascist nations, defeated in war, seem to have embraced (or have been obliged to embrace) liberal democracy. Moreover, the book on communism closed in 1989, even if authoritarianism and radical nationalism then took root in many "liberated" areas. Liberal democratic capitalism is now the predominant form of governance in the advanced areas of the planet. Could it be that the social and economic structures that underpin Moore's argument have changed in major ways? And, if this is the case, might it be that these changes cast the future of liberal democracy in new terms?

We can be more precise. Beginning two decades ago a set of international economic phenomena—increased trade, more intense international competition, shorter and more volatile product cycles, rapid dissemination of fundamental technological innovation, the effects of the precocious internationalization of capital flows, and a global market in cultural goods, among other things—have had dramatic impact on the institutions, policy agendas and patterns of representation in advanced capitalist societies.[2] Capitalism as a

---

[1] His realism, in stark contrast to many of his peers and rivals, also endowed him with the pessimism needed to understand the pathologies of liberal democracy (predatory relationships with less developed and less powerful parts of the world, persistent inequalities, and elite domination) along with those of other national "paths" without buying into the prophetic hopes of socialists and Marxists.

[2] Scholars disagree about this contention. It is clear that capitalism is much more globalized today in terms of the salience of international trade to particular nations than it was during the years of the postwar boom from 1945 to the mid-1970s, when particularly national strategies for economic development were widely pursued. The salience of international trade for advanced capitalist societies in the 1990s may not be a great deal more than it was in certain earlier periods like the 1890s. The argument about new globalization does not rest simply on the implication of particular nations in international trade in gross terms, however. Quite as important are matters such as the extraordinary internationalization of financial exchanges, greatly

system has thus "globalized," as the slogan of the day goes. Largely because of this, confident postwar national quests for economic security—within an optic assuming that steady growth, near full employment levels, and the widespread institutionalization of insurance against market harshness were possible—have given way to less confident searches for new international competitiveness. Nation-states, even the most powerful, have found their autonomy greatly constrained. Has this globalization challenged the patterns of national path dependency and international political realism that lay at the center of Moore's intellectual universe in *Social Origins?* Quite as important, how has the global-ization of advanced capitalism affected the workings of liberal democracy?

It is much too soon to propose answers with the authority of those advanced by Moore in *Social Origins.* Still, because much depends upon the answers, even tentative indicators are important. The case study that follows examines Europe's recent efforts, beginning in the mid-1980s, to master the large changes brought by recent economic globalization. In these efforts European nation-states sought supranational solutions through the European Com-munity (or European Union [EU] as it became in 1993).[3] These states en-gaged in uniquely transnational political activities in pursuit of their quest and upset the delicate equilibria upon which liberal democracy within particular countries was premised. Closer scrutiny of this extraordinary episode may provide us with some of the indicators we seek.

Pooling Sovereignty and Promoting Transnationality: European Integration

Whatever the ultimate outcomes of globalization-induced changes for Eu-rope, recent efforts undertaken at the EU level to develop new *regional* re-sponses to globalization phenomena have been striking. Few would have predicted them, given the past history of European integration. The EU took off rapidly after the Rome Treaty of 1957, amidst all manner of high talk about the transcendence of national interests and, indeed, of nationality itself. The major initial result, beyond the construction of European-level institutions, was a customs-free area including the six original EU members. This "com-mon market" was a circumscribed and protected playing field for trade, involv-ing the pooling of limited, carefully chosen areas of sovereignty, designed less to transcend national sovereignty than to help EU member states pursue

---

enhanced by technological change, plus the emergence of transnational firms as global actors (with which nation-states must negotiate, often as near equals).

[3] The acronym EU will hereafter be used to simplify the text. Readers will note that it is an anachronism, however. The term "common market" was most often used prior to the 1970s. It was then replaced by EC or "the Community" until the ratification of the Maastricht Treaty in 1993. EU has been used since that time.

national growth strategies. Beyond the common market there were "common policies" in agriculture, common representation in international trade negotiations and a few other areas of integrated action. The EU's scope was quite limited.

None of this should be surprising. European integration began exactly as Western European nations entered "golden age" reconstruction and unprecedented economic growth, which eventually produced consumerist societies and massive social change. Within the constraints of the Cold War and American hegemony, it was the profoundly *national* focus of golden age developmental models that was most striking. Between 1947 and 1973 governments learned to control important macroeconomic policy parameters (usually adopting some version of Keynesianism) and consolidated protective welfare states. In varying ways, there was rapid economic growth and an institutionalization of capital-labor relations. The liberal democratic political envelope in which this occurred promoted patterns of exchange dominated by large producer groups (employers and unions) and powerful state agencies, primarily concerned with the distribution of boom-time profits among private firms, expanded taxation, higher wages, and enhanced social security. In general, golden age Western Europe, warts and all, was a triumph for profoundly national forms of liberal democracy, particularly compared to the area's past. In this context European integration should be understood as an arrangement that provided useful services to European nation-states where the action that counted took place. The greatest loss of sovereignty in the first quarter century of European integration was not to the EU but to NATO and American financial hegemony.[4]

If European integration settled into providing services to national capitalist developmental models, the political forms it assumed were nonetheless significant. Europe's designers, beginning with the pioneering Jean Monnet, plotted European integration by political stealth.[5] The "Monnet model," developed for the European Coal and Steel Community and used again for the EU, involved agitation for further integration by specific supranational institutions, "functionalism," and decision making by diplomatic methods. For the EU, an appointed European Commission was empowered to propose changes as long as they could be grounded in the founding treaties. Functionalist hopes were

[4] It should be noted that golden age developmental models varied significantly in their forms and their points of emergence. The changes described here, it must also be noted, occurred in polities that were flawed in any number of ways. Restricted elites dominated decision making; large, organized and powerful group interests were the predominant real "citizens" in political exchange, political parties were dominated by bureaucrats and "insiders" and, in general, patterns of representation were skewed against the weak and poor.

[5] Francois Duchene's excellent biography of Monnet, *Jean Monnet, The First Statesman of Interdependence* (New York: Norton, 1994) is the best source on the development of the Monnet method.

premised on the hypothesis that once significant parts of economic sovereignty were integrated, underlying interdependencies would create new needs for further integration and new constituencies to advocate it. "Spillover," in the jargon of the academic literature, was action which implied more thorough market integration and ultimately more regulatory and political integration.[6] Decisions to implement spillover measures would be taken in the EU Council of Ministers. The leaders and officials who made these decisions would proceed diplomatically, in much the same way all "foreign affairs" matters were decided, in camera, with little information provided to the public.[7]

The "Monnet model," institutionalized in the EU from the beginning, therefore envisaged a progressive pooling of sovereignty by EU member states occurring by and large external to national democratic processes. To be sure, the national leaders and officials periodically had to face their electorates, who might judge their Euro-level actions on results. But without much knowledge and in the absence of transparent decision making and open debate, such judgments would usually be ill-informed and too late to make much difference. European integration was thus meant as a "Saint-Simonian" affair. Enlightened officials would decide what was good for the people without fully informing them. Monnet himself was quite lucid about this. If European integration had to proceed through national democratic processes it would not occur.

European integration was thus born with the "democratic deficit" which characterizes it to this day. Even though there was debate and protest about the issue from the beginning, it was muted because the EU served as an auxiliary to flourishing, and quite self involved, national developmental models during its first decades. Thus what really counted to people happened nationally, and the EU did not impinge notably on these issues. When, in the early 1960s, an activist Commission tried too hard to promote spillover beyond the first common market stage, the French created a crisis which quickly led to a stalemate in which no further forward action could occur without unanimity among member states.[8] This de facto change turned the EU into a completely intergovernmental affair where it became virtually impossible to

6 "Functionalism" was the predominant academic view on European integration in the early years. Spillover is one of its key concepts. See Ernst Haas, *The Uniting of Europe* (Stanford: Stanford University Press, 1958) and idem, *Beyond the Nation State* (Stanford: Stanford University Press, 1964).

7 Foreign affairs, almost universally, have been understood as an executive prerogative in democracies, usually shielded, when not completely hidden, from full domestic democratic political scrutiny.

8 The move towards this new situation was led by French President de Gaulle and it eventuated in what came to be called the "Luxembourg compromise." De Gaulle, for once, was not speaking only for the French and himself, however. Many, if not most, EU member states went along.

expand the European agenda because nothing could be done without every member agreeing. From the mid-1960s, therefore, the EU settled down to a confederal institutional system in which a lowest common denominator of member state positions dictated the logic of EU action, confirming the predictions of realist theories.

Thereafter, until the mid-1980s, there was no lack of ambitious "Europeanizing" proposals, but minimal accomplishment.[9] Among the rare changes were those designed to address the "democracy" problem. The original treaties had included a European-level consultative assembly composed of members appointed by member state governments from among national parliamentarians; this group eventually became the European Parliament. Initially it had next to no power except to pontificate about matters on the EU table. No one paid much attention, therefore. In the early 1970s, however, the Parliament acquired some new power in the EU budgeting process, giving it definable jobs and making it the object of some lobbying. Later on in the 1970s the Council of Ministers passed legislation for the direct election of members of the Parliament, with the first elections held in 1979. Since this particular change was not accompanied by any change in the Parliament's prerogatives, its major result was a parliament composed of ambitious politicians lobbying constantly for an expansion in their powers, hence a permanent lobby for one particular "solution" to the problems of democratic deficit, namely turning the European political system into a national parliamentary democracy writ large. In the meantime, however, this Europarliament without power over legislation, without majorities and minorities competing over governmental policies (because there was no government), and with a host of obscure committees and procedures, produced more confusion than democracy.[10]

More generally, the premise of a Europe which provided needed, but relatively modest, services for its member states collapsed in the 1970s with the golden age models it had pursued. Growth slowed, stagflation occurred, unemployment began to rise, and Europe's international competitiveness declined. By the early 1980s, with European economies in a shambles and the

---

[9] The few important changes in the 1970s—the European Monetary System (EMS) and the European Council, for example—flowed clearly from an interstate-confederal approach to agenda setting and originated outside the EC altogether. The European Council is a twice yearly summit of EC heads of state and government begun in 1979. See Simon Bulmer and Wolfgang Wessels, *The European Council, Decision-Making in European Politics* (London: Macmillan, 1987); see also Wessels, "The EC Council: The Community's Decisionmaking Center," in Robert Keohane and Stanley Hoffmann, eds., *The New European Community* (Boulder, Colo.: Westview Press, 1991). On EMS see Peter Ludlow, *The Making of the European Monetary System* (London: Allen and Unwin, 1977).

[10] On the issue of Europarliamentary power see Shirley Williams' excellent essay in Robert Keohane and Hoffmann, *New European Community*.

EU in incessant gridlock over petty issues, the dream of European integration seemed far away. "Europessimism" was the rule.

Renewal: European Institutions and European Integration

Things changed dramatically after 1985. Supranational actors reappeared, often with quasi-federalist goals. In contrast to ordinary international organizations the EU had been set up to contain a supranational motor, the European Commission, to press member states toward *more* integration. These states had a single legislator in the Council of Ministers. In the minds of the EU's founders, the Commission was not to be simply a "delegated agent" of member states, but a "proposition force" constantly prodding member states toward greater integration. The European Commission lost most of this capacity during the EU's first quarter century however, and member states, constitutionally designated as the EU's "big citizens," became the EU's central actors. Beginning in the mid-1980s, however, environmental changes made it possible for the European Commission to take new transnational initiatives.

The most important environmental changes were new economic problems. The oil shocks, stagflation, the end of the postwar boom, globalization, and the effects of policy-induced deflation of the earlier 1980s—largely imposed by the United States—recast Europe's economic setting. All this prodded greater convergence in economic management outlooks among key EU member states. In particular, the 1982–83 French retreat from a nation-centered program of planning, nationalization, and redistribution to a renewed commitment to the EU was critical. From that moment, French and German purposes coincided much more closely, giving new life to the Franco-German European couple that had traditionally been the key to European integration. It then became much easier for EU members to convince one another of the need for new European solutions to common problems and to circumvent residual opposition.[11]

The existence of a more favorable diplomatic setting did not automatically imply a renaissance of European integration, however, let alone determine its directions. Actors, the European Commission in the first instance, had to make this renaissance happen. In formal terms, it was the job of the new Commission appointed in 1985 to produce new ideas, just as it was its job to be the major political advocate for a federalizing Europe. The fact that it had been very difficult and demoralizing for recent Commissions to do this job undoubtedly created more incentives for it to try and make its mark. Moreover, the new Commission President, Jacques Delors, a front-ranking

---

[11] The problem member state was the United Kingdom.

European political figure of great strategic capacities, was a convinced and knowledgeable European, well connected to the French and German leaders whose political decisions were essential. He had reasons to be unhappy with the EU as it stood, and he had a good practical sense about intelligent and potentially successful initiatives for change. Finally, Delors was imbued with great personal ambitions.[12]

The new Commission needed a launching pad project which had to fit the EU's constitutional bias toward economism. Its creation was the 1985 White Paper to complete the single market within eight years (two Commission terms), the "1992" program. The White Paper contained a long list of propositions to eliminate the nontariff barriers to inter-EU trade which had theretofore allowed the perpetuation of as many separate national markets as the EU had members.[13] Needless to say, the construction of a *single* EU market had huge implications for the national economic policy autonomy, which was the very glue of national sovereignty.

The idea of completing the internal market, along with most of the Delors Commission's subsequent initiatives, had in fact been around for some time, stored in the EU's large closet of unfulfilled but solemnly declared policy promises.[14] The Commission and its allies understood that generating forward movement on such ground was much easier than beginning de novo. There were numerous ideological resources in the environment for the Commission to tap. Regardless of past EU history, completing the single market as a program, with its deregulatory logic, fit extremely well with the newly liberal consensus of member state governments in the mid-1980s. It also coincided perfectly with the inclinations of much of European big business, eager for a plausible way out of an economic morass and sensitive to the argument that a larger market would offer new opportunities and incentives. And, as already noted, the diplomatic setting had also shifted. The French had moved closer to the Germans—their own strategy of competitive deflation targeted on alignment with the DM and toward the new liberal consensus—while the British, eternally blocking any EU forward movement, could be seduced by a program presented in liberal market-building terms.

The immediate next step involved negotiations in the context of the Inter-Governmental Conference (IGC) called at the Milan European Council (the biannual summit of heads of state and government) in the spring of 1985. The IGC was convened to suggest the treaty modifications necessary to implement

[12] For an approachable discussion of Delors' biography see Charles Grant, *Delors* (London: Nichlas Brealey, 1994).

[13] Delors briefly describes the ways in which he decided upon the "1992" option in his preface to Paolo Cecchini, *The European Challenge* (Aldershot: Wildwood House, 1988).

[14] David Cameron provides a useful overview of the evolution of the single market notion in his chapter in Alberta Sbragia, ed., *Europolitics* (Washington, D.C.: Brookings, 1991).

the Commission's White Paper on completing the Single Market. IGCs are designed to prepare final bargaining documents for a European Council, where binding deals are struck intergovernmentally. But the vast bulk of deliberations of the Milan Council's IGC proceeded from initial papers presented by the Commission, which, although present legally only as an observer, argued forcefully for its ideas.[15] Here perhaps the shrewdest move was linking the single market to a fundamental change in prevailing EU decision-making procedures. Because the internal market program was so ambitious, the Commission argued, the Luxembourg compromise that had enjoined unanimity from the 1960s had to give way to decisions by a "qualified majority."[16] Henceforth in single market areas member states might very well have to accept legislation they did not desire. Using similar arguments about the necessity for complementary policies to "frame" the single market, the Commission also proposed a newly extended list of EU "competences"—new areas in which the EU acquired a legal basis to act—in research and development, regional policy, and the environment and foreign policy cooperation, and it advocated increased powers for the European Parliament.

Single European Act treaty revisions, allowing qualified majority Council voting on most single market matters and consecrating the end of the first period of de facto intergovernmentalism in EU history, substantially opened up the Commission's political opportunity structure. The constraint of searching for a member state consensus was thereby lightened. The Commission and its allies could henceforth politic in a more open setting and strategize linkages, packages, and coalitions to their advantage. That Spain and Portugal joined the EU at the same time had also expanded the range of divergence and interests among member states, a process driving in the same direction.[17]

From a political point of view the instant public opinion successes of the Single Market Program itself were essential. To the surprise of virtually everyone, "1992" struck fire. "Selling the product," to use Brussels's language, was nonetheless necessary, and the Commission was also central in this. Placing a symbolic time limit on the implementation of the White Paper created a slogan—"1992" which greatly simplified a complex cluster of policy initia-

[15] See, in particular, Emile Noel, "The Single European Act," *Government and Opposition* 22, no. 1 (Winter 1987:3–12). Also *Bulletin of European Communism* (October 1985); 7–9. For the Luxemburg European Council see *Bulletin of the European Commission,* no. 11 (1985): 7–21, no. 12 (1985):7–15.

[16] Under the decision-making rules of "qualified majority" votes are assigned to member states in accordance with their size. This system makes it impossible for the big EC members to unite and carry issues over the wishes of smaller states while also allowing a "blocking" coalition of two large members and one small one.

[17] Single European Act changes also created what was called the "cooperation" procedure among Commission, Council, and Parliament, which allowed the European Parliament new powers of amendment on Single Act legislation, an important increase in the Parliament's powers.

tives, and was essential in generating interest and enthusiasm from a wide range of publics.[18] Specific and assiduous Commission efforts were made to generate support from more targeted constituencies as well—the European parliament, business, and labor, in particular.[19] The Commission's influential "Cecchini Report" detailing "the costs of non-Europe" was also important.[20] Perhaps most important, the period around the conclusion of the Single Act saw the first signs of a substantial European economic recovery from which "1992" profited greatly. Commission leaders were quick to give "1992" the credit for the new jobs created. Finally, Jacques Delors became a widely known international statesman who could deploy his own political clout to aid the Commission.

Reinvesting Success: The Russian Dolls Period

As the Delors Commission's activities unfolded after 1985, they quickly assumed a certain strategic logic, labeled "Russian dolls" by Delors's Brussels team.[21] This involved iterated initiatives to exploit the nested nature of its programs—"engineering spillover" in the vocabulary of the Monnet method. The hope was that the success of each initiative would accumulate political capital, which the Commission could quickly reinvest in new, usually broader, initiatives, with the ultimate goal of mobilizing a "cycle" of "Europeanizing" change, which in turn could lead to a point of no return for European integration in which the national sovereignty of EU members was largely eclipsed. Resource returns to this Russian dolls approach depended greatly on the shrewd design of each move—how well the Commission analyzed and deployed its resources and how intelligently it evaluated the evolving political opportunity structure. Above all, the Commission had to make absolutely sure that its proposals stood a strong chance of approval by key member states.

[18] Jacques Delors used the target date of 1992 in his initial speech to the European Parliament in January 1985, only a few days after he had assumed office and well before the program itself had been designed. This speech, along with excerpts from most of Delors's important speeches from 1985 through 1992, is reproduced in Jacques Delors, *Le Nouveau Concert européen* (Paris: Odile Jacob, 1992).

[19] Business enthusiasm for the Single Market seems to have been rather more a product of the policy program than one of its primary causes, and it may well be that much initial business support, including its organizational expression, may have been drummed up by the Commission. See Wayne Sandholtz and John Zysman's "1992: Recasting the European Bargain," *World Politics* 42, 1 (October 1989): 95–129.

[20] The "cost" arguments were detailed in the original Cecchini report published by the Commission and in the abridgments and paraphrases which quickly circulated. Here the Commission's administration demonstrated a deft touch in mobilizing academic commentators, particularly economists.

[21] On the centrality of this team, see George Ross, *Jacques Delors and European Integration* (New York: Oxford University Press, 1994). See also George Ross, "Inside the Delors Cabinet," *Journal of Common Market Studies* 32, no. 3 (December 1994): 499–518.

The Commission first "turned over" the resources and power gained in its White Paper–Single Act initiatives to promote the Delors budgetary package of 1987. Using the initial argument that a new financial package was necessary to implement the Single European Act, the Commission proposed an innovative three-tiered program. The first part substituted five-year financial programming for yearly budget discussions, thereby granting the Commission freedom from resource-sapping annual budget fights. The second part brought changes to the Common Agricultural Policy (CAP), including a five-year program of guidelines for spending that would keep squabbles about agriculture off the table until 1993. Third, under the label of "economic and social cohesion" came a new set of financial transfers to help raise Europe's less developed areas to levels comparable to those of its rich core, the first really new European-level commitment to planned redistribution since the CAP itself. Better-off EU members would thus put more into the EU than they received in order to compensate poorer regions for the asymmetry of costs created by the Single Market.[22] Moreover, this "reform of the structural funds" was designed to enhance the Commission's architectural and directive power over regional development funding.

Success of the *Paquet Delors*, which depended ultimately upon German willingness to use its checkbook, opened the way for the Economic and Monetary Union (EMU), the most important Russian doll. The architectural hand of the Commission on EMU was undeniable. The strategic use of accumulated resources was directed, this time, toward dispossessing member states of the bulk of their autonomy in monetary and macroeconomic policy—hardly a small affair. Needless to say, it was also a European state-building proposal in important ways, since economic and monetary steering, once removed from the national level, would settle to a transnational one. Initially, the EMU initiative was remarkably successful. The Delors Committee, established at Hanover in 1988 worked so that the Commission President was able to structure plans for EMU and bring Central Bank Governors "on board" to support those plans. This support, in turn, was an essential beachhead for getting European political leaders behind the program. At the Madrid European Council in 1989 the British announced their intention to refuse participation in much of the plan, but nonetheless allowed the Delors Committee report to move forward.[23] EMU was to involve the progressive unification of much

[22] The sums involved, if modest in absolute terms, would be substantial in reationship to the investment needs of poorer EC countries. Delors took to comparing the program with the Marshall Plan. For detail on 1989, see the *Rapport annuel sur la mise en oeuvre de la réforme des fonds structurels*, (Luxembourg: CEE, 1991); for 1990, see Com(91) 400, December 4, 1991. See also EC Commission, *Les Régions dans les années 1990* (Luxembourg: CEE, 1991); Yves Doutriaux, *La Politique régionale de la CEE* (Paris: Presses Universitaires de France, 1991).

[23] See Committee for the Study of Economic and Monetary Union, *Report on Economic and Monetary Union in the European Community* (Luxembourg: EC, 1989). Delors wrote the report himself.

member state economic policy and the eventual creation of a central European Banking system and single currency.

The final major initiative of the Russian doll period, the "social dimension," had fewer positive outcomes. In the neoliberal atmosphere of the mid-1980s, proposing social programs was problematic.[24] The Social Charter of May 1989 was a "solemn commitment" by eleven member states—the British gave furious opposition—to a set of "fundamental social rights" for workers. The charter, which proposed no legal additions to the treaties, was designed to make good on the unfulfilled social promises that the EU's treaty base already contained. The action program that followed proposed a flood of new EU legislation. Some forty-seven different instruments were prepared and submitted to the Council of Ministers by January 1, 1993.[25] But only those proposals whose treaty base allowed for a qualified majority (Article 118a on health and safety and Article 119 on equal treatment) had much of a chance of passing. The British government stopped or slowed everything else.

The social dimension initiatives had multiple purposes. The initiatives were meant to calm some of the fears which "1992" aroused in the European labor movement and help the Commission acquire labor support for its strategies. Moreover, to the degree to which action could not be produced in support of Social Charter promises, the Commission could count on a substantial mobilization of indignant voices (including the large socialist bloc in the European Parliament) to spread the message about "Social Europe" in the media and the member states. The Commission was thus hoping to generate public pressure for a future change in the European agenda, and ultimately in the EU treaty itself, which was needed for greater EU activism in social policy. Finally, persistent British blockages on social matters—as well as on other issues— isolated the British, a situation which was important for the Commission's position in the internal politics of the EU.

The logic of the Social Charter was ultimately connected to the Commission's other major social policy priority, "social dialogue," an attempt to bring European-level employers' associations and labor unions together periodically to debate important matters.[26] The initial purpose was confidence building,

[24] Key documents are Delors's speech to the 1988 Stockholm Conference of the European Trade Union Confederation (ETUC), reproduced in Delors, *Le Nouveau Concert européen*, Patrick Venturini, *Un Espace social européen a l'horizon 1992* (Luxembourg: EC, 1988), and those found in the 1988 special edition of *Social Europe*, "The Social Dimension of the Internal Market."

[25] See Com(89) 568, Brussels, November 29 1989 for the full text. A table of the proposed initiatives is presented in *Social Europe* 1(1990): 52–76. A record of their progress can be found in Annex II of the EC's social *Green Paper* of 1993 (Brussels: EC Commission, 1993).

[26] The Single European Act included a new Article 118B stating that "the Commission shall endeavour to develop the dialogue between management and labour at the European level which could, if the two sides consider it desirable, lead to relations based on agreement." The relaunching of social dialogue was in fact Delors's first social policy step, taken in January 1985. But initial discussions among UNICE, the employers' association, the European Trade Union

engaging employers and unions in habits of discussion which, in time, might create mutual trust and eventuate in more substantial "contractual" conclusions and, additionally, help transform the actors themselves into agents with the power to deal.[27] Discussion quickly ran up against labor and capital's contradictory purposes. The European Trade Union Confederation (ETUC) wanted concrete proposals while the Union of Industrial and Employers' Confederation of Europe (UNICE), the employers' association, accepted only large principles. Moreover, all actors were obliged to keep their eyes on what was going on in the member states before saying much of anything, since imprudent remarks at the European level could upset delicate, and more essential, national-level discussions.

In the period around the Maastricht Treaty in 1991, things became clearer. The Commission, with some member state support, proposed broadening the EU treaty to allow greater EU social policy activity. Simultaneously, however, it also proposed that the "social partners" might try to negotiate instead of relying on legislation in those areas where the Commission announced its intention to act. After very complicated politicking, this proposal was embodied in a "Social Protocol" to the new treaty, engaging everyone but the British, who opted out. Achievements were limited, but the first genuine European-level collective agreement, over parental leave, was signed in 1994.

The strategic logic that underlay these large Russian dolls was followed in other areas. In the immediate wake of the end of the Cold War in 1989, the Commission and its allies proceeded similarly and invested considerable effort in trying to shape an approach for restructuring the EU's foreign political postures. In this area—that of interstate dealing par excellence—the Commission's reach and potential success rate were subject to great constraints. The imprimatur of Commission agenda-setting was clear in the EU dealings with the European Free Trade Association (EFTA), which led to the European Economic Area treaty.[28] The EU's first real "Eastern" crisis, born of the collapse of the German Democratic Republic, provided yet another example of Commission agenda-setting in foreign affairs. When the possibility of German unity became clearer, the Commission decided to welcome unification and to propose the rapid incorporation of the former GDR into the EU

Confederation (ETUC), and the public sector trade association did not get very far.

[27] There was considerable distance to travel, since neither the ETUC nor UNICE—both essentially Brussels lobbies—was empowered to negotiate.

[28] The success of the 1992 program finally made it clear to remaining EFTA members that they needed a piece of Single Market action. The solution proposed by the EU, the European Economic Area, was conceived as an antechamber to keep EFTA members from applying for full EU membership, however. They would get more or less full access to the Single Market, but without political control over future EU decisions. Most EFTA countries quickly applied to join the EU because of the liability they would suffer if they did not, and three—Austria, Finland and Sweden—became members in 1995.

itself.[29] New relationships between the EU and the former socialist countries of Central and East Europe (CEECs) were also largely structured by Commission action.[30]

The strategy behind all of these new ventures was to parlay new international dealings into enhancement of the EU's foreign policy capabilities—more engineered spillover, in other words. Given the end of the Cold War, Soviet decline, and America's domestic problems, a window of opportunity had opened for Europe to occupy new international political space, and this situation had provoked the Commission and French and German leaders toward new state-building efforts. De facto accumulation of foreign policy roles allowed the Commission to agitate for de jure change toward a genuine common foreign policy.

The Descending Cycle

It is possible to argue about the details of what happened in, and to, Europe between 1985 and 1990, but the deeper outline of events is clear. In response to challenges of economic globalization and given the preexisting institutional framework of the European Union, the deep interdependencies of European nation-states led EU members to substantial new sacrifices of economic sovereignty, taken in the interests of creating a more coherent regional economic bloc in the EU area to buffer European competitiveness and economic and political power. The European Commission, a transnational political actor, was quite as central in all this as EU member states.

It was unquestionable that the evolution of capitalism had, by 1990, pushed European countries to begin Europeanizing their national interests in ways that diminished their autonomy and capacities as nation-states. If one assumes that these resources are central to the perpetuation of the strong national value that are at the core of the world described in *Social Origins,* then, on the evidence of Europe in the later 1980s, advancing capitalism in Europe had begun transcending this world. The issue of democracy which accompanied this transcendence was less clearly confronted, however. Sovereignty had been "pooled" at the European level, but popular scrutiny and control over these transfers of power fell behind.

[29] The Commission president took the lead in this, distinguishing himself from Margaret Thatcher and François Mitterrand who were both much more cautious. See European Commission, *The Impact of German Unification on the European Community* (Luxembourg: EC, 1990).

[30] Following complex and skillful maneuvering by Commission insiders "at the top," the Community was given responsibility for coordinating G-24 (and Community) aid to Poland and Hungary at the July 14, 1989, Paris G7 Summit. The task was later expanded to include the rest of the CEECs.

The story was far from over in 1991, however. Two processes had interacted to get the EU up and moving after 1985. A changing environment altered political opportunities, and legitimate actors emerged with the skills to take advantage of these changes, the European Commission especially. Since the logic of European integration was the pooling of sovereignty, the EU's motion was in the direction of allocating national powers and prerogatives to the market and to transnational institutions. The upward cycle ended in 1991, however, and a descending cycle began.

The Downward Spiral

The events contributing to this new EU decline are well known. The first signs that the climate had turned chilly emerged during the negotiations for the Maastricht Treaty in 1991. Its promoters had intended Maastricht to be a point of no return for the new integrated Europe. By constitutionalizing Economic and Monetary Union, EU member states would pool the vast bulk of their monetary and economic policy powers in transnational authorities and mechanisms. By negotiating a Common Foreign and Security Policy, greater democratic legitimacy (that is, increased powers for the European parliament), and new or enhanced competencies for the EU, the shift of control from nations to the new European Union would be decisive. The realities of Maastricht were different.

The EMU proceedings produced agreement on mechanisms to create a European Central Banking System and, ultimately, a European single currency while imposing strict constraints on price stability on all EU member states. Alas, this approach, which summarized the policy orthodoxies of the 1980s, was decreed just as the 1990s turned toward a recession that made it essential for nations to maintain their ability to stimulate economic activity. Attempts to expand EU competencies met with limited success, and to the degree to which new matters could become European in scope, as on matters of immigration policy and police cooperation, this would happen in carefully limited inter-governmental ways. In the name of "democratic legitimacy" the European parliament gained new powers, but in ways which increased the opacity of European institutions to public vision. The fate of the proposed Common Foreign and Security Policy was even more problematic. Little more than polite formalities could be agreed on and substantial collaboration on foreign policy and defense remained years away. This was underlined by member state disagreements about the most important practical foreign policy matter to face them in the aftermath of 1989: what to do about the dissolution of the Yugoslav Republic. Europe thus granted an opening to Serbian aggression, and the terrible bloodshed which followed occurred at exactly the same moment when Europe's foreign ministers talked of greater foreign policy cooperation.

In general, it became evident in the Maastricht discussions that there existed growing divisions between EU member state governments and elites about how much further to go toward creating EU supranational authority. The result was a Maastricht treaty that substantively fell far short of the turning point for which the Commission and its allies had hoped. That the text was extremely difficult to understand—one journalist claimed that trying to get through it was like "reading the London bus schedule"—made its public reception more problematic and made popular understanding of what a united Europe was all about more difficult.

This last failing prompted the next step in the EU's fall from the heights. The Maastricht document had to be ratified by all twelve EU members before coming into effect and, in a few cases, this meant national referenda. The first hammer blow fell when the Danes narrowly rejected ratification in June 1992 (they would later vote again favorably). The French referendum that followed in September passed, saving the treaty politically, but the "petit oui" of barely 1% indicated that nearly half of the French opposed Maastricht. Opinion polls in other EU member states all reported strong reservations about the treaty and the "new Europe," with ordinary citizens being the most reticent.

The new Europe was unpopular. The first reason for this had to do with the impact of its policies. During the Russian Dolls period the EU's successes, in particular the single market, had been largely psychological. The new programs had sent signals to key decision makers, particularly capitalists, that action was finally being taken to move Europe out of the morass. These signals, in the context of an economic upturn, then stimulated renewed optimism that translated into investments and growth. The actual policies of "1992" took quite a bit longer to implement, however. A huge amount of legislation had to be written, passed, transposed into national law and put into practice. When all this occurred, the "1992" policies turned out to have real teeth, creating a degree of new economic uncertainty for ordinary Europeans as companies and public services restructured and rationalized. Unfortunately for Maastricht, the delayed effects of these policies on the daily lives of European citizens coincided with the ratification season in 1992–93.

The second source of unpopularity was political, rejoining the democratic deficit issue. Following the Monnet method, integrating Europe had always been an elitist affair, created by political executives and technocrats behind closed doors and consecrated by legal documents and institutional procedures that few could follow. As long as the results were positive and/or far from the concerns of ordinary citizens, as they had been during the EU's first quarter century, this approach was feasible. When conditions changed, as they had by the early 1990s, Europe began to suffer seriously from its "democratic deficit."

The EU was clearly responsible for policies that made a visible difference to the daily lives of people. Yet these policies had been decided behind closed doors through processes of dubious political legitimacy that escaped the democratic norms, however flawed, that existed on nation state level. Europe, per se, as distinct from European nations, had no specific democratic distinctiveness, yet it was rapidly becoming a major source of public control over European citizens.

It was the third source of unpopularity which was most devastating. After 1985 the EU's policy innovations had been marketed as remedies to Europe's problems of economic decline. The Single Market and its sequels would free up economic dynamism and creativity and, above all, create jobs, for the major symptom of these problems was a disquieting rise in unemployment. One of the Commission's favorite ways of generating support had been to claim credit for the jobs created in the boomlet of the later 1980s. That this was a tactical mistake became clear when the economic boomlet gave way, in 1991–92, to Europe's worst recession since the war. To many, the Commission that had been so eager to take credit for earlier good times should now shoulder much of the blame for the new bad times. Worse still, a combination of political uncertainty, new economic problems and bad monetary tactics led, in 1992–93, to a cycle of currency speculation and devaluation that tore the European Monetary System inside out and came perilously close to destroying the only dimension of Maastricht that had seemed relatively solid, plans for Economic and Monetary Union.[31]

The environment around European integration had once again severely deteriorated. As we have earlier noted, it took a situation in which favorable environments and a strategically daring and skillful Commission coexisted to make Europe move forward. Deterioration in the environment dramatically undercut opportunities for further European-level action. Delors, his Commission team, and their allies were obliged to take a strategic retreat—pushing through whatever they could as discreetly as possible. Thus the Common Agricultural Policy was reformed, a second Delors budgetary package was approved and the hugely complicated GATT Uruguay Round negotiations concluded. These were signal successes by any measure, but they occurred in a very gloomy broader setting. The Commission, increasingly scapegoated by member states as meddlesome "Brussels bureaucrats," had little choice but to lie low. Its last major act, the 1993 White Paper on *Growth, Competitiveness and Employment* demonstrated that it had lost little of its imagination. Forced to admit that it, along with everyone else, had vastly underestimated Europe's

[31] The most exhaustive review of the ERM events of 1992–93 is in David Cameron's "British Exit, German Voice, French Loyalty: Defection, Domination and Coooperation in the 1992–93 ERM Crisis" (Paper delivered at the 1993 Meeting of the American Political Science Association, Washington, D.C., August 1993).

economic difficulties, it proceeded to outline an ambitious new approach designed to promote competitiveness while preserving what could be preserved of the European welfare state.[32]

The Roots of Decline—Contingencies and Contradictions

Even at the moment of its greatest successes the post-1985 strategy to push European integration forward was contingent on three favorable contextual variables. The first was member state receptivity to European-level solutions to problems. Resort to European, as opposed to national, problem solving had to make sense in the abstract and be congruent with domestic political vectors. The strategy's first triumphs, following the announcement of the "1992" programs, were largely cost-free for ordinary Europeans, since success followed more from communicating signals to elite actors than from actual impact of policies, which would only follow their implementation. The initial moments when the Commission and its allies reinvested returns from Single Market successes into new programs—the high point of the Russian dolls period—were thus relatively easy going compared to what came later. Once the policies began to bite, EU politics would become more complicated and difficult. Given predictable lags in actual impact of the early programs, any initially negative effect on ordinary EU citizens, might well occur at just that moment when Delors, Mitterrand, Kohl, and allies were making their critical "turning point" moves.

This important matter of political timing was correlated with political circumstances in key member states. The mid-1980s, when the Delors strategy began its successful ascent, was a moment when the most important EU governments were in the hands of powerful leaders at the peaks of careers. François Mitterrand, Helmut Kohl, Margaret Thatcher, and Felipe Gonzales had all become legends; the Christian Democrats remained in firm control of Italy; and figures like Ruup Lubbers, Paul Schluter, and Andreas Papandreou had solid positions in smaller states. Such propitious circumstances could not last forever. What might happen to the strategy if governments in the most important EU member states like Germany, France, the UK, and Italy were weakened by domestic political problems? The answer to this is simple. The longer the strategy was pursued the more difficult it would become to pursue it further. This was tremendously important in the light of the logics of key actors. Delors and allies sought to pyramid resources gained from the success of the easiest programs to promote to move from market building to political integration ("state building"). Later, when the great turning point toward

---

[32] Commission of the European Communities, *Growth, Competitiveness, Employment: The Challenges and Ways Forward into the 21st Century,* Bulletin of the European Communities, Supplement 6/93 (Luxembourg: EC, 1993).

state building occurred (Maastricht), it was quite possible that the impact of earlier policies on ordinary Europeans and the declining support that beset all the long-sitting political elites in democracies would combine to lessen member state willingness to sustain it.

The international change that occurred after 1989 was the second major contextual contingency. German unification, the promarket revolutions of Central and Eastern Europe, and the disaggregation of former Communist federal states were huge, unpredictable events. Changing American behaviors in consequence was important as well. It was not surprising that great new uncertainty created unsure footing for the Commission and other key actors. Even if it was not alone, however, the Commission responded overconfidently in anticipating the rapid success of benign Eastern European transitions and the effectiveness of marketization. And if it was politically essential and morally courageous for it to support rapid German unification it thereby accepted the dangerous consequences of the ways in which unification was worked out. It is clear that the primary motivations of the Commission President were to use the international changes to enhance the foreign political stature and role of the EU. It is also clear that Delors and the Commission were under strong pressure from both the French and Germans to do what they did.

It is quite wrong to assert that these international changes were *the* causes of the Commission's difficulties in the early 1990s. They were significant mainly as part of a cluster of causes that disrupted and added great new complexity to a strategy for integration already stretched to its limit. Even before the world around it changed, the EU had already assumed a staggering number of difficult tasks. Putting Eastern Europe and the divisive idea of an EU foreign and defense policy on the table was thus tempting fate. The new issues raised questions about the EU's responsibilities in organizing an entirely new set of continental interdependencies in market, political, and geostrategic realms. The new capitalist and democratic Eastern European societies needed help, integration in some way into the EU's market system, promises of ultimate EU membership, some kind of participation in EU decision making, and last but not least, a redesigned security order. Any one of these matters would have challenged the EU's ongoing agenda. Taken together, they threatened an overload that could interfere with clear discussion and provoke new conflict.

The third, and undoubtedly most important, contingency was economic. Initial Commission successes coincided with an upturn in the business cycle in the later 1980s, the first to occur after the "Eurosclerosis" period ending in 1979. The contrast between earlier recession and renewed growth coming simultaneously with the enunciation of the "1992" program was great. The renewal of European integration helped stimulate the return of economic optimism which, in turn, provided a major boost for the Commission's strategy. It was easy to be misled by what happened and conclude that the EU's new initiatives had solved Europe's economic problems and brought a return to steady growth and prosperity. When the business cycle later turned down, however, Europe and the Commission strategy would both inevitably be hurt. Ordinary Europeans were quite capable of concluding that the multiple promises made by their leaders, national and European, had not been kept.

It was a commonplace that European integration could only thrive in moments of economic optimism and growth. When the economy goes bad in a democracy, domestic politics becomes volatile as people seek to protect themselves. In EU Europe, in large part because of the "democratic deficit," the leverage which the people possessed, such as it was, was national. National-level protection made bad economic moments equally bad for European integration. The crisis of the early 1990s turned out even worse, however. It was a moment of truth for elites and ordinary citizens, which underlined the fact that the good times of the postwar boom were gone, never to return. To the degree to which the new Europe had been marketed, and understood, as a vehicle to make the good times return, it was bound to suffer.

There were three fundamental contradictions in the Delors Commission/Franco-German strategic vision, and the contingencies just reviewed intensified them. The first contradiction was a function of the strategy's attempt at sequential unfolding from market to state building. Market building, largely through "1992," was to be a launching pad for state building. The strategy gambled that a combination of evidence and argument about the functional need for new "Euroregulation" plus persuasive political mobilization in favor of "organizing" the new Single Market would be enough to move strongly into state building, working from the success of "1992." This was a high stakes bet, however, and odds against complete success were great. There were plans other than Commission's on the field. A number of member states, not only the British, had little interest in European state building and would try to keep new European integration confined within the EU's traditional trade-market mandate. Even among the member states who wanted European state-building there were important disagreements over its extent and the forms which it should take. The Germans, many smaller EU members, and the Delors team were federalists. But the all-important French, strong advocates for more Europe, were avid confederalists. Finally, to the degree to which state building touched upon foreign policy and defense it, touched another set of divisive issues, among them NATO and ties to the United States.

All this meant that market building stood a greater chance of succeeding than state building. In the worst case this could leave Europe economically liberalized but underregulated, the Commission's least preferred outcome. Something close to this was what happened. The strategy was a high-stakes gamble. If its state-building initiatives failed or fell short of their goals, which was much more likely to occur than failure at market integration, then outcomes would not only involve "more market" relative to supranational regulation, but more market relative to *national* regulation as well. This is because of the great likelihood that economic flows in a single market relatively open to the world will be more powerful than the capacities of any individual member state to regulate them.

A second contradiction lurked in the EU's democratic deficit. The Monnet method, deeply inscribed in the political system that had been built at the European level, was consciously elitist. For everyone to benefit, European construction had to proceed in the shadows of democratic accountability as ordinarily understood. After 1985 the Commission and others had little choice but to work within a European institutional system reflecting this philosophy. There was an appointed Commission empowered with sweeping powers of policy proposition. There were secretive and opaque councils of ministers, an imperious European Council, and a powerful European Court of Justice. Then there was an impotent talking-shop of a parliament. Connections among these institutions and any mass European political culture were tenuous. Moreover, they were all knit into a system whose operations were perplexingly complicated and largely unfathomable to nonspecialists.

The danger was not abstract. Success at the level of post-1985 ambitions meant that new EU policies would impact seriously on ordinary people. The more this was true, the more likely ordinary people would demand an accounting. The Commission could hope that the weight of new EU activities would be largely benign and that this accounting would lead both to an enhancement of the EU's reputation and a deepening of trans-European political culture. But it was in the nature of things that many of the EU's new programs would work their benign effects over the medium term, even if things turned out well. The strategy might bring substantial disruption in the short run, particularly in the realm of employment. When member state publics came to confront such matters, it would be difficult to avoid an EU crisis. This was indeed what happened toward the end of the Delors Commission's tenure.

The third contradiction was inherent in the strategy's purpose of pyramiding one advance onto another as rapidly as feasible, a strategy complicated by the end of the Cold War. It seems strange in retrospect, but the Commission and its allies had few provisions for handling the quite likely eventuality of the cessation of forward movement, for consolidating and administering the EU's new successes. Jacques Delors, the Commission President, an indefatigable and militant reformist, was convinced that Europe had only a very few years to work very large changes and that these changes had to be built one upon the other. When powerful member states then decided to add or impose upon the Commission's own program there was little that the Commission President or anyone else could do to stop them. In general there was a risk of a programmatic overload, of putting more things on the table than the EU's various systems could handle. This also occurred in the early 1990s, particularly as the EU's own European environment changed.

Globalization, Democracy, and Transnational Politics

What is to be made of this dense story? We had two initial queries, the first about the appropriateness of Moore's international "realism" to new times, and the second, a related one, about the unfolding of democracy as the millennium approached. First, with the nation-state–centered arguments of *Social Origins* in mind, could contemporary economic globalization challenge national sovereignty sufficiently to lead nation states to divest themselves of central dimensions of this sovereignty? Second, if a reconsideration of Moore's realist premises was in order, as seemed likely from knowledge of recent European integration, what did it imply for the evolution of liberal democracy?

Keeping in mind the uniqueness of European integration—to use language that Moore would reject, "we have an N of 1"—evidence from the EU since 1985 provides tentative answers to both questions. During this period the EU has been on a roller coaster ride ending far short of the consolidation of any solid transnational political entity. It is nonetheless clear from what has been undertaken that Europe will emerge integrated in new, largely unprecedented ways. Skeptics will contend that within this new Europe, the Germans, the French, and others will remain visibly pushing away in pursuit of their particular national goals. This is true. The renaissance of European integration after 1985 and its subsequent downward plunge after 1991, were the products of national leaders making decisions on grounds of national interest, aided and prodded to do so by Euro-level institutions. But this answer is inadequate, for the *product* of these decisions transcends their origins. Europe, per se, exists as a structured, institutionalized environment which now places great constraints on the nature and ways in which the pursuit of national interests by EU member states can be carried on.

The Germans, the French, and the others have, over time, surrendered considerable portions of their sovereignty, particularly in the economic realm, in order to be able to "play" in this new environment. They did so, to be sure, in a quest to solve important national problems. But in so doing they accepted important limitations in their future autonomy and resources to pursue the kinds of nation-state–based strategies that characterized the trajectories explored in *Social Origins*. The nature of the present EU environment is an indicator of modifications in the character of sovereignty. The completion of the Single Market, to take only one large example, removes an entire toolbox of traditional techniques for controlling national economic spaces. Governments can no longer resort to nontariff barriers to protect national activities.

Beyond certain points they cannot subsidize national industries. They must observe a wide range of European-level norms and standards, including regulations concerning workplace health and safety. They cannot limit capital flows. They must open most of their public procurement to genuine transnational competitive bidding. They must "harmonize" their indirect tax systems, including VAT taxes. They must observe the rulings about competition law and about mergers and acquisitions which are rendered from Brussels. And the list, which could be much longer, will expand dramatically with Economic and Monetary Union. EMU will bring the loss of most traditional nation-state monetary policy prerogatives. Adjustments to changed economic conditions through currency revaluations will then no longer be possible, implying that EMU members will be obliged to adjust by lowering wages and social protection levels.

More broadly, transnational EU institutions have clearly *mattered* in the post-1985 EU story. The Commission, which we have discussed, and the Court of Justice, which we have not, have set agendas, shaped frameworks of analysis and exercised real power. They will undoubtedly continue to do so, despite the EU's current difficulties. Slow movement toward transnational economic blocs elsewhere—the North American Free Trade Association (NAFTA) and the embryonic arrangements in Latin America and Asia—indicates that regional collaboration involving pooling of economic sovereignty is one contemporary response to globalization. The nature of the European EU/Union as a *political* system makes the EU story distinctive and atypical, however. The EU was founded in the wake of World War II ostensibly for trade-market objectives, but its architects had far broader ambitions. The EU was constitutionally designed from the beginning to open toward patterns of transnational governance. That the contemporary EU has promoted major changes in the nature of its member states' definition of sovereignty seems evident. But the uniqueness of EU institutionally means that the causes for this cannot be "read out" in any quasi-functionalist way from underlying tendencies toward economic globalization. Globalization may have been as much a pretext for EU political institution builders to go to work as the cause of what they attempted to build.

The implication of what has happened for the evolution of liberal democracy is somewhat less clear, but equally challenging. If the root causes of recent European integration are connected to a new, transnationalizing stage, in the development of capitalism—and the jury is still out on such questions—then what is happening to liberal democracy in Europe because of integration becomes an important datum. Conclusions are grim indeed. Earlier we discussed the lack of democratic commitment in the Monnet method. Periodic attempts to create new democratic institutions and procedures to limit and compensate for the Monnet method have been quite unsuccessful to date.

They have primarily involved establishing a European Parliament, initially without significant powers, and then incrementally granting it more prerogatives and new grounds for legitimizing its actions through direct election. The Parliament also acquired extensive powers of amendment in 1987 and then, with Maastricht, new powers of "codecision" (that is, the ability to decide, in conjunction with the Council of Ministers, upon the fate of European legislation). Maastricht also gave the Parliament enhanced powers over the appointment of new European Commissions. It still does not have power to initiate legislation, full budgetary control, or the capacity to "defeat" Europe's other governing bodies (the Commission and Council) by majority vote, as opposed to blocking particular measures, but it does have considerable power to scrutinize and investigate. However, the exercise of this particular mixture of prerogatives is shrouded in a fog created by the complexity of Europe's decision rules. There are upwards of twenty different ways to pass a directive, for example, and very few of them are fully understood by anyone except EU insiders. Such opacity is itself a huge barrier to democracy.

Beyond all this, exactly how fundamental issues of democratic deficit might be addressed remains disputed. Profound issues of political philosophy remain open. The EU's legitimacy was originally built on the premise that the Council of Ministers, which signed off on European legislation, was composed of delegates from duly elected member state governments. Moreover, EU legislation was possible only if the EU treaties provided for it, and these treaties had been signed by democratically elected representatives of member states. This doctrine has ceased to be persuasive, however. Should the legitimacy of EU Europe be built on a transnational European political culture focussed upon the European Parliament? Such a structure is the answer promoted without any previous planning towards it throughout the history of European integration. It is not the only answer. Should EU legitimacy follow from a full "Europeanization" of national parliamentary lives and political cultures? This option of bringing European issues into national democratic politics has the merit of building upon existing habits. Is there some hybrid form waiting to be invented?

No option has been pursued far enough yet to understand its implications, and today there exists little but confusion. There is virtually no trans-EU political culture to support the "Europarliamentist" strategy and, with few exceptions, the Europeanization of national parliamentary lives and political cultures has barely begun.[33] At present, therefore, there is no satisfactory resolution of the democratic deficit problem in sight.

The major and permanent transfers of sovereignty from member states to

---

[33] The range of options and problems is well discussed in Mario Telo, ed., *Democratie et construction europeenne* (Brussels: Editions de l'Universite de Bruxelles, 1995).

the European level that have already occurred create significant areas for decision making which largely escape classic democratic control. Moreover, one cannot ignore that these transfers have mainly occurred through use of the Monnet method which was explicitly designed to avoid such control. These are even more disturbing conclusions than they seem at first sight. European nation-states faced a set of grave economic problems in the 1980s. These problems, connected with globalization and other economic changes, would not have been easy to solve in national contexts, particularly given the neoliberal perspectives that European leaders had adopted. Deregulation, budgetary austerity and cutbacks in social protection programs, threats to group positions that had been consolidated in the golden age, and a host of other matters were, in most circumstances, guaranteed political losers if pursued within national boundaries. In fact, what then happened was that these painful solutions, if indeed they are solutions, were off-loaded by national governments onto the EU. That the EU largely escaped the kinds of democratic accountability that existed at the national level made such off-loading an even more convenient course. In the absence of anything resembling a genuine European mass political life many, if not most, member state regimes could then routinely play exculpatory political games with the EU, using it as a scapegoat for the difficult decisions, particularly in the economic realm, that "Europe demanded." One consequence was that it opened the way for to ambitious politicians to break into the limelight by invoking nationalism against the "Brussels bureaucrats," hence intensifying national populist fears.

In all, it is difficult to avoid the observation that in Europe, where the most propitious circumstances exist for the democratic resolution of such difficult problems, responses to globalization have involved a flight away from democratic responsibilities and procedures. Major matters concerning the daily lives and security of European citizens are now decided at the European level without these citizens being fully consulted. One frightening implication can be drawn. Globalization, if it is a new stage in the evolution of capitalism, could constitute a significant threat to liberal democracy.

The story is far from finished, but we know enough to wonder whether the trajectories to democracy that Moore, with all of his skepticism, found so important in *Social Origins* may find themselves menaced in the future. Europe may be engaged in a historic transition, even if the outcomes are not yet visible. *Social Origins* accounted for an earlier epoque. It will take a great deal more than we currently know to discern the deep lines of causality and the trajectory of the course we are presently taking. But what if the centuries-long narratives recounted by *Social Origins* have come to an end? What if, at least for the major centers of global economic activity, these markets have finally begun to constrain the essential attributes of the most powerful nation-states rather than coinciding with them? And what if these developments have begun threatening cherished and altogether too-limited earlier victories for democracy? Arrant foolishness about the "end of history" is clearly out of order, as realists like Moore have always known. Monsters will not cease to populate the dark nights of the next millennium. But realism surely cannot exclude the possibility that they will be different kinds of monsters from those whose roots were so magisterially laid bare by Barrington Moore, Jr., in *Social Origins*.

Notes on the Contributors

BRIAN M. DOWNING studied for a Ph.D. in Political Science at the University of Chicago. His dissertation won the Gabriel Almond Award of the American Political Science Association, and was then turned into his first book, *The Military Revolution and Political Change: Origins of Democracy and Autocracy in Early Modern Europe* (Princeton University Press, 1992).

EDWARD FRIEDMAN is the Hawkins Chair Professor in the Department of Political Science at the University of Wisconsin, Madison. His co-authored *Chinese Village, Socialist State* (Yale University Press, 1991) was selected by the Association for Asian Studies as the best book on modern China. He edited the volume *The Politics of Democratization: Generalizing East Asian Experiences* (Westview, 1994) and wrote *National Identity and Democratic Prospects in Socialist China* (M. E. Sharpe, 1995).

PETER ALEXIS GOUREVITCH is a Professor at the Graduate School of International Relations and Pacific Studies and the Department of Political Science at the University of California at San Diego (UCSD). He is the author of *Politics in Hard Times: Comparative Responses to International Economic Crises* (Cornell University Press, 1986), *Paris and the Provinces: The Politics of Local Government Reform in France* (University of California Press, 1980), and numerous articles on international and comparative political economy. Gourevitch is co-editor with David Lake of *International Organization* and is doing research on the globalization of international production networks.

GEORGE ROSS is Morris Hillquit Professor in Labor and Social Thought at Brandeis University, Senior Associate at the Minda de Gunzburg Center for European Studies at Harvard University, and Chair of the Council for European Studies. His most recent book is *Jacques Delors and European Integration* (Oxford University Press, 1995). Other books include *Workers and Communists in France: From Popular Front to Eurocommunism* (University of California Press, 1982); *The View from Inside: A French Communist Cell in Crisis*, with Jane Jenson (University of California Press, 1984); *Unions, Crisis, and Change*, vol. 1, with Peter Lange and Maurizio Vannicelli (Allen and Unwin, 1982), and vol. 2, with Peter A. Gourevitch (1984); *The Mitterrand Experiment*, edited with Stanley Hoffmann and Sylvia Malzacher (Oxford University Press, 1987); and *Searching for the New France*, with James F. Hollifield (Routledge, 1991).

REBECCA J. SCOTT is Frederick Huetwell Professor of History at the University of Michigan. As an undergraduate at Radcliffe College she completed a senior thesis under the direction of Barrington Moore, Jr., on the consequences of U.S. foreign assistance to Bolivia. She later went on to study economic history at the London School of Economics and to complete a doctorate in Latin American history at Princeton University. In 1985 Princeton University Press published her monograph *Slave Emancipation in Cuba: The Transition to Free Labor, 1860–1899*, which has subsequently been translated into Spanish and Portuguese. She is currently completing a book entitled *Degree of Freedom: Society after Slavery in Louisiana, Cuba, and Brazil*, which examines questions of race, labor, and citizenship.

THEDA SKOCPOL is Victor S. Thomas Professor of Government and Sociology at Harvard University. She received her Ph.D. from Harvard in 1975, having studied with Barrington Moore as a graduate student. Her first book, *States and Social Revolutions: A Comparative Analysis of France, Russia, and China* (Cambridge University Press, 1979), won the 1979 C. Wright Mills Award of the Society for the Study of Social Problems and was co-winner of the 1980 American Sociological Association Award for a Distinguished Contribution to Scholarship. Subsequently, Skocpol co-edited *Vision and Method in Historical Sociology* (Cambridge University Press, 1984) and *Bringing the State Back In* (Cambridge University Press, 1985). For the past decade, Skocpol has worked on U.S. politics and social policy in historical and comparative perspective. Her recent book, *Protecting Soldiers and Mothers: The Political Origins of Social Policy in the United States* (Harvard University Press, 1992) won five major scholarly awards, including the Woodrow Wilson Foundation Award of the American Political Science Association and the Ralph Waldo Emerson Award of Phi Beta Kappa.

TONY SMITH is the Jackson Professor of Political Science at Tufts University. His books include *The French Stake in Algeria, 1945–1962* (Cornell University Press, 1976), *The Pattern of Imperialism: The United States, Great Britain, and the Late Industrializing World Since 1815* (Cambridge University Press, 1981), *Thinking Like a Communist: State and Legitimacy in the Soviet Union, China, and Cuba* (Norton, 1987), and *America's Mission: The United States and the Worldwide Struggle for Democracy in the Twentieth Century* (Princeton University Press, 1994). He is currently completing a book on ethnic groups and U.S. foreign policy.

CHARLES TILLY. The unlikely pair of George Homans and Barrington Moore co-directed Charles Tilly's Harvard doctoral dissertation in sociology (completed in 1958). Tilly has held appointments of a year or more at Delaware, Princeton, Harvard, MIT, Toronto, Michigan, the Center for Advanced Study in the Behavioral Sciences, and the Institute for Advanced Study. Until he resigned in 1996 in protest against cutbacks in their graduate programs, he was University Distinguished Professor and director of the Center for Studies of Social Change at the New School for Social Research. He then became Joseph L. Buttenwiesser Professor of Social Science at Columbia University. His most recent books are *Popular Contention in Great Britain, 1758–1834* (Harvard University Press, 1995), the edited volume *Citizenship, Identity, and Social History* (Cambridge University Press, 1995), and *Durable Inequality* (University of California Press, forthcoming). He is now writing books on the emergence of mass national politics in Western Europe and (with his son Chris Tilly) on capitalist work and labor markets.

JUDITH EISENBERG VICHNIAC is Director of Social Studies and a senior lecturer for the Committee on Degrees in Social Studies at Harvard University. Barrington Moore, Jr., helped found this program in 1960. She is also an affiliate at the Center for European Studies. She recently published "French Socialists and Droit à la Difference" in *French Politics and Society,* and also a book entitled *The Management of Labor: The British and French Iron and Steel Industries, 1860–1918* (JAI Press, 1990).

MICHAEL WALZER is the UPS Foundation Professor of Social Science at the Institute for Advanced Study in Princeton, New Jersey. Among his many books are *The Revolution of the Saints: A Study in the Origins of Radical Politics* (Harvard University Press, 1965); *Just and Unjust Wars: A Moral Argument with Historical Illustrations* (Basic Books, 1977); *Spheres of Justice: A Defense of Pluralism and Equality* (Basic Books, 1983); *Exodus and Revolution* (Basic Books, 1985); *What It Means to Be an American* (Marsilio/Rizzoli, 1992); and *Thick and Thin: Moral Argument at Home and Abroad* (University of Nore Dame Press, 1984).

Index

absolutism: Caroline period of, 41–46; class balance in, 132; collapse of French, 32–34, 35; vs. constitutionalism, 212–13; development of, 27–29, 47; disaffection with, 45–46; gentry as obstacle to, 51–54; Jewish emancipation and, 172, 176, 182, 187–88; popular support for, 44–45; unlikely in Netherlands, 46–50. *See also* authoritarianism; dictatorship

Adenauer, Konrad, 201–2

advanced industrial countries: economy of, 211, 214–15, 231–32; fragmented politics and, 228. *See also specific countries*

African Americans: militia for, 148–49, 153–54; pensions for, 99. *See also* color line; plantation systems; race; slavery

Afro-Cubans: arrests of, 156; leaders of, 159. *See also* Cuba; plantation systems

agnosticism, as revolutionary option, 127–28

agriculture: commercialization of, 9, 13, 33, 212–13, 230–31; EU's policies on, 233, 240; in India, 104; Jewish role in, 180–81; land distribution concerns in, 113, 147–48, 153, 155, 184–85, 203, 224; role of, 223; state management of, 28; subsidies for, 222; Swedish control of grain trade, 41; trade barriers in, 215n9. *See also* peasant communities; plantation systems; sugar production

Agrupación Independiente de Color (Cuba), 161–62

Akbar (emperor of India), 108

Akira Iriye, 205–6

Albania, democratization in, 110, 116

Algeria, industrialization of, 103

Alliance for Progress, 103

Almond, Gabriel, 3

Alsace (France), Jewish status in, 173, 175, 177–80, 182

American occupation policy: constitutional development under, 201–2; democracy as goal of, 196–202, 207–8; economic development and reconstruction under, 202–7; liberalism and, 191–92; long-term effects of, 207–9; purges fostered in, 199–200; skepticism toward, 196

American Political Science Association, 7, 12

American Revolution: French debt crisis after, 66; role of, 73–74; veterans' benefits after, 100

American Sociological Association, 7

anticlericalism, 34

anti-Semitism: new type of, 186–87; persistence of, 169–70, 180–81; varied impacts of, 16

antitrust policy, 220, 226

Arendt, Hannah, 136, 175–76

Arrears of Pension Act (U.S.), 86, 88–93, 95, 99

Asia: vs. Europe, 108–9, 116; financial crisis in, 217–18, 228; fragmented politics and, 228. *See also* East Asia; *specific countries*

Athens, freedom in, 108

Austria: alliances of, 52–53; European inte-

The Wilder House Series in Politics, History and Culture

A Series Edited by David Laitin and George Steinmetz

Democracy in Translation: Understanding Politics in an Unfamiliar Culture
by Frederic C. Schaffer
Democracy, Revolution, and History
edited by Theda Skocpol
State/Culture: State-Formation after the Cultural Turn
edited by George Steinmetz
"We Ask for British Justice": Workers and Racial Difference in Late Imperial Britain
by Laura Tabili
Gifts, Favors, and Banquets: The Art of Social Relationships in China
by Mayfair Mei-hui Yang